# Web Development with MongoDB and NodeJS

*Second Edition*

Build an interactive and full-featured web application
from scratch using Node.js and MongoDB

**Mithun Satheesh**

**Bruno Joseph D'mello**

**Jason Krol**

[PACKT] open source*
PUBLISHING     community experience distilled

BIRMINGHAM - MUMBAI

# Web Development with MongoDB and NodeJS
## *Second Edition*

Copyright © 2015 Packt Publishing

First published: October 2015

Production reference: 1261015

Published by Packt Publishing Ltd.
Livery Place
35 Livery Street
Birmingham B3 2PB, UK.

ISBN 978-1-78528-752-7

www.packtpub.com

# Credits

**Authors**

Mithun Satheesh

Bruno Joseph D'mello

Jason Krol

**Reviewers**

Huseyin Babal

Luke P. Issac

Alexandru-Emil Lupu

Suhas Hoskote Muralidhar

Sandeep Pandey

Oddur Sigurdsson

**Commissioning Editor**

Nadeem Bagban

**Acquisition Editors**

Neha Nagwekar

Reshma Raman

**Content Development Editor**

Zeeyan Pinheiro

**Technical Editor**

Deepti Tuscano

**Copy Editor**

Merilyn Pereira

**Project Coordinator**

Suzanne Coutinho

**Proofreader**

Safis Editing

**Indexer**

Tejal Soni

**Production Coordinator**

Manu Joseph

**Cover Work**

Manu Joseph

# About the Authors

**Mithun Satheesh** is an open source enthusiast and a web developer from India. He has over five years of web development experience and specializes in JavaScript, Ruby, PHP, and other frontend engineering technologies. He is the author of a couple of libraries on Node.js, which are available as opensource via npm. One of these is called node-rules, which is a forward-chaining rule engine implementation written initially to handle transaction risks on bookmyshow.com, one of his former employers. Node rules have a considerable user following both on npm and GitHub. Apart from this, he has also served as an individual contributor to many open source projects on GitHub.

He is a regular on programming sites such as Stack Overflw and loves contributing to the open source world. Apart from programming, he is also interested in experimenting with various cloud platform solutions. He has a number of applications listed in the developer spotlight of platform-as-a-service providers such as RedHat's OpenShift.

You can follow him on Twitter at @mithunsatheesh.

I would like to thank my parents for all the support they have given me. I am thankful to all my teachers for whatever knowledge I have gained in my life.

**Bruno Joseph D'mello** is a web application engineer currently working at Built.io. He is a JavaScript enthusiast and has a keen interest in different web technologies and the programming paradigms implemented in them.

Thanks to my family for their patience and encouragement.

**Jason Krol** is a passionate web developer with over 15 years of professional experience creating highly interactive web applications using the latest in both client and server technologies.

Over the past few years, Jason has been focusing on developing Single-Page Applications using JavaScript in the full stack with Node.js, MongoDB, and Backbone.js. After co-owning and running a successful web development agency for a number of years, Jason recently joined AWeber Communications, an e-mail marketing service provider in the suburbs of Philadelphia.

When he isn't writing code for work or side projects, Jason blogs about his development experiences and opinions at `KrolTech.com`. Jason loves spending his free time with his wife and 8-year-old son.

A very special thank you to my wonderful wife for putting up with me and for always being there to push me whenever I doubt myself.

# About the Reviewers

**Huseyin Babal** is an enthusiastic full stack developer since 2007. He mainly develops web applications using Java, Node.js, and PHP on the backend, AngularJS, and Twitter Bootstrap on the frontend, and Elasticsearch and MongoDB for some research projects. He is the author of `NodeJS in Action in Udemy` with over 1,500 students. He is also interested in DevOps engineering and applies continuous delivery principles to his projects. He writes tutorials about full stack development on Tuts+ and Java Code Geeks and shares his experiences at public conferences.

Besides the computer world, he lives in Istanbul with his wonderful wife and two cockatiels. He likes to spend his spare time with his wife by walking at least an hour per day, visiting different places, watching cartoons, and going on summer holidays.

**Luke P. Issac** is a full stack JavaScript developer with bachelor's of technology degree (Hons.) in computer science engineering. He has also been a technical writer for the past two years for `www.thegeekstuff.com` where he keeps on sharing his works with the world in a simplified form and mentors an active technical discussion on the blog.

His experience over the last four years involves his contribution to several successful e-commerce implementations around the globe. He believes that technology is not a bar and continues to research different technology stacks to find efficient and optimized solutions for the continuously evolving Web. Thus, he has hands-on experience with live e-commerce implementations on the MEAN stack and the LAMP stack, which makes him very versatile in web development.

He had his thankful contribution on behalf of the Author in reviewing and adding content for *Getting Started with Flurry Analytics, Packt Publishing*.

> I want to thank my parents, Mr. Issac P. L. and Mrs. Sisily Issac, who worked hard for my education, and all my friends for their continuous support and inspiration to explore more and share it with the world.

**Alexandru-Emil Lupu** is a CTO and Ruby on Rails developer at `2Performant.com`. Alex has about 10 years of experience in the web development industry, during which time he learned a lot of skills from e-commerce platforms implementation and presentation sites, to online games code writing. He is one of the developers who are constantly learning new programming languages and he has no problem understanding Ruby, PHP, Python, JavaScript, and Java code.

Alex is very passionate about programming and computer science; when he was a teenager, he did not have his own computer or an Internet connection (hard to believe, but true). He would go to an Internet cafe to read about his programming problems and would then struggle to implement them at home. He fondly remembers those days and hopes he's the same guy from 10 years ago with much more experience. For him, *passion* is the word that describes the challenge he faced while learning. Trust me, it is not easy to be a youngster, but also willing to learn new stuff. Coming home at 2-3 A.M, determined to install Linux just to learn about it, is not as easy as it sounds. I had a Pentium I at 133 MHz in the Pentium IV at 1800 MHz era!

He is constantly learning and likes to stay close to well-trained and passionate people who better motivate him every day! This is the reason he joined the 2Performant (2Parale) team, to face a challenge. He likes teams that work intelligently and are energetic.

Proof of his perseverance is that he is a Certified Scrum Master and is passionate about Agile development. His resume also includes four years at `eRepublik.com`, an online game, where he was responsible for a long list of tasks including feature development, performance optimization, but also was the tech lead on an internal project. He learned the necessarily skills to fulfill his day-to-day tasks at `2Performant.com` the hard way.

In the little spare time he has developed small personal projects or reads technical or project management books or articles. When relaxing, he enjoys watching thriller movies and playing shooter or strategy games.

He doesn't talk too much, but is willing to teach others programming. If you meet him at a cafe prepare to be entertained, as he likes to tell a lot of contextual jokes.

His LinkedIn profile is at `https://www.linkedin.com/in/alecslupu`. Interact with him on `http://github.com/alecslupu`.

**Suhas Hoskote Muralidhar** is a computer enthusiast and is extremely interested in learning and exploring new technologies. After receiving his undergraduate degree in computer science, he worked at Intel Corporation as a full stack web developer. He is currently pursuing his master's degree at the University of Illinois at Urbana-Champaign. He has kept in sync with his passion for web development by working as a research assistant at the university by being involved in building full stack e-learning web applications. He also developed a strong interest in machine learning and big data analytics and has that as his main research focus. Besides optimizing his code, he enjoys playing the guitar and going on road trips.

**Sandeep Pandey** is a full-stack developer for Practo.com, India, and builds products for doctors and patients. In the past, he worked with CISCO as a consultant on learning products (`https://www.youtube.com/watch?v=dYMAD_L2kkM`). He has been actively involved in design and development of solutions using Node.js as a tech stack. Some of the solutions he has contributed to include a social media platform (`https://flikstak.com`) and an LMS adaptor at CLKS.

Sandeep enjoys working as a full stack developer and providing complete end-to-end solutions, including UI frameworks such as Ember.js and Node frameworks such as Experss.js, Restify.js, and so on. Apart from daily development activities, he enjoys teaching and discussing things related to Node.js via an instructor-led training website (`http://learnsocial.com`).

**Oddur Sigurdsson** is a full-stack JavaScript developer who's passionate about cutting-edge experiences for the Web and sharing this knowledge with others. After spending time as a teaching fellow at Fullstack Academy, an immersive JavaScript program, he now works at Hoefler & Co. in New York, where he contributes to an array of solutions that provide developers and designers with beautiful typography for the Web.

Many thanks to Mithun Satheesh, Suzanne, and the excellent team at Packt Publishing for giving me the opportunity to contribute to this wonderful book.

# www.PacktPub.com

## Support files, eBooks, discount offers, and more

For support files and downloads related to your book, please visit www.PacktPub.com.

Did you know that Packt offers eBook versions of every book published, with PDF and ePub files available? You can upgrade to the eBook version at www.PacktPub.com and as a print book customer, you are entitled to a discount on the eBook copy. Get in touch with us at service@packtpub.com for more details.

At www.PacktPub.com, you can also read a collection of free technical articles, sign up for a range of free newsletters and receive exclusive discounts and offers on Packt books and eBooks.

https://www2.packtpub.com/books/subscription/packtlib

Do you need instant solutions to your IT questions? PacktLib is Packt's online digital book library. Here, you can search, access, and read Packt's entire library of books.

## Why subscribe?

- Fully searchable across every book published by Packt
- Copy and paste, print, and bookmark content
- On demand and accessible via a web browser

## Free access for Packt account holders

If you have an account with Packt at www.PacktPub.com, you can use this to access PacktLib today and view 9 entirely free books. Simply use your login credentials for immediate access.

# Table of Contents

# Preface

Node.js and MongoDB are quickly becoming very popular tech stacks for the Web. Powered by Google's V8 engine, Node.js caters to easily building fast, scalable network applications while MongoDB is the perfect fit as a scalable, high-performance, open source NoSQL database solution. Using these two technologies together, web applications can be built quickly and easily and deployed to the cloud with very little difficulty.

The book will begin by introducing you to the groundwork needed to set up the development environment. Here, you will quickly run through the steps necessary to get the main application server up and running. Then, you will see how to use Node.js to connect to a MongoDB database and perform data manipulations.

From here on, the book will take you through integration with third-party tools for interaction with web apps. It then moves on to show you how to use controllers and view models to generate reusable code that will reduce development time. Toward the end of the book, we will cover tests to properly execute the code and some popular frameworks for developing web applications.

By the end of the book, you will have a running web application developed with MongoDB and Node.js along with their popular frameworks.

## What this book covers

*Chapter 1*, *Welcome to JavaScript in Full Stack*, introduces you to Node.js and the advantages of writing Javascript on the backend. In addition to this, it will explain the overall architecture of the application you are going to build using this book.

*Chapter 2*, *Getting Up and Running*, explains how to set up the development environments for Node.js and MongoDB. You will also be verifying that everything is set up properly by writing a sample app and running it.

*Chapter 3*, *Node and MongoDB Basics*, teaches you about the fundamental concepts of JavaScript, Node.js, and MongoDB in this chapter. It will introduce you to NodeJS and the various concepts around it, as well as MongoDB and its basic shell for CRUD operations.

*Chapter 4*, *Introducing Express.js*, introduces you to the Express framework and its various components It also walks you through how you will be organizing the basic application you are building with this framework. It will give you a detailed overview of the MVC components of Express.js too.

*Chapter 5*, *Templating with Handlebars*, introduces you to the concept of using a templating engine and handlebars. Also, it shows you how to use handlebars in your application as a templating engine.

*Chapter 6*, *Controllers and View Models*, shows you how to organize the code for the sample application you build into the controllers and views of Express. It will introduce you to the MVC concepts indirectly via introducing the need of separating the code into various modules and utilizing the Express framework.

*Chapter 7*, *Persisting Data with MongoDB*, shows you how to connect to the MongoDB server from the Node.js application you are building. It will also introduce you to the concept of ODM, the most popular one being Mongoose.

*Chapter 8*, *Creating a RESTful API*, introduces you to RESTful APIs. Also, it shows you the importance of RESTful wrapper for the application. Then, it will teach you how to can change the current application to a REST API based application.

*Chapter 9*, *Testing Your Code*, shows you why you need testing incorporated with your application and also what you should keep in mind for the testability of the code written.

*Chapter 10*, *Deploying with Cloud-Based Services*, discusses the options for hosting the Node.js MongoDB application you are building. It also compares the various PaaS solutions available in the market.

*Chapter 11*, *Single-Page Applications with Popular Frontend Frameworks*, discusses Single Page Applications. Also, you will analyze the popular frontend frameworks available. You will have a look at other frontend aspects such as the automation tools and transpilers available.

*Chapter 12*, *Popular Node.js Web Frameworks*, covers the various web frameworks available on Node.js, other than Express, which you will be using to build the application in this book. You will analyze various web frameworks such as Meteor, Sails, Koa, Hapi, and Flatiron.

# What you need for this book

You will need:

- A computer running OS X, Windows, or Linux
- Samba 4.x Server software

# Who this book is for

This book is designed for JavaScript developers of any skill level that want to get up and running using Node.js and MongoDB to build full-featured web applications. A basic understanding of JavaScript and HTML is the only requirement for this book.

# Conventions

In this book, you will find a number of text styles that distinguish between different kinds of information. Here are some examples of these styles and an explanation of their meaning.

Code words in text, database table names, folder names, filenames, file extensions, pathnames, dummy URLs, user input, and Twitter handles are shown as follows: "The function that actually logs Three is known as a callback to the setTimeout function."

A block of code is set as follows:

```
console.log('One');
console.log('Two');
setTimeout(function() {
    console.log('Three');
}, 2000);
console.log('Four');
console.log('Five');
```

When we wish to draw your attention to a particular part of a code block, the relevant lines or items are set in bold:

```
<div class="panel panel-default">
    <div class="panel-heading">
        <h3 class="panel-title">
            Newest Images
        </h3>
    </div>
```

```
<div class="panel-body">
    {{#each images}}
        <div class="col-md-4 text-center" style="padding-bottom:
1em;"><a href="/images/{{ uniqueId }}"><img src="/public/upload/
{{filename}}" alt="{{title}}" style="width: 175px; height: 175px;"
class="img-thumbnail"></a></div>
    {{/each}}
    </div>
</div>
```

Any command-line input or output is written as follows:

```
$ command -parameters -etc
```

**New terms** and **important words** are shown in bold. Words that you see on the screen, for example, in menus or dialog boxes, appear in the text like this: " You should see **The image:index controller testing123** on the screen!"

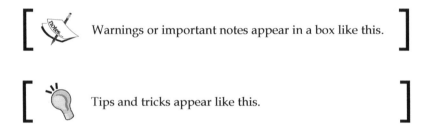

Warnings or important notes appear in a box like this.

Tips and tricks appear like this.

# Reader feedback

Feedback from our readers is always welcome. Let us know what you think about this book—what you liked or disliked. Reader feedback is important for us as it helps us develop titles that you will really get the most out of.

To send us general feedback, simply e-mail feedback@packtpub.com, and mention the book's title in the subject of your message.

If there is a topic that you have expertise in and you are interested in either writing or contributing to a book, see our author guide at www.packtpub.com/authors.

# Customer support

Now that you are the proud owner of a Packt book, we have a number of things to help you to get the most from your purchase.

# Downloading the example code

You can download the example code files from your account at http://www.packtpub.com for all the Packt Publishing books you have purchased. If you purchased this book elsewhere, you can visit http://www.packtpub.com/support and register to have the files e-mailed directly to you.

# Errata

Although we have taken every care to ensure the accuracy of our content, mistakes do happen. If you find a mistake in one of our books—maybe a mistake in the text or the code—we would be grateful if you could report this to us. By doing so, you can save other readers from frustration and help us improve subsequent versions of this book. If you find any errata, please report them by visiting http://www.packtpub.com/submit-errata, selecting your book, clicking on the **Errata Submission Form** link, and entering the details of your errata. Once your errata are verified, your submission will be accepted and the errata will be uploaded to our website or added to any list of existing errata under the Errata section of that title.

To view the previously submitted errata, go to https://www.packtpub.com/books/content/support and enter the name of the book in the search field. The required information will appear under the **Errata** section.

# Piracy

Piracy of copyrighted material on the Internet is an ongoing problem across all media. At Packt, we take the protection of our copyright and licenses very seriously. If you come across any illegal copies of our works in any form on the Internet, please provide us with the location address or website name immediately so that we can pursue a remedy.

Please contact us at copyright@packtpub.com with a link to the suspected pirated material.

We appreciate your help in protecting our authors and our ability to bring you valuable content.

# Questions

If you have a problem with any aspect of this book, you can contact us at questions@packtpub.com, and we will do our best to address the problem.

# 1

# Welcome to JavaScript in the Full Stack

What an exciting time to be a JavaScript developer! What was once only considered a language to add enhancements and widgets to a web page has since evolved into its own fully-fledged ecosystem. As of the beginning of 2015, it stands as the second most popular language in terms of questions tagged on stack overflow, next to only Java, with around a million questions tagged on it. There are tons of frameworks and environments to make it possible to run JavaScript almost anywhere. I believe Atwood's law says it best:

> *"Anything that can be written in JavaScript will eventually be written in JavaScript!"*

While this quote dates back to 2007, it's never been more true than today. Not only can you use JavaScript to develop a complete single-page application such as Gmail, but you will also see how we can achieve the following projects with JavaScript in the coming chapters of the book:

- Completely power the backend using Node.js and Express.js
- Persist data with a powerful document oriented database such as MongoDB
- Write dynamic HTML pages using Handlebars.js
- Deploy your entire project to the cloud using services such as Heroku and **Amazon Web Services (AWS)**

With the introduction of Node.js, JavaScript has officially gone in a direction that was never even possible before. Now you can use JavaScript on the server and you can also use it to develop full-scale, enterprise-level applications. When you combine this with the power of MongoDB and its JSON-powered data, you can work with JavaScript in every layer of your application.

Let's quickly go through some basic concepts of Node.js and MongoDB, which would be helpful for you to follow the rest of the chapters in this book.

# A short introduction to Node.js

One of the most important things that people get confused about while getting introduced to Node.js is to understand what exactly it is. Is it a different language altogether, is it just a framework on top of it, or is it something else? Node.js is definitely not a new language, and it is not just a framework on JavaScript. It can be considered as a runtime environment for JavaScript built on top of Google's V8 engine. So, it provides us with a context where we can write JavaScript code on any platform where Node.js can be installed. Anywhere!

Now a bit about its history! Back in 2009, Ryan Dahl gave a presentation at JSConf that changed JavaScript forever. During his presentation, he introduced Node.js to the JavaScript community. After a roughly 45-minute talk, he concluded it, receiving a standing ovation from the audience in the process. He was inspired to write Node. js after he saw a simple file upload progress bar on Flickr, the image-sharing site. Realizing that the site was going about the whole process the wrong way, he decided that there had to be a better solution.

Now let's go through the features of Node.js, which makes it unique from other server-side programming languages.

# The advantage that the V8 engine brings in

The V8 engine was developed by Google and was open sourced in 2008. As we all know, JavaScript is an interpreted language and it will not be as efficient as a compiled language, as each line of code gets interpreted one by one while the code gets executed. The V8 engine brings in an efficient model here, where the JavaScript code will be compiled into machine-level code and the executions will happen on the compiled code instead of interpreting the JavaScript. But even though Node. js is using the V8 engine, Joyent, which is the company that is maintaining Node. js development, it does not always update the V8 engine to the latest versions that Google actively releases. This has led to the new branch named io.js, which we will discuss later in this chapter.

# Node.js is single threaded!

You might be asking, how does a single threaded model help? Typical PHP, ASP. NET, Ruby, or Java-based servers follow a model where each client request results in the instantiation of a new thread or even a process. When it comes to Node. js, requests are run on the same thread with even shared resources. A common question that is often asked is what will be the advantage of using such a model? To understand this, we should understand the problem that Node.js tries to resolve. It tries to do asynchronous processing on a single thread to provide more performance and scalability for applications that are supposed to handle too much web traffic. Imagine web applications that handle millions of concurrent requests; if the server makes a new thread for handling each request that comes in, it will consume a lot of resources and we would end up trying to add more and more servers to increase the scalability of the application. The single threaded asynchronous processing model has its advantage in the previous context, and you can process much more concurrent requests with less number of server-side resources. However, there is a downside to this approach; Node (by default) will not utilize the number of CPU cores available on the server it is running on without using extra modules like pm2.

The point that Node.js is single threaded doesn't mean that it doesn't use threads internally. It is just that the developer and the execution context that the code has exposure to have no control over the threading model internally used by Node.js.

If you are new to the concept of threads and process, we would suggest you to go through some preliminary articles about these topics. There are plenty of YouTube videos as well on the same topic. The following reference could be used as a starting point:

```
http://www.cs.ucsb.edu/~rich/class/cs170/notes/
IntroThreads/
```

# Non-blocking asynchronous execution

One of the most powerful features of Node is that it is event-driven and asynchronous. So how does an asynchronous model work? Imagine you have a block of code and at some *nth* line you have an operation that is time consuming. So what happens to the lines that follow the *nth* line while this code gets executed? In normal synchronous programming models, the lines that follow the *nth* line will have to wait till the operation at that line completes. An asynchronous model handles this case differently. To handle this scenario in an asynchronous approach, we need to segment the code that follows the *nth* line into two sections. The first section is dependent on the result of the operation at the *nth* line and the second section is independent of the result.

We wrap the dependent code in a function with the result of the operation as its parameter, and register it as a callback to the operation on its success. Once the operation completes, the callback function will be triggered with its result. Meanwhile, we can continue executing the result-independent lines without waiting for the result. In this scenario, the execution is never blocked for a process to complete. It just goes on with callback functions registered on each ones completion. Simply put, you assign a callback function to an operation, and when Node determines that the completion event has been fired, it will execute your callback function at that moment.

We can look at an example to understand the asynchronous nature in detail:

```
console.log('One');
console.log('Two');
setTimeout(function() {
    console.log('Three');
}, 2000);
console.log('Four');
console.log('Five');
```

In a typical synchronous programming language, executing the preceding code will yield the following output:

```
One
Two
... (2 second delay) ...
Three
Four
Five
```

However, in an asynchronous approach, the following output is seen:

```
One
Two
Four
Five
... (approx. 2 second delay) ...
Three
```

The function that actually logs Three is known as a callback to the setTimeout function.

 If you are still interested in learning more about asynchronous models and the callback concept in JavaScript, **Mozilla Developer Network (MDN)** has many articles that explain these concepts in detail.

# npm – the Node Package Manager

Writing applications with Node is really enjoyable when you realize the sheer wealth of information and tools at your disposal! Using Node's built-in package manager npm, you can find literally tens of thousands of modules that can be installed and used within your application with just a few keystrokes! One of the reasons for the biggest success of Node.js is npm, which is one of the best package managers out there with a very minute learning curve. If this is the first ever package manager that you are getting exposed to, then you should consider yourself lucky!

On a regular month, npm handles more than a billion downloads and it has around 150,000 packages currently available for you to download. You can view the library of available modules by visiting www.npmjs.com. Downloading and installing any module within your application is as simple as executing the npm install package command. Have you written a module that you want to share with the world? You can package it up using npm and upload it to the public www.npmjs.org registry just as easily! If you are not sure how a module you installed works, the source code is right there in your projects' node_modules/ folder waiting to be explored!!

 Package versions of modules in npm follow semantic versioning, such as major.minor.patch order.

# Sharing and reusing JavaScript

While you develop web applications, you will always end up doing the validations for your UI both at the client and server sides, as the client-side validations are required for better UI experience and server-side validations are needed for better security of app. Think about two different languages in action: you will have the same logic implemented in both the server and client side. With Node.js, you can think of sharing the common function between server and client, reducing the code duplication to a large extent.

Ever worked on optimizing the load time for client-side components of your Single-Page Application (SPA) loaded from template engines such as underscore? You would end up thinking about a way we could share the rendering of templates in both server and client at the same time—some call it hybrid templating. Node.js resolves the context of duplication of client templates better than any other server-side technologies, just because we can use the same JS templating framework and the templates both at server and client.

If you are taking this point lightly, the problem it resolves is not just the issue of reusing validations or templates on the server and client. Think about an SPA being built; you will need to implement the subsets of server-side models in the client-side MV* framework also. Now, think about the templates, models, and controller subsets being shared on both client and server. We are solving a higher scenario of code redundancy.

# Not just for building web servers!

Node.js is not just to write JavaScript in the server-side. Yes, we have discussed this point earlier. Node.js sets up the environment for the JavaScript code to work anywhere it can be installed. It can be a powerful solution to create command-line tools as well as fully-featured, locally run applications that have nothing to do with the Web or a browser. Grunt.js is a great example of a Node-powered command-line tool that many web developers use daily to automate everyday tasks such as build processes, compiling CoffeeScript, launching Node servers, running tests, and more.

In addition to command-line tools, Node is increasingly popular among the hardware crowd with the Node bots movement. Johnny-Five and Cylon.js are two popular Node libraries that exist to provide a framework to work with robotics. Just search on YouTube for Node robots and you will see a lot of examples. Also, there is a chance that you might be using a text editor developed on Node.js. GitHub's open source editor named Atom, which is hugely popular, is an example.

# Real-time web application with Socket.io

One of the important reasons behind the origin of Node.js was to support real-time web applications. Node.js has a couple of frameworks built for real-time web applications, which are hugely popular: Socket.io and sock.js. These frameworks make it very simple to build instant collaboration-based applications such as Google Drive and Mozilla's together.js. Before the introduction of WebSockets in the modern browsers, this was achieved via long polling, which was not a great solution for real-time experience. While WebSockets is a feature that is only supported in modern browsers, Socket.io acts as a framework, which also features seamless fallback implementations for legacy browsers.

 If you need to understand more on the use of WebSockets in applications, here's a good resource on MDN that you can explore:

```
https://developer.mozilla.org/en-US/docs/Web/
API/WebSockets_API/Writing_WebSocket_client_
applications
```

# Networking and file IO

In addition to the powerful non-blocking asynchronous nature of Node, it also has very robust networking and filesystem tools available via its core modules. With Node's networking modules, you can create server and client applications that accept network connections and communicate via streams and pipes.

# The origin of io.js

As we mentioned earlier in this chapter, io.js is nothing but a fork of Node.js created to be updated with the latest development on both V8 and other developments in the JS community. Joyent was taking care of the releases in Node.js and the process that was followed in taking care of the release management of Node.js lacked an open governance model. It leads to scenarios where the newer developments in V8 as well as the JS community were not incorporated into its releases. For example, if you want to write JavaScript using the latest **EcmaScript6** (**ES6**) features, you will have to run it in the harmony mode. Joyent is surely not to be blamed for this, as they were more concerned about stability of Node.js releases than frequent updates in the stack. This led to the io.js fork, which is kept up to date with the latest JavaScript and V8 updates. So, it's better to keep your eyes on the releases on both Node and io.js to be up to date with the Node.js world.

# A simple server with Node.js

To see an example of just how lightweight Node can be, let's take a look at some sample code that starts up an HTTP server and sends **Hello World** to a browser:

```
var http = require('http');
http.createServer(function (req, res) {
  res.writeHead(200, {'Content-Type': 'text/plain'});
  res.end('Hello World\n');
}).listen(8080, 'localhost');
console.log('Server running at http://localhost:8080');
```

A few basic lines of code are all it takes to write a complete Node application. Running it with a simple Node `app.js` command will launch an HTTP server that is listening on port 8080. Point any browser to `http://localhost:8080`, and you will see the simple output **Hello World** on your screen! While this sample app doesn't actually do anything useful, it should give you a glimpse of the kind of power you will have while writing web applications using Node.js. If you don't have the initial Node.js development environment set up, we will discuss it in the next chapter.

# When to use Node.js?

You should have heard of this proverb:

*"If all you have is a hammer, everything looks like a nail!"*

This makes a lot of sense in this context. Node.js is not a technology to depend on all the application problems that you intend to solve and if not chosen wisely, the decision will backfire. Node.js is well suited for applications that are expected to handle a huge amount of concurrent connections. Also, it should be noted that it is most suited for applications where each incoming request requires very few CPU cycles. This means that if you intend to do computation-intensive tasks on requests, it will end up blocking the event loop—thereby impacting other requests concurrently processed by the web server. Node.js is well suited for real-time web applications, such as chat rooms, collaboration tools, online games, and so on. So when deciding whether to use or not use Node.js, we should analyze the application context seriously and figure out whether Node.js really suits the context of the application.

It is quite hard to debate over the use cases of Node.js in a detailed manner. However, the following stackoverflow thread does this so effectively and we strongly recommend you to go though the answers on this post if you are more interested in the use cases of Node.js: http://stackoverflow.com/questions/5062614/how-to-decide-when-to-use-node-js

As we have briefly gone through the features and concept of Node.js, now let's look into the NoSQL and MongoDB side.

# The NoSQL movement

Let's start by exploring the answers to the question, what exactly is a NoSQL database? NoSQL is a common term for database technologies that deviate from the traditional **Relational Database Management System (RDBMS)** concepts. The common reason for these database solutions to deviate from RDBMS database standards is to achieve and set a better standard of availability and partitioning capabilities than traditional RDBMS solutions.

To introduce you to this concept, we should have a look at the Brewer's theorem, which is otherwise known as the CAP theorem:

*"It is impossible for a distributed computer system to simultaneously provide all three of the following guarantees: Consistency, Availability, and Partition tolerance."*

Traditional RDBMS solutions are good at consistency and compromise a little once it comes to providing better availability (data reads) and partitioning capabilities. Most of the NoSQL solutions have been evolved in this direction to achieve better heights in data availability and partitioning.

As this is a common term for any database technology that deviates from the concepts followed by RDBMS solutions such as MySQL, PostgreSQL, and so on, there are various subsets for NoSQL databases. Most popular subsets of NoSQL are document stores, key-value stores, and graph-based database solutions. MongoDB, which is the one we are going to try out, falls in the document store category. There are many more NoSQL solutions available in the market apart from MongoDB, such as Cassandra, Redis, Neo4j, Hbase, and so on.

# A short introduction to MongoDB

As we discussed in the previous paragraph, MongoDB falls into the document store category of NoSQL databases. MongoDB is being actively developed by 10gen, which was later renamed to MongoDB I.inc. MongoDB is open source and its source is available on various platforms such as GitHub.

# Features of MongoDB

One of the most important reasons for the popularity of MongoDB is that it is a JSON-friendly database. It means that documents are stored and retrieved from MongoDB as JavaScript objects. Internally, this JSON data gets converted to BSON format while getting persisted to the system. So, this gives an extreme flexibility where we can use the same data format from client to server and eventually to the database.

A typical document (record) in a MongoDB collection (table) might look like the following code:

```
$ mongo
> db.contacts.find({email: 'jason@kroltech.com'}).pretty()
{
    "email" : "jason@kroltech.com",
    "phone" : "123-456-7890",
    "gravatar" : "751e957d48e31841ff15d8fa0f1b0acf",
    "_id" : ObjectId("52fad824392f58ac2452c992"),
    "name" : {
        "first" : "Jason",
        "last" : "Krol"
    },
    "__v" : 0
}
```

Another important feature of MongoDB is its schemaless nature. With a relational database, you are required to define (ahead of time) the exact structure of the data being stored, which is termed as the schema. This means that you must have defined the exact number of columns, length, and data type for every field in a table, and that each field must always match that exact set of criteria. Mongo provides a flexible nature where the documents that you store into the database need not follow any schema unless the developer enforces it through the application level. This makes MongoDB a great fit for Agile-based development, as you could carry out modifications on the application schema on fly.

Other than the JavaScript-friendly nature, one other resemblance of MongoDB with Node.js is that it is also designed with highly concurrent applications with heavy read operations in mind.

MongoDB also introduces the concept of sharding, which makes it possible to scale the database horizontally as well as vertically. If the application owner needs to increase the database capabilities, they could add up more machines into the stack. This is a cheaper option compared to investing on RAM of a single machine, which will be the case in RDBMS solutions.

All the advantages that we discussed come with some impact on the consistency, as MongoDB does not strictly adhere to the RDBMS standards like ACID transactions. Also, if you end up creating a data model that might need too many JOIN operations, then MongoDB won't make a good fit as it is not designed with too many aggregations even though the aggregations are possible via the MongoDB aggregation framework. MongoDB may or may not be the right solution for your application. You should truly weigh the pros and cons of each technology before making a decision to determine which technology is right for you.

# Node and MongoDB in the wild

Both Node and MongoDB are extremely popular and active in the development community. This is true for enterprises as well. Some of the biggest names in the Fortune 500 space have fully embraced Node to power their web applications. This is due in large part to the asynchronous nature of Node, which makes it a great alternative for high traffic, high I/O applications such as e-commerce websites and mobile applications.

Here's just a small list of some big companies that are working with Node:

- PayPal
- LinkedIn
- eBay

- Walmart
- Yahoo!
- Microsoft
- Dow Jones
- Uber
- New York Times

MongoDB's use in the enterprise sector is equally as impressive and widespread, with an increasing number of companies adopting the leading NoSQL database server. Here's just a small list of some big companies that are working with MongoDB:

- Cisco
- Craigslist Inc.
- Forbes
- FourSquare
- Intuit
- McAfee
- MTV
- MetLife
- Shutterfly
- Under Armour

# What to expect from this book

The remainder of this book is going to be a guided tour that walks you through creating a complete data-driven website. The website we create will feature almost every aspect of a typical large-scale web development project. The app will be developed using a popular Node.js framework called Express, and it will persist data using MongoDB. In the first few chapters, we will cover the groundwork involved in getting the core of the server up and serving content. This includes configuring your environment so you are up and running with Node and MongoDB, and a basic introduction to the core concepts of both technologies. Then, we will write a web server from scratch powered by ExpressJS, which will handle serving all of the necessary files for the website. From there, we will work with the Handlebars template engine to serve both static and dynamic HTML web pages. Diving deeper, we will make the application persistent by adding a data layer where the records for the website will be saved and retrieved via a MongoDB server.

We will cover writing a RESTful API so that other people can interact with your application. Finally, we will go into the details to see how to write and execute tests for all of your code. A summary is given in the following figure:

Wrapping up, we will take a brief detour as we examine some popular, merging frontend technologies that are becoming increasingly popular while writing SPAs. These technologies include Backbone.js, Angular, and Ember.js.

Last but not least, we will go into details about how to deploy your new website to the Internet using popular cloud-based hosting services such as Heroku and Amazon Web Services.

**Downloading the example code**

You can download the example code files from your account at http://www.packtpub.com for all the Packt Publishing books you have purchased. If you purchased this book elsewhere, you can visit http://www.packtpub.com/support and register to have the files e-mailed directly to you.

# Summary

In this chapter, we reviewed what is to be expected throughout the rest of this book. We discussed the amazing current state of JavaScript and how it can be used to power the full stack of a web application. Not that you needed any convincing in the first place, but I hope you're excited and ready to get started writing web applications using Node.js and MongoDB!

Next up, we will set up your development environment and get you up and running with Node, MongoDB, and npm as well as write and launch a quick Node app that uses MongoDB!

# 2
# Getting Up and Running

In this chapter, we will cover the necessary steps to set up your development environment. These will include the following:

1. Installing Node.js on your machine
2. Installing MongoDB on your machine
3. Verifying whether everything is set up properly

Follow these sections carefully, as we need the development environment to be up and running before we jump into the chapters where we dive into actual coding. For the remainder of this book, it's going to be assumed that you are using either a Mac with OS X, Linux, or Windows 7 / Windows 8. You will also need super user and/or administrator privileges on the computer, as you will be installing the Node and MongoDB server. The code and examples after this chapter will all be OS agnostic and should work in any environment, assuming you have taken the steps I have outlined earlier to be prepared ahead of time.

You will need a proper text editor to write and edit the code. While any text editor you choose will serve this purpose, choosing a better text editor will hugely improve your productivity. Sublime Text 3 appears to be the most popular text editor regardless of the platform at this moment. It is a simple, lightweight editor with unlimited plugins made available by developers around the world. If you are on a Windows machine, then Notepad++ is also a good candidate. Also, there are JavaScript-based open source editors such as Atom and Brackets, which are also worth a try.

Finally, you're going to need access to the command line. Linux and Mac have access to the command line via the Terminal program. A great alternative on the Mac is iTerm2 (`http://iterm2.com`). For Windows, the default command-line program works, but isn't the best. A great alternative there is ConEmu (`http://conemu.codeplex.com`). For the remainder of this book, any time I reference a command line or command prompt, it will look like the following:

```
$ command -parameters -etc
```

# Installing Node.js

The Node.js installer can be easily obtained by visiting the official Node website and accessing the downloads section. Once there, be sure to download the correct version depending on your OS and CPU (32 bit or 64 bit). As an alternative, you can also use OS-specific package managers to install this. Depending on the OS you are using, just jump into the specific subsection below to get more details on the steps to be followed.

 You can jump into the Node.js download sections by following the link `http://nodejs.org/download`.

# Mac OS X

There is a universal installer available from the Node website specifically for OS X.

We need to follow these steps to install Node.js on a Mac:

1. Visit the download page of the Node.js official website as mentioned earlier and click on the Mac OS X installer, which is independent of the processor type (32 or 64 bit).

2. Once the download is complete, double-click on the `.pkg` file, which will launch the Node installer.

3.  Proceed through each step of the wizard that should be fairly self-explanatory.

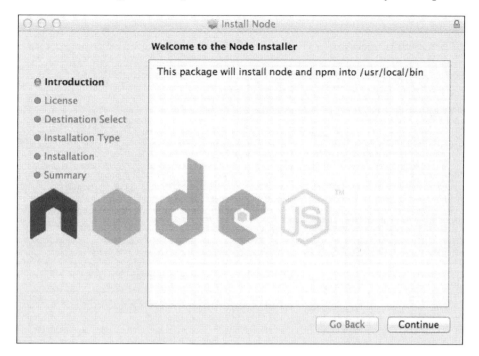

 Also, note that if you have any of the OS X package managers installed, then you don't need to manually download the installer. You may install Node.js via the respective package manager.

You may install Node.js via the respective package manager:

- Installation using Homebrew

  ```
  brew install node
  ```

- Installation using Mac ports

  ```
  port install nodejs
  ```

 The installation of Node.js via either an installer or via the package managers will include npm alongside. So, we don't need to install it separately.

# Windows

To install Node.js on Windows, we will follow these steps:

1. We need to determine your processor type, 32 or 64 bit. You can do this by executing the following command at the command prompt:

   ```
   $ wmic os get osarchitecture
   ```

   The output is as follows:

   ```
   OSArchiecture

   64-bit
   ```

2. Download the installer depending on the result of this command.

3. Once the download is complete, double-click on the `.msi` file, which will launch the Node installer.

4. Proceed through each step of the wizard.

5. When you get to the custom setup screen, you should notice that the installation wizard will install not only the Node.js runtime, but also the npm package manager, and configure a PATH variable.

6. So once the installation is done, Node and npm can be executed from any folder via the command line.

Also, if you have any of the Windows package managers installed, then you don't need to manually download the installer. You may install Node.js via the respective package manager:

- Using chocolatey

```
cinst nodejs.install
```

- Using scoop

```
scoop install nodejs
```

# Linux

Because there are so many different flavors and distributions of Linux available, installing Node isn't quite as straightforward. However, if you're running Linux to begin with, then you are more than aware of this and probably comfortable with a few extra steps.

Joyent has an excellent wiki on how to install Node on Linux using the many different package manager options available. This covers almost all the popular deb and rpm based package managers. You can read that wiki by visiting:

```
https://github.com/joyent/node/wiki/Installing-Node.js-via-package-
manager
```

For Ubuntu 12.04 and above as an example, the steps to install Node would be as follows:

```
$ sudo apt-get update
$ sudo apt-get install python-software-properties python g++ make
$ sudo add-apt-repository ppa:chris-lea/node.js
$ sudo apt-get update
$ sudo apt-get install nodejs nodejs-dev npm
```

Once these steps have been completed, both Node and npm should be installed on your system.

# Testing whether Node.js is installed properly

Now that Node has been installed on your system, let's run a quick test to ensure everything is working properly.

Access a command line via your terminal program and execute the following command:

```
$ node --version
v0.10.35

$ npm --version
2.1.14
```

Assuming that your Node installation was successful, you should see the version number that was installed as an output on the screen right below the command you executed.

 Note that your version numbers will most likely be more recent than those printed earlier.

You can also launch the Node `repl`, a command-line shell that lets you execute JavaScript directly:

```
$ node
> console.log('Hello world!')
Hello World!
Undefined
[press Ctrl-C twice to exit]
```

# Online documentation

You'll want to be sure to point your browser to the online documentation for Node and bookmark it, as it will undoubtedly become a resource that you will want to access on a regular basis. It is not mandatory that you should go through each and every section of it, but once you start writing code in Node.js, you will need to refer to this document frequently to understand more on the `apis` exposed by Node.js. The document is available at: `http://nodejs.org/api/`.

Also, check out the npm registry available at `http://npmjs.com` where you can find tens of thousands of modules available for Node developers.

# Installing MongoDB

MongoDB can also be easily downloaded by visiting the official MongoDB website and accessing the downloads section from http://www.mongodb.org/downloads.

Once there, be sure to download the correct version depending on your OS and CPU (32 or 64 bit). For Windows users, you can opt to download the MSI installer file, which will make the installation much simpler.

 Depending on the version of MongoDB you downloaded, you will want to replace <version> in the following sections with the appropriate version number that matches your file.

# Mac OS X installation instructions

If you are using the Homebrew package manager, MongoDB can be installed using the following two commands:

```
$ brew update
$ brew install mongoDB
```

The remainder of this chapter assumes you are not using Homebrew and need to install MongoDB manually. If you are installing MongoDB via Homebrew, you can proceed directly to the testing MongoDB installation section.

After completing the download, open and extract the contents of the .tgz file. You will want to move the extracted contents to a destination folder /mongodb. You can do this either via the Finder or the command line, whichever you prefer, as follows:

```
$ mkdir -p /mongodb
$ cd ~/Downloads
$ cp -R -n mongodb-osx-x86_64-2.4.9/ mongodb
```

You will want to ensure that the locations of the MongoDB binaries are configured in your environment PATH so that you can execute mongod and mongo from any working directory. To do this, edit the .profile file in your home folder (~/) and append the location for MongoDB to it. Your .profile file should look something like the following:

```
export PATH=~/bin:/some/of/my/stuff:/more/stuff:/mongodb/bin:$PATH
```

If you don't have this line or are missing `.bash_profile` completely, you can create one easily by executing the following command:

```
$ touch .bash_profile
$ [edit] .bash_profile
export PATH=$PATH:/mongodb/bin
```

You will more than likely have a lot more than what I have in the preceding lines of code. The important thing is that you append `:/mongodb/bin` before the `$PATH` at the end. The `:` is a delimiter between different paths (so it's likely that you will be adding your path to the end of an existing list but before the trailing `$PATH`).

 Here, `mongod` refers to the MongoDB server instance that you need to invoke and `mongo` refers to the Mongo shell, which will be the console through which you will be interacting with the database.

Next, you need to create a default `data` folder that MongoDB will use to store all data documents. From the command line, execute the following:

```
$ mkdir -p /data/db
$ chown `id -u` /data/db
```

Once the files have been properly extracted to the `/mongodb` folder and the data folders created, you can now start the MongoDB database server by executing the following command from the command line:

```
$ mongod
```

This should dump a bunch of log statements while the server starts up, but ultimately ends with:

```
Sun Mar 16 12:26:58.885 [initandlisten] waiting for connections on
port 27017
```

That's it! Your MongoDB server is up and running. You can type `Ctrl-C` to cancel and shut down the server.

# Windows 7 / Windows 8 installation instructions

After completing the download, the MongoDB website will automatically redirect you to a landing page with a link to a Windows Quick Start guide at `http://docs.mongodb.org/manual/tutorial/install-mongodb-on-windows/`.

It is highly recommended that you follow that guide, as it will be the most up to date and will generally be more detailed than what I can provide here.

Extract the ZIP file that was downloaded to the root `c:\` destination. By default, this should extract a folder named `mongodb-osx-x86_64-2.4.9`. Depending on the tool you are using for extraction, you can leave this as is or change the destination folder to simply `mongodb`. If you don't change the destination during extraction, you should rename the folder once complete. Either way, be sure that the files that are extracted reside in a folder named `c:\mongodb`.

Next, you need to create a default `data` folder that MongoDB will use to store all data documents. Using Windows Explorer or Command Prompt, whichever you are most comfortable with, create the folder `c:\data` and then `c:\data\db` by using the following command:

```
$ md data
```

```
$ md data\db
```

Once the files have been properly extracted to the `c:\mongodb` folder and both the data folders subsequently created, you can now start the MongoDB database server by executing the following command from a prompt:

```
$ c:\mongodb\bin\mongod.exe
```

This should dump a bunch of log statements while the server starts up, but will ultimately end with:

```
Sun Mar 16 16:58:05.182 [initandlisten] waiting for connections on
port 27017
```

That's it! Your MongoDB server is up and running. You can type `Ctrl-C` to cancel and shutdown the server.

# Linux installation instructions

Once again, we will face a slightly more challenging installation process with Linux versus Windows or Mac. The official website `http://docs.mongodb.org/manual/administration/install-on-linux/` has great instructions on how to install MongoDB on a number of different Linux distributions.

We will continue to use Ubuntu as our flavor of choice and use the APT package manager for the installation.

```
$ sudo apt-key adv --keyserver hkp://keyserver.ubuntu.com:80 --recv
7F0CEB10
```

```
$ echo 'deb http://downloads-distro.mongodb.org/repo/ubuntu-upstart
dist 10gen' | sudo tee /etc/apt/sources.list.d/mongodb.list
```

```
$ sudo apt-get update
```

```
$ sudo apt-get install mongodb-10gen
```

Once these steps are completed, MongoDB should be installed and ready to run on your system. Execute the following command in the terminal to be sure. This gets the MongoDB daemon up and running, listening for connections:

```
$ mongod
```

```
Sun Mar 16 12:04:20 [initandlisten] waiting for connections on port
27017
```

Success! Your MongoDB server is up and running. You can type Ctrl-C to cancel and shut down the server.

> It's important to note that as you are performing local development on your development machine and not a production server, you don't need the MongoDB server to always be up and running. This will be an unnecessary strain on your machine for the majority of the time you're not developing against the server. Because of this, throughout the remainder of this book it will always be a requirement that you manually launch the server every time you launch code that expects to connect to a MongoDB server. If you want, you can certainly configure MongoDB to run locally as a service and be always up, but the instructions to do so are beyond the scope of this chapter.

# Confirming successful MongoDB installation

Now that MongoDB has been installed on your system, let's run a quick test to ensure everything is working properly.

Access a command line via your terminal program and execute the following command:

```
$ mongod --version
```

```
db version v2.4.8
```

```
Sun Mar 16 14:17:18.280 git version: a123b456c789d012e345f678
```

```
$ mongo --version
```

```
Mongod shell version 2.4.8
```

Assuming that your MongoDB installation was successful, you should see the version number that was installed as an output on the screen right below the command you executed.

 Note that your version numbers will most likely be more recent than those printed earlier.

## Bookmark the online documentation

You'll want to be sure to point your browser to the online documentation for MongoDB available at `http://docs.mongodb.org/manual/` and bookmark it as it will undoubtedly become a resource that you will want to access on a regular basis.

# Writing your first app

Now that you have everything installed and confirmed that it's all working, you can write your first quick app that will use both Node and MongoDB. This will prove that your environment is good to go, and you're ready to get started. In addition, it will give you a brief taste of the world of Node and MongoDB development! Don't worry if a lot of the following is confusing or just doesn't make sense to you—it will all be made clear throughout the rest of the book!

To begin with, we need to create a folder for our application where this application's specific code will reside, as follows:

```
$ mkdir testapp
$ cd testapp
```

## Creating the sample application

The `testapp` folder that we just created will be the root of our sample Node application. Even though it's not necessary, it's important and also a best practice that we should create the `package.json` file for our Node app, which will hold the necessary data regarding the application such as its version, name, description and development, and runtime dependencies. This can be done by issuing the following command from the `testapp` folder root:

```
$ npm init
```

This command will follow up by asking you a few questions such as the name and version number of your newly created application. It is not necessary that you fill in all the details in one go, and you can skip the steps by pressing *Enter* and the default values will be entered, which you may update later.

## Getting the dependent modules in place

Before we start to write any Node.js code, we need to get our dependencies in place by using npm. Since this is a basic app, we will be using it to test our Node.js connectivity with the MongoDB server. So, the only dependent module that we need is the native MongoDB client for Node.js. We can easily install that by executing the following command:

```
$ npm install mongodb --save
```

After npm installs the MongoDB driver, you can list the contents of the directory and notice that a new folder was created, node_modules. This is where, surprisingly enough, all Node modules are stored whenever you install them from npm. Inside the node_modules folder should be a single folder named mongodb. Also, you will notice that the package.json file of our sample application will be updated by this new dependency entry.

# Adding the application code

Now, let's write the simple application code to test things out. This app is going to basically connect to our locally running MongoDB server, insert a few records as seed data, and then provide the output on whether or not the data was inserted properly into MongoDB.

You can download a Gist of the code via the URL: http://bit.ly/1JpT8QL.

Using your editor of choice, create a new file named app.js and save it to the application root, which is the testapp folder. Just copy the content of the above Gist on to the app.js file.

# Understanding the code

Now, let's go through and explain what each section of the code is doing.

```
//require the mongoClient from mongodb module
var MongoClient = require('mongodb').MongoClient;
```

The preceding line requires the MongoDB Node driver that we installed via npm. This is the required convention used in Node.js for bringing in external file dependencies to the current file in context. We will explain more about this in the coming chapters.

```
//mongodb configs
var connectionUrl = 'mongodb://localhost:27017/myproject',
    sampleCollection = 'chapters';
```

In the preceding code, we declare the variables for the database server information and collection we want to work with. Here, myproject is the database we want to use and chapters is the collection. In MongoDB, if you reference and try to use a collection that doesn't exist, it will automatically be created.

The next step would be to define some data that we can insert into MongoDB to verify whether everything is fine. So, we create an array of chapters here, which can be inserted into the database and collections we set up in the previous steps:

```
//We need to insert these chapters into mongoDB
var chapters = [{
    'Title': 'Snow Crash',
    'Author': 'Neal Stephenson'
},{
    'Title': 'Snow Crash',
    'Author': 'Neal Stephenson'
}];
```

Now, we can take a look at the rest of the code where we insert this data into the MongoDB database:

```
MongoClient.connect(connectionUrl, function(err, db) {
  console.log("Connected correctly to server");
  // Get some collection
  var collection = db.collection(sampleCollection);
  collection.insert(chapters,function(error,result){
    //here result will contain an array of records inserted
    if(!error) {
      console.log("Success :"+result.ops.length+" chapters
inserted!");
    } else {
      console.log("Some error was encountered!");
    }
    db.close();
  });
});
```

Here, we initiate a connection with the MongoDB server, and if the connection was proper, the db variable will have the connection object that we can use for further operations:

```
MongoClient.connect(url, function(err, db) {
```

Look at the preceding code closely, do you remember something that we learned in *Chapter 1*, *Welcome to JavaScript in the Full Stack*. We are using a callback for the connection call that we are making here. As discussed in the first chapter, this function will be registered as a callback to trigger once the connection attempt is completed. Upon connection completion, this will be triggered with either an error or a db object depending on whether we were able to make proper connectivity or not.

So, if you look at the code in the callback function, we are not checking whether any error was raised in the connection attempt before logging connected correctly to the server. Now, that's your task to add and check while we try to run this app! Take a look at the following code block in this section:

```
var collection = db.collection(sampleCollection);
collection.insert(chapters, function(error, result){
```

This does nothing but use the db object we got in the connection call and get the collection named chapters. Remember that we set that value to sampleCollection at the beginning of the code. Once we get the collection, we make an insert call to put the chapters we have defined in the array chapters. As you can see, this insert call is also done via an asynchronous call by attaching the callback function. This callback function will be triggered once the insert operation is completed by the code residing inside the MongoDB native client, which we required as a dependency.

Next, we will take a look at the code inside the callback function, which we passed to the insert function call.

```
if(!error) {
  console.log("Success :"+result.ops.length+" chapters
            inserted!");
} else {
  console.log("Some error was encountered!");
}
db.close();
```

Here, we process the values passed via the callback to find out whether the insert operation succeeded or not and the data related to the records which have been inserted. So, we check whether there was an error, and, if not, proceed to print the number of records that got inserted. Here, the result array will contain the records that we inserted into MongoDB, if the operation was a success.

Now we can go ahead and try to run this code, as we have understood what it does.

# Launching the sample app

Once you have the complete code saved to `app.js`, it's time to execute it and see what happens. However, before you can launch an app that clearly relies on a connection to MongoDB, you need to first boot up the MongoDB daemon instance:

```
$ mongod
```

 In Windows, if you haven't set a PATH variable for `mongod`, you may need to use the full path while executing MongoDB, which is `c:\mongodb\bin\mongod.exe`. For your needs, the remainder of this book will refer to the `mongod` command, but you may always need to execute the full path in each instance.

Now, to launch the app itself, execute the following command after moving to the root folder where `app.js` is located:

```
$ node app.js
```

When the app first executes, you should see the following:

```
Connected correctly to server
Success :2 chapters inserted!
```

# Checking the actual database

Let's take a quick look at the database itself to see what happened during the execution of the app. Since the server is currently up and running, we can connect to it using the Mongo shell—a command line interface to the MongoDB server. Execute the following commands to connect to the server using Mongo and run a query against the chapters collection. As you can see in the upcoming code, Mongo shell connects to a default database named `test` initially. We need to manually specify the database name to switch to, if its something other than `test`:

```
$ mongo
Mongod shell version: 2.4.8
connecting to: test
> use myproject
> show collections
chapters
system.indexes
> db.chapters.find().pretty()
```

Here `pretty` is used as part of the command to format the result from the `find` command. This is used only in a shell context. It does more of a prettification task for the JSON.

You should see something similar to the following output.

```
{
    'id' : ObjectId("5547e734cdf16a5ca59531a7"),
    'Title': 'Snow Crash',
    'Author': 'Neal Stephenson'
},
{
    'id' : ObjectId("5547e734cdf16a5ca59531a7"),
    'Title': 'Snow Crash',
    'Author': 'Neal Stephenson'
}
```

 If you run the Node app again, the records will be inserted into the Mongo server again. So, if you repeat the command multiple times, the result will have more records in the output. We are not handling this case in this chapter as we intend to have only specific code, which will be simple enough to understand.

# Summary

In this chapter, we took time to make sure your development environment was properly configured with both the Node runtime environment as well as the MongoDB server. After making sure both were properly installed, we wrote a basic app that utilized both technologies. The app connected to a locally running MongoDB server, and inserted sample records.

Now that the tedious but necessary tasks of setup and installation are out of the way, we can move on to some fun and start learning!

In the next chapter, we will review a primer on the JavaScript language and understand the basics of Node. Then we will review the basic CRUD (`create`, `read`, `update`, `delete`) operations with MongoDB using the Mongo shell.

# 3

# Node and MongoDB Basics

Before we dig in and start building a full-blown web application using Node and MongoDB, it's important that we review some of the basics first. This chapter will give you a crash course on the syntax and important topics. It is broken down into two parts, where the first half focuses on JavaScript or Node, and the second half covers MongoDB. You will gain insight into some of the more common and powerful tools available to you, and a lot of sample code will be reviewed to get you up to speed.

In this chapter, we will review the following topics:

- Fundamentals of the JavaScript language
- The basics of Node.js
- Node's package manager, npm
- The basics of MongoDB

By the end of this chapter, you should have a solid understanding of the syntax and how to use both Node and MongoDB. There's a lot to cover, so let's get started.

## A JavaScript primer

As we already know Node.js is not just another language, but JavaScript. The language syntax and tools you are used to while coding JavaScript on the browser will work verbatim on the server. Node.js has additional tools that are only available on the server, but the language and syntax again are the same as JavaScript. I'm assuming you have a general understanding of the basic JavaScript syntax, but I will introduce JavaScript to you with a very brief primer on the language just in case.

In general, JavaScript is a fairly simple language when it comes to syntax, and you only need to know a few important elements.

# Syntax basics

The most basic thing you can do in pretty much any programming language is declare a variable. Unlike most other languages, JavaScript is a dynamically typed language, which means when you declare a variable, its value can be of any type and can change during the course of its lifetime. However, in contrast, a strongly typed language dictates that a variable defined as a type `string` must always be a string and must always have a value of a string.

To declare a variable in JavaScript, simply use the var keyword before your variable name:

```
var myVariable;      // declaring a variable with no value
var myFirstName = "Jason";
var myLastName = "Krol";
var myFullName = myFirstName + ' ' + myLastName;
// => Jason Krol
```

The preceding code snippet shows how we declare variables and define them with initial values alongside their declarations. The + operator is used for string concatenation.

Also, we use camel case for the variable names. It is not mandatory that you use camel case for variable naming, but it is more common in object-oriented languages to follow camel case as opposed to the underscore-based approach.

> JavaScript won't complain if you forget to put a semicolon at the end of each statement. Instead it will attempt to put the semicolons for you if there are proper statement terminations missing. This can lead to unexpected results. The rules of semicolon insertion are explained in this article at `http://bclary.com/2004/11/07/#a-7.9.1`.

Apart from `var`, ES6 introduced two more keywords for variable declarations, namely `let` and `const`, which we will not be discussing in this chapter to avoid confusion.

In the preceding example, the variables we created held string values. JavaScript supports a number of data types along with string. Let's take a look at them.

# Data types

Data types are the base of any language. The data types available in JavaScript are as follows:

- Number
- String
- Boolean
- Object
- Null
- Undefined

In our code, every variable we declare will contain values that belong to any of the types above. Number, string, and Boolean types are quite straightforward to understand. These come under the primitive data types supported by the language. Here, one important point is to note that JavaScript has no distinction between integers or floating points at its type level.

Types such as array, function, regex, and date come under the object data type. They are considered to be composite data types. So the functions that you define in your code will also be nothing but objects.

Null and undefined are two special types supported by JavaScript. Null points to a deliberate non-value, whereas undefined points to an uninitialized value. So when you just declare a variable and haven't yet initialized it with a value, the variable will be of undefined type.

# Understanding the scope of variables

Understanding the scope of variables is very important in JavaScript to gain a better hold of the language. Scope may be referred to as a bucket in which your variable or your function exists. Unlike Java and other popular languages, JavaScript follows function-level scoping as opposed to block-level scoping. So this means that the variables you define will be limited to a scope that is bound to its parent function.

Consider the following code snippet:

```
var outer = 10;
function myFunction() {
   var inner = 2;
   console.log(inner);// 2
   console.log(outer);// 10
}
```

As you can see, the scope of the inner variable is limited to the parent function named myFunction. It won't be accessible outside it. Also, the variables available in outer scopes are available in function scopes, and you don't need to make any extra effort to access them, as you have seen with the variable named outer in the preceding example.

An important thing to discuss in this context is the use of the var keyword. JavaScript won't complain if you missed var while declaring a new variable. But things can get really bad if that happens. See the following example:

```
(function (){
    (function (){
        a = 10;
    })();
})();
console.log(a);// 10
```

Here, as the var keyword was skipped along with the variable declaration inside the inner function, JavaScript considered that this variable should be searched in its parent scopes, then attached it to the global scope, and ended up making it available everywhere. So, to avoid such issues with the code, it is always useful if you pass your code through code quality tools such as JSHint. The preceding code may have confused you, as it used self-invoked functions just to induce scopes. So let's take a look at the various ways to define and use functions, arrays, and objects.

## Operators and flows

JavaScript supports similar control structures to other languages in the C family. Conditional statements are written with if and else, and you can chain together the statements using else-if ladders.

```
var a = "some value";
if(a === "other value") {
  //do something
} else if (a === "another value") {
  //do something
} else {
  //do something
}
```

Control statements can be written using `while`, `do-while`, `for`, and `switch` statements. One important thing to consider while writing conditions in JavaScript is to understand what equates to `true` and/or `false`. Any value greater or less than zero, not null, and not undefined equates to `true`. Strings such as 0, null, undefined, or empty strings equate to `false`.

Some sample examples using `while`, `do-while`, `for` and `switch` statements are given below.

```javascript
// for loop example

var myVar = 0;
for(var i = 0; i < 100; i += 1) {
  myVar = i;
  console.log(myVar); // => 0 1 ... 99
}

// do while example
var x = 0;
do {
  x += 1;
  console.log(x); // => 1 2 ... 100
} while (x < 100);

// while example
while (x > 90) {
  x -= 1;
  console.log(x); // => 99 98 ... 90
}
//switch example

var x = 0;
switch(x) {
  case 1 :
console.log(""one"");
break;
  case 2 :
console.log("two"");
break;
  default:
console.log("none");

} // => "none"
```

Another important thing will be to understand the basic difference between the comparisons using == and ===. The == comparisons should be used where the type of variable is not your concern; and if the data type of the variables also should be compared, then you should opt for a === comparison symbol as given in the following command:

```
var a = '5';
var b = 5;
if(a == b) {
  //do something
}
if(a === b) {
  //do something
}
```

Here in the code snippet, the first condition evaluates to true while the second doesn't. So while you code, it's always safer to depend on strict (===) equality checks as a best practice.

> It's always advised to run your code through code quality tools such as JS Hint before you approve them for your application. You can automate the code quality checks via task runners such as Grunt so that each time we make a change in your code, the code quality tool runs and presents if there are any potential issues with the code that has been written.

# Understanding objects

In JavaScript objects, the arrays and even functions we create fall into the same data type: Object. Declaring an object is a fairly straightforward process:

```
var myObject = {};    // that's it!
```

You may add properties or attributes to this object, which may belong to any type. It means you can add arrays, functions, or even other objects as properties of this object. Adding a new property to this object can be done in any of the two ways shown here:

```
var person = {};
person.firstName = 'Jason';    // via dot operator
person['lastName'] = 'Krol';   // via square brackets
```

Let's look at an example where we add arrays and functions as properties of
this object:

```
var person = {};
person.firstName = 'Jason';      // properties
person.lastName = 'Krol';
person.fullName = function() {  // methods
  return this.firstName + ' ' + this.lastName;
};
person.colors = ['red', 'blue', 'green'];  // array property
```

You can see in the preceding code that we defined a basic object called `person` and
assigned it some properties and a function. It's important to note the use of the `this`
keyword in the `fullName` function. The `this` keyword refers to the object that the
function is a part of. So via the `this` keyword, the function will be able to access the
other properties that are part of the object it belongs to.

Apart from the approach of adding properties after the object creation, we can also
attach the initial object properties as part of its creation, as follows:

```
// define properties during declaration
var book = {
  title: 'Web Development with MongoDB and NodeJS',
  author: 'Jason Krol',
  publisher: 'Packt Publishing'
};
console.log(book.title);
// => Web Development with MongoDB and NodeJS
book.pageCount = 150;      // add new properties
```

In the preceding example, we are creating objects without specifying any class from
which they should be created by using {}. So, this results in the creation of this new
object from the `Object` base class from which other composite types such as Arrays
and Functions are extended. So when you use {}, it is equivalent to a new `Object()`.

> Here, the objects we create via use of the object literal {} are instances of
> the `Object` class. To define custom classes for our application, we will
> need to use functions and prototypes. Mozilla has a fairly good tutorial
> on introducing this whole point, available at `https://developer.`
> `mozilla.org/en-US/docs/Web/JavaScript/Introduction_`
> `to_Object-Oriented_JavaScript`.

# Understanding arrays

Arrays work the same way in JavaScript as they do in pretty much any other language. They are zero indexed, and you can declare a variable as an empty array or a pre-populated array. You can manipulate the items in an array, and arrays are not fixed in length:

```
var favFoods = ['pizza', 'cheeseburgers', 'french fries'];
var stuff = [];          // empty array
var moreStuff = new Array();        // empty array
var firstFood = favFoods[0];     // => pizza

// array functions:
favFoods.push('salad');     // add new item

// => ['pizza', 'cheeseburgers', 'french fries', 'salad']
favFoods.pop();          // remove the last item
// => ['pizza', 'cheeseburgers', 'french fries']
var first = favFoods.shift();     // remove the first item
// => first = 'pizza';
// => favFoods = ['cheeseburgers', 'french fries']
```

To be more precise, you can consider arrays as extended child classes of the base `Object` class with extra implementations of `Array` functions.

# Understanding functions

Functions are first-class citizens in JavaScript. What this means is that a `function` by itself is an object, so it can be treated as such and extended with properties and additional functions to the base `Object` class. We will see a lot of situations where we pass functions as parameters to other functions and return functions from other function calls.

Here, we will take a standard function (in this case, `myFunction`). We will assign this function a `timesRun` property, just like we do for any other object during its execution, and see how to refer to that property later:

```
var myFunction = function() {
  if(this.timesRun)
    this.timesRun += 1;
  else
    this.timesRun = 1;
  // do some actual work
```

```
    console.log(this.timesRun);
};
myFunction();
// => 1;
myFunction();
// => 2;
myFunction();
// => 3;
```

As we have seen in the preceding example, by using the var keyword, we can define functions in the same way as variables:

```
function sayHello() {
    console.log('Hello!');
}
// or
var sayHello = function() {
  console.log('Hello!');
};
```

Both methods are almost identical in the preceding sample code. The first method is the most common way to define a function, and is called the named function approach. The second method discussed here is the function expression approach, where you assign the unnamed function as a reference to a variable and keep it unnamed.

The single most important difference between these two approaches is related to a concept called JavaScript hoisting. Basically, the difference is that when you adopt a function expression strategy, the function will not be available in its containing scope till the point in its definition statement gets executed. In the named function approach, regardless of the position you define it at, the function will be available throughout the containing scope as given in the following code:

```
one();//will display Hello
two();//will trigger error as its definition is yet to happen.

function one() {
    console.log('Hello!');
}

var two = function() {
  console.log('Hello!');
};
two ();//will display Hello
```

In the preceding sample code snippet, function one can be invoked from anywhere in this parent scope. But function two will not be available before the point where its expression is evaluated.

JavaScript hoisting is the process by which the function definitions and variable declarations are moved to the top of the containing scope by the JS interpreter before the script is executed. So in the previous case of named functions, the definition was moved to the top of the scope. However, for the function expression, only the declaration of the variable moved to the top of the scope, setting it to undefined till the point in the script where it was actually executed. You can read more about the concept of hoisting at http://code.tutsplus.com/tutorials/javascript-hoisting-explained--net-15092.

# Anonymous functions and callbacks

Often, you will need to use a temporary function that you don't necessarily want to declare ahead of time. In this type of scenario, you can use an anonymous function, which is simply a function that is declared at the time you need it. This is similar to the function expression context we explored earlier, with a simple difference that the function isn't assigned to a variable so it has no way of being referenced to later. The most common use of anonymous functions is when they are defined as a parameter to another function (most notably when used as a *callback*).

One of the most common places to use an anonymous function (which also acts as a callback even if you didn't realize it) is with setTimeout or setInterval. These are two standard JavaScript functions that will execute code after a specified delay (in milliseconds) or repeat the execution of code every specified delay. Here is an example of one of them, setTimeout, using an anonymous inline function:

```
console.log('Hello...');
setTimeout(function() {
  console.log('World!');
}, 5000);
// => Hello...
// (5000 milliseconds i.e. 5 second delay)
// => World!
```

You can see that the anonymous function was passed as the first parameter to setTimeout because setTimeout expects a function. You can, if you so desire, declare the function ahead of time as a variable and pass that to setTimeout instead of the inline anonymous function:

```
var sayWorld = function() {
  console.log('World!');
}
setTimeout(sayWorld, 5000);
// (5 second delay)
// => World!
```

The anonymous function just acts as a clean inline disposable function.

Callbacks are important because one of the most powerful (and confusing) features of JavaScript is that it's asynchronous. This means that every line executes sequentially, but it doesn't wait around for code that might be taking longer than it should (even if by design). We have explored this via an example in the first chapter while looking into the asynchronous nature of Node.js.

> Mozilla has a detailed tutorial on JavaScript concepts, which we advise you to go through once you finish this chapter. The tutorial includes highly advanced concepts, such as closures, that were not covered in this chapter due to the depth of the topic. So refer to this Mozilla Development Network article at `https://developer.mozilla.org/en-US/docs/Web/JavaScript/A_re-introduction_to_JavaScript`.

# JSON

**JavaScript Object Notation (JSON)** is the standard syntax used when dealing with data in JavaScript as well as most other languages and web services. The basic premise of JSON is that it looks exactly like a standard JavaScript object with a few strict exceptions:

- JSON is pure text. There are no data types with properties; that is, date values are stored as strings and so on.
- All names and string values must be in double quotes.
- There can be no functions as properties.

Let's take a quick look at a pretty standard JSON object:

```
{
  "title": "This is the title",
  "description": "Here is where the description would be",
  "page-count": 150,
  "authors": [
    { "name": "John Smith" },
    { "name": "Jane Doe" },
    { "name": "Andrea Johnson" }
  ],
  "id": "1234-567-89012345"
}
```

If you are at all familiar with XML, JSON is somewhat similar, except it is much easier to read and make sense out of. As described best by the ECMA, *JSON is a text format that facilitates structured data interchange between all programming languages.*

# The basics of Node.js

With the basics of JavaScript out of the way, let's focus on some of the basics of Node.

## Event-driven

At its core, one of the most powerful features of Node is that it is event-driven. This means that almost all the code you write in Node is going to be written in a way that is either responding to an event or is itself firing an event (which in turn will fire other code listening for that event).

Let's take a look at the code that we'll write in a later chapter that handles connecting to a MongoDB server using Mongoose, a popular Node.js MongoDB **Object Document Mapper (ODM)** module:

```
mongoose.connect('');
mongoose.connection.on('open', function() {
console.log("Connected to Mongoose...");
});
```

First, we tell our `mongoose` object to connect to the server provided as a string parameter to the function. Connecting will take an undetermined amount of time though, and we have no way of knowing how long. So, what we do is bind a listener to the `open` event on the `mongoose.connection` object. With the use of the on keyword, we are indicating that when the `mongoose.connection` object triggers an `open` event, it executes the anonymous function that was passed in as the parameter.

## Asynchronous execution

Earlier, we reviewed the idea of asynchronous JavaScript code in the browser using `setTimeout` — the principles apply more strongly in the world of Node. As you may be making a number of network-dependent connections to different REST API services, database servers, and anything else, it is important that your code can execute smoothly and has proper callback usage in place whenever each service responds.

# The module system

In an effort to make the code as modular and reusable as possible, Node uses a module system that allows you to better organize your code. The basic premise is that you write a code fulfilling a single concern, and export this code as a module that serves that single purpose. Then, whenever you need to use that code elsewhere in your code base, you will require that module:

```
// ** file: dowork.js
module.exports = {
  doWork: function(param1, param2) {
    return param1 + param2;
  }
}

// ** file: testing.js
var worker = require('./dowork'); // note: no .js in the file

var something = 1;
var somethingElse = 2;

var newVal = worker.doWork(something, somethingElse);
console.log(newVal);
// => 3
```

Using this system, it is simple to reuse the functionality in a module (in this case, the dowork module) in a number of other files. Furthermore, the individual files of a module act as a private namespace. Any variables declared and used within the module file are private to that module and not exposed to any code that uses the module via require().

This system extends infinitely as well. Within your modules, you can require other modules and so on and so forth.

# The Node.js core

The Node.js core literally has hundreds of modules available for you to use while writing your applications. These include the following:

- Events
- Filesystems
- HTTP
- Net

- Streams
- Timers

 Definitely make sure to check out the online docs on Node (at http://nodejs.org/api) to see the full list of modules available in Node's core and see plenty of sample code and explanations.

# Installing modules using npm

The module system in Node is so powerful that consuming a third-party module written by other developers is a piece of cake. Node includes its own package manager called npm, which is a registry that currently contains over 60,000 unique modules written in Node. These modules are completely open source and available to you via a few short commands. In addition, you can release your own personal modules via npm and allow anyone in the world to use your feature!

Let's say you wanted to include a popular web framework, Express, in your project (the one we will be using later in this book). There are simply two steps required to download a module and use it in your code:

```
$ npm install express
// ** file: usingnpm.js
var express = require('express');
```

And that's it! Literally, it's that simple! From the command-line of the folder where your project is located, simply execute npm install package-name, and the package will be downloaded from npm and stored in a folder called node_modules within your project. If you browse through the node_modules folder, you will find a folder for the package you installed, and within that folder, you will find the raw source code for the package itself. Once the package is downloaded, it's as simple as using require() from within your code.

There may be times when you want to install a Node package globally, for example, when using a popular command-line build tool called Grunt.js. To install an npm package globally, simply include the -g or --global flag, and the module will be installed as a global executable instead. When installing npm packages globally, the source files for the package are not stored within the node_modules folder of a specific project, but instead within a node_modules folder in a system directory of your machine.

A really powerful feature of npm is that it allows a quick, easy, and consistent way for other developers to boot up your code in their local environment. Node projects typically include a special file called package.json that includes information about the project as well as a list of all npm packages that the project depends on. A developer with a copy of your local code can simply execute npm install to have every dependency downloaded and installed locally using this file.

The npm install flag --save or --save-dev is required if you want the dependency you are installing to be saved to the package.json file. If you are starting a new project and don't want to create a package.json file by hand, you can simply execute npm init and answer a few quick questions to get a default package.json file quickly set up. You can leave every question blank during init and accept the default values if you want:

```
$ npm init

$ npm install express --save
$ npm install grunt --save-dev
$ cat package.json
{
  "name": "chapter3",
  "version": "0.0.0",
  "description": "",
  "main": "index.js",
  "scripts": {
    "test": "echo \"Error: no test specified\" && exit 1"
  },
  "author": "",
  "license": "ISC",
  "dependencies": {
    "express": "^3.5.1"
  },
  "devDependencies": {
    "grunt": "^0.4.4"
  }
}
```

Note that the dependencies and devDependencies sections have express and grunt listed. The difference between these two sections is that the dependencies section is absolutely critical for the app to function properly. The devDependencies section has only packages that need to be installed for a developer to use during the development of the project (such as Grunt for various build steps, testing frameworks, and so on).

 If you are confused about the use of the ^ symbol in the package versions, its used to update the dependency to the most recent minor version or patch version (the second or third number). ^1.2.3 will match any 1.x.x release including 1.3.0, but will hold off on 2.0.0. So in our case ^3.5.1 of Express.js will look for the most recent minor version of Express but will not take 4.0.0, as it's a major version.

# The basics of MongoDB

Since MongoDB is largely powered by JavaScript, the Mongo shell acts as a JavaScript environment. In addition to being able to execute regular Mongo queries, you can also execute standard JavaScript statements. Most of the items mentioned earlier in the JavaScript primer apply directly to the Mongo shell as well.

In this next section, we will focus primarily on the various ways to perform standard **create, read, update, delete (CRUD)** operations via the Mongo shell.

# The Mongo shell

To access the Mongo shell, simply execute mongo from any terminal. The Mongo shell requires the mongod server to be currently running and available on the machine, as the first thing it does is connect to the server. Use the following command to access the Mongo shell:

```
$ mongo
MongoDB shell version: 2.4.5
connecting to: test
>
```

By default, when you first launch Mongo, you are connected to the local server and set to use the test database. To display a list of all databases on the server, use the following command:

```
> show dbs
```

To switch databases to any of those listed in the output of `show dbs`, use the following command:

```
> use chapter3
switched to db chapter3
```

An interesting thing to note is that if you use `use` on a database that doesn't exist, one is created automatically. If you are using an existing database and want to view a list of collections in the database, execute the following command:

```
> show collections
```

In the case of my `chapter3` database, I had no existing collections since it was automatically generated as a new database for me. Collections in MongoDB are similar to the tables in a relational database.

# Inserting data

Since we are working with the `chapter3` database, which is brand new, there are currently no collections in it. You can use any collection (table) you want by simply referring to a new collection name with the `db` object:

```
> db.newCollection.find()
>
```

Performing a `find` operation on an empty collection simply returns nothing. Let's insert some data so we can experiment with some queries:

```
> db.newCollection.insert({ name: 'Jason Krol', website:
'http://kroltech.com' })
> db.newCollection.find().pretty()
{
  "_id" : ObjectId("5338b749dc8738babbb5a45a"),
  "name" : "Jason Krol",
  "website" : "http://kroltech.com"
}
```

After we perform a simple insertion (basically of a JavaScript JSON object), we perform another find operation on the collection and get our new record returned, this time with an additional `_id` field added. The `_id` field is Mongo's method for tracking a unique identifier for every document (record). We also chained the `pretty()` function to the end of the find, which outputs the results a little more nicely.

Go ahead and insert a few more records so you have some data to play with in the next section when we go over querying.

# Querying

Querying and searching for documents in a MongoDB collection is pretty straightforward. Using the `find()` function by itself with no parameters will return every document in the collection. To narrow down the search results, you can provide a JSON object as the first parameter with as much or as little specific information to match against as you wish, as shown in the following code:

```
> db.newCollection.find({ name: 'Jason Krol' })
{ "_id" : ObjectId("533dfb9433519b9339d3d9e1"), "name" : "Jason
Krol", "website" : "http://kroltech.com" }
```

You can include additional parameters to make the search more precise:

```
> db.newCollection.find({ name: 'Jason Krol', website:
'http://kroltech.com'})
{ "_id" : ObjectId("533dfb9433519b9339d3d9e1"), "name" : "Jason
Krol", "website" : "http://kroltech.com" }
```

Note that with each result set, every field is included. If you want to only return a specific set of fields with the result, you can include a map as the second parameter to `find()`:

```
> db.newCollection.find({ name: 'Jason Krol' }, { name: true })
{ "_id" : ObjectId("533dfb9433519b9339d3d9e1"), "name" : "Jason Krol"
}
> db.newCollection.find({ name: 'Jason Krol' }, { name: true, _id:
false })
{ "name" : "Jason Krol" }
```

Note that the `_id` field will always be included by default unless you specifically state that you don't want it included.

Additionally, you can use query operators to search for things that are within ranges. These include greater than (or equal to) and less than (or equal to). If you want to perform a search against a collection of homework, and you want to find every document with a score within the B range (80–89), you can execute the following search:

```
> db.homework_scores.find({ score: { $gte: 80, $lt: 90 } })
```

Finally, you can use `regex` while performing a search to return multiple matching documents:

```
> db.newCollection.find({ name: { $regex: 'Krol'} })
```

The preceding query will return every document that contains the word `Krol`. You can get as advanced as you want with `regex` statements.

If you know that you are going to be returning multiple documents on a query and only want the first result, use `findOne()` in place of a regular `find()` operation.

# Updating data

To update a record, use the `update()` function, but include a find query as the first parameter:

```
> db.newCollection.update({ name: 'Jason Krol' }, { website:
                        'http://jasonkrol.com' })
```

There's a bit of a catch here. If you perform a new `find({ name: 'Jason Krol' })` operation, something strange happens. No data is returned. What happened? Well, the second parameter in the `update()` function is actually the new version of the complete document. Since you only wanted to update the `website` field, what actually happened was that the document that was found was replaced with the new version that consists of only the `website` field. To reiterate, the reason this happens at all is because with NoSQL such as MongoDB, the document does not have a set number of fields (as a relational database does). To fix this problem, you should use the `$set` operator instead:

```
> db.newCollection.update({ name: 'Jason Krol' }, { $set: { website:
'http://jasonkrol.com'} })
```

There may be a time when you want to update a document, but the document itself may or may not exist. What happens when the document does not exist, and you'd like a new one to be created instantly based on the updated values you provide? Well, there's a handy function just for that. Pass `{upsert: true}` as the third parameter to the `update()` function:

```
> db.newCollection.update({ name: 'Joe Smith' }, { name: 'Joe Smith',
                    website: 'http://google.com' }, { upsert: true })
```

If we have a document with a `name` field that matches `Joe Smith`, the `website` field will be updated (and the `name` field preserved). However, if we do not have a matching document, a new one will be created automatically.

# Deleting data

Deleting documents works almost exactly like `find()`, except instead of finding and returning results, it deletes those documents that match the search criteria:

```
> db.newCollection.remove({ name: 'Jason Krol' })
```

If you want the nuclear option, you can use the `drop()` function, which will remove every document in a collection:

```
> db.newCollection.drop()
```

# Additional resources

For additional learning with JavaScript, I suggest you check out some of the following resources:

- Mozilla Developer Network at `https://developer.mozilla.org/en-US/docs/Web/JavaScript`
- *Secrets of the JavaScript Ninja, John Resig, Bear Bibeault, Manning*
- *Learning JavaScript Design Patterns, Addy Osmani, O'Reilly*
- *JavaScript: The Good Parts, Douglas Crockford, O'Reilly*

The Node API online documentation is going to be your best bet for fully understanding everything that's available within the Node core set of modules. The Node API docs can be found at `http://nodejs.org/api`.

Additionally, there is a great website that teaches Node using actual programming problems that you must solve. The emphasis with these exercises is to understand the nuts and bolts of how Node works and get down into the fundamentals of working with streams, asynchronous I/O, promises, and more. Node school can be found at `http://nodeschool.io`.

Finally, the creators of MongoDB offer an amazing 7–8 week online training and certification program completely free of charge, where you will learn everything you need to be a true MongoDB master. This can be found at MongoDB University at `https://university.mongodb.com`.

Now it's time to dive in and start writing some real code!

# Summary

In this chapter, you took a crash course on the basics of JavaScript, Node.js, and MongoDB. In addition, you learned about Node's package manager, npm. For further learning, additional resources were provided for JavaScript, Node.js, and MongoDB.

In the next chapter, you will write your first Node web server using Express.js and get started with creating a complete web application.

# 4
# Introducing Express

When we need to build a full-fledged web application, writing the whole application from scratch is not the best approach to take. We can think of using a well-maintained and well-written web application framework to build our application to reduce the development effort and increase the maintainability.

In this chapter:

- We will explore the Express.js web application framework
- We will explore the various elements of Express.js
- We will develop the necessary code to bootstrap a web application using Express

## Web application frameworks

Simply put, a web framework makes it easier to develop a web application. Consider the aspect of breaking down commonly used functionality into reusable modules. That is exactly what frameworks do. They come with a lot of reusable modules and enforce a standard structure for the code so that it will be easier for developers across the world to go through and understand the application. Apart from all these advantages, web frameworks mostly get maintained by lots of developers across the world. So, the effort of developers in incorporating the newer bug fixes and features of underlying languages is minimized to a step where we just need to upgrade the framework version that is being used by the application. So, the use of web frameworks for building web applications brings a lot of advantages to the development and maintenance phases of an application.

The Express.js framework, which we are going to use throughout this book, is a Model View Controller (MVC) based web application framework. MVC is just an architectural design pattern:

- **Models** are used to represent the data or entities of the web application. They lie more close to the instances, which store the data of the application—typically a database or a web service.

- **Views** are responsible for how the application gets presented to the end user. So, a view can be considered as the presentation layer of the application.

- Now, you may be wondering about the role of **controllers** in the web application. Well, the role of controllers is nothing but to just glue together the models with the respective views and to take care of the request from the user for a particular web page in our application end to end.

This may be a bit hard for you to grasp if you are hearing this concept for the first time. But after going through this chapter, you will get used to these concepts while we present the various examples to you.

# What is Express.js?

As described perfectly on its home page, Express is a minimal and flexible Node.js web application framework, providing a robust set of features for building single, multi-page, and hybrid web applications. In other words, it provides all the tools and basic building blocks you need to get a web server up and running by writing very little code. It puts the power to focus on writing your app and not worry about the nuts and bolts that go into making the basic stuff work in your hands.

The Express framework is one of the most popular Node-based web frameworks and one of the single most popular packages available in npm. It is built based on the Sinatra web framework, which is quite popular in the Ruby world. There are a lot of frameworks across languages that take inspiration from Sinatra's simplicity such as PHP's Laravel framework. So Express is the Sinatra-based web framework in the Node.js world.

If you look at a sample piece of code, one of the most basic implementations of Express, you can see how easy it is to get a web server up and running, for example:

```
var express = require('express');
var app = express();
app.get('/', function(req, res){
    res.send('Hello World');
});
app.listen(3300);
```

The beauty of Express is that it makes building and maintaining the server code for a website simple.

# Building a complete web application

Beginning with this chapter, we are going to build a complete web application. The web application that we build will be a clone of a popular social image-sharing site, imgur.com. We'll call our site **imgPloadr.io**.

# Designing the web application

The requirements of the site are as follows:

- The home page will allow visitors to upload an image as well as browse the existing uploads, which will be ordered based on newest to oldest.

- Each uploaded image will be presented via its own page that shows its title, description, and a large image display. Visitors will be able to like the image and post comments.

- A consistent shared sidebar will be visible on both pages and will showcase some general statistics about the site, the most popular images, and the most recent comments.

The site will use Bootstrap, so that it has a nice professional design and is responsive on any device.

The following screenshot is from the home page of the completed site:

The next screenshot is an image's details page from the site:

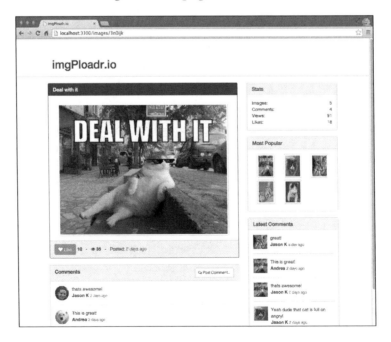

# Organizing the files

Before you start writing any code, we want to make sure that you have a project folder set up correctly with the proper folder structure to house all of the various files that you will be creating. Get started by creating a new folder for your project, and name it anything you like. Then, inside that folder, create additional folders to match the following structure:

```
/(project root)
---/helpers
---/controllers
---/public
------/css
------/img
------/js
------/upload
---/server
---/views
------/layouts
------/partials
```

Each of these folders will contain important modules that we will write throughout the remainder of this chapter and book.

 If you use an Express-based generator through Yeoman, you will get the necessary folder structure and the dependencies imported with boilerplate code. However, as our intention is to understand this framework, we will skip this. Visit `http://yeoman.io/` for more information on the features of Yeoman.

You are going to need a `package.json` file for this project, and the easiest way to create one of these is by simply executing the following command from the root of the project folder:

```
$ npm init
```

Respond to each of the questions as you are prompted or simply press *Enter* repeatedly to accept the default values. Now, let's install Express and its necessary dependencies via npm:

```
$ npm install express morgan body-parser cookie-parser method-
override errorhandler express-handlebars --save
```

This will install the Express framework in the node_modules folder and also add Express to the package.json file in the dependencies section. Note that at the time of writing this book, Express.js is in its 4.x.x versions. Here, as you can see, Express is a completely decoupled framework that doesn't come with a lot of packaged modules within itself. Instead, you can figure out the dependencies of your application and plug in and out of the application anytime. If you have been following Express development from the beginning, you must have noted that these changes where introduced as part of the Express 4.x.x versions. Prior to this version, Express used to come with a lot of built-in modules bundled within it. Here, the modules we installed alongside Express are the various dependencies our application has when we start building the complete web application. We will discuss the use of each module in a later section of this chapter!

# Creating the application's entry point

The next step in developing the application after installing Express and the necessary dependencies will be to create a file, which will serve as the default entry point of this application. We will be executing this file to start our web application and it will contain the necessary code to require dependent modules and boot up the application to listen to a specified port in the development server.

We are going to name the entry point file server.js for now and will keep it pretty lean so that its contents are quite self-explanatory. Any major logic that is going to be executed within this file will actually be deferred to external modules hosted within other files.

Before we can do anything within server.js, we require a few modules that we're going to work with, specifically Express:

```
var express = require('express'),
// config = require('./server/configure'),
app = express();
```

In the preceding code, we are assigning the express module to the express variable. The config module is actually going to be our own module that we will write shortly, but for now, since it doesn't exist, we will leave that line commented out. Finally, we will declare a variable called app that is actually what the Express framework returns when it is executed. This app object powers our entire app application, which is how it was so cleverly named.

Throughout this chapter and the remainder of the book, I may include commented out code in the samples (code that starts with //). This is so that following along will be easier when we use the commented lines as reference points, or we can enable those features by simply uncommenting the code.

Next up, we will set a few simple settings via the app object using the app.set() function. These settings are really just a way for us to define some app-level constants that we can use throughout the rest of our code as handy shortcuts:

```
app.set('port', process.env.PORT || 3300);
app.set('views', __dirname + '/views');
// app = config(app);
```

The code is explained as follows:

- The first two lines of the preceding code use built-in constants in Node. The process.env.PORT constant is an environment setting that is set on the actual machine for the default port value to the server. If no port value is set on the machine, we will hardcode a default value of 3300 to use in its place.

- After that, we set the location of our views (HTML templates) to __dirname + '/views' or, using another Node constant, the /views folder from within the current working directory.

- The third line of code is referencing the config module, which we haven't written yet, so that the line is commented out.

- Last but not least, we will create a HTTP server using our app object and tell it to listen for connections:

```
app.get('/', function(req, res){
   res.send('Hello World');
});
app.listen(app.get('port'), function() {
    console.log('Server up: http://localhost:' + app.get('port'));
});
```

Here, we set a route in our application to respond with a Hello world message. If any user requests for the root of our application, it will respond with a Hello World message. The last section of the code is to call the listen() function on our app that tells it which port to listen to and to pass in a simple anonymous callback function that will execute once the server is up and listening by executing a simple console.log() message. That's it! Again, make sure to save this file with the name server.js within the root of the project. You're ready to run your server and see if it works.

# Booting up the application

Let's take your server for a spin and see how you're doing so far:

```
$ node server.js
```

```
Server up: http://localhost:3300
```

Perfect! At this point, your server doesn't actually do anything great. Try pointing your browser to http://localhost:3300. You should receive a pretty basic message that says Hello World! If you request any other routes on the port, such as http://localhost:3300/, it will respond with a cannot get response. This is because you haven't configured any routes or any actual logic in your server to say how to handle certain requests, but only a GET request to the default route of /. Before you set up your routes, we should understand the concept of middleware in Express, which will be essential to understanding how the modules that are custom dependencies of our application, get integrated with our normal application flow.

> You can set any number of environment variables right from the command line before you run your server by executing something like the following command:
>
> ```
> $ PORT=5500 node server.js
> ```
>
> ```
> Server up: http://localhost:5500
> ```
>
> You can also set environment variables in your environment settings permanently. This can be done typically by editing your .profile file or equivalent.

# Using and understanding middleware

One of the most powerful features available with Express is the concept of middleware. The idea behind middleware is that it acts like a stack of filters that every request to your server passes through. Since every request passes through each filter, each filter can perform a specific task against the request before it passes through to the next filter. Typically, these filters are used for tasks such as cookie parsing, form field handling, session handling, authentication, and error handling and logging. The list goes on and on and you can use hundreds of third-party modules as well as simply write your own.

The order that the middleware is called in is very important. Again, using the concept of filters, as a request passes through each filter, you want to be sure that they are performing their responsibilities in the correct order. A great example of this is implementing a cookie parser before a session handler—since sessions typically rely on cookies to maintain state with a user between requests.

Another great example of how the order of middleware is important involves error handling. If any of your middleware encounters an error, they will simply pass that error along to the next middleware in the stack. If the last middleware, regardless of what it is, doesn't gracefully handle that error, it will basically show up in your application as a stack trace (and that's bad). Having an error handler configured as one of the last middleware is like saying *if everything else fails, and at any point in the previous middleware a failure occurs, deal with it gracefully.*

The various dependencies we have installed to use in this application are going to be integrated into our code as middlewares. We are going to carry out this task of integrating the various middlewares through the `config` module as it will help us to make our `server.js` file leaner to add more readability to the code base.

# The configure module

Since we are leaving our `server.js` file very lean, there is still a fair amount of logic that is required in configuring our server. For this, we will defer to a custom module that we'll create called `configure`. To get started, create a `configure.js` file in the `server` folder. We have already installed the custom dependencies when we were installing Express in the first place.

Now that the module is installed and ready to be used, let's start writing the `configure.js` file. First, like any of our modules, we will declare our dependencies:

```
var path = require('path'),
    routes = require('./routes'),
    exphbs = require('express-handlebars'),),
    express = require('express'),
    bodyParser = require('body-parser'),
    cookieParser = require('cookie-parser'),
    morgan = require('morgan'),
    methodOverride = require('method-override'),
    errorHandler = require('errorhandler');

module.exports = function(app) {
app.use(morgan('dev'));
    app.use(bodyParser.urlencoded({'extended':true}));
    app.use(bodyparser.json());
    app.use(methodOverride());
    app.use(cookieParser('some-secret-value-here'));
    routes(app);//moving the routes to routes folder.
```

```
    app.use('/public/', express.static(path.join(__dirname,
        '../public')));

if ('development' === app.get('env')) {
    app.use(errorHandler());
}
    return app;
};
```

In the preceding code, we declared variables for each of the modules that we will be using in our custom `configure` module. Then, we defined the actual module that will be exported by this code file, more specifically a function that accepts our `app` object as a parameter as well as returns that same object (after we make some configuration modifications to it).

 You should see that we require Connect, which is actually installed by default with Express.js as it's one of its core dependencies. Connect is a popular third-party middleware framework that we will learn more about later in this chapter.

Let's take a look at each of the Connect middleware we have used in the preceding code:

- `morgan`: This is the module responsible for logging. This is very helpful for debugging your Node server.

- `bodyParser`: This helps facilitate the packing of any form fields that are submitted via a HTML form submission from a browser. Form fields that are submitted via a POST request will be made available via the `req.body` property.

- `methodOverride`: For older browsers that don't properly support REST HTTP verbs, such as UPDATE and PUT, the `methodOverride` middleware allows this to be faked using a special hidden input field.

- `cookieParser`: This allows cookies to be sent and received.

- `errorHandler`: This handles any errors that occur throughout the entire middleware process. Typically, you would write your own custom `errorHandler` that might render a default 404 HTML page, log the error to a data store, and so on.

- `Handlebars`: This is the templating engine we are going to use with the views. We will explain more about integrating it in the upcoming sections.

The `routes(app)` line is a special component of Express that says you are actually using a router with your server, and you can respond to requests such as GET, POST, PUT, and UPDATE. Since you are using the Express router as one of the last middleware, we will also define the actual routes in the next section.

Finally, the `express.static()` middleware is used to render static content files to the browser from a predefined static resource directory. This is important so that the server can serve up static files, such as `.js`, `.css`, images, and regular `.html`, as well as any other files you might need to serve up. The static middleware will serve up any static files from the public directory like the following code:

```
http://localhost:3300/public/js/somescript.js
```

```
http://localhost:3300/public/img/main_logo.jpg
```

It's important that your static middleware is defined after the `app.router()` so that static assets aren't inadvertently taking priority over a matching route that you may have defined.

## Activating the configure module

Now that your `configure.js` file is complete, you're ready to call it from your main `server.js` file. If you recall, we included two lines of code that were commented out for our `configure` module. It's time to uncomment these two lines so that when you run your server, your `configure` module will do its part. The two lines should now look like this:

```
config = require('./server/configure'),
app = config(app);
```

Boot up your server again by executing the `server.js` node and everything should still be running smoothly. Now, it's time to incorporate more routes into our application in addition to the `Hello World` route we added earlier.

## Routers and controllers

So far, you have your `server.js` file and a `configure` module that is used to wire up all of the necessary middleware for the application. The next step is to implement proper routers and the necessary controllers.

The router is going to be a map of each of the available URL paths for the app. Every route on the server will correspond to a function in a controller. Here is what our routes table will look like for the particular application we are writing:

```
GET  /(index) - home.index (render the homepage of the site)
GET  /images/image_id - image.index (render the page for a specific
image)
POST /images - image.create (when a user submits and uploads a new
image)
POST /images/image_id/like - image.like (when a user clicks the Like
button)
POST /images/image_id/comment - image.comment (when a user posts a
comment)
```

You can see that we are handling two different GET requests and three different POST requests. In addition, we have two main controllers: home and image. Controllers are really just modules with different functions defined that match up with the corresponding routes. As pointed out earlier, they are called controllers in the **Model View Controller (MVC)** design pattern. Typically, every route will correspond to a controller. This controller will more than likely render a view, and that view will more than likely have its own model (any data that is displayed in the view).

Let's write our router as its own module, matching the table I outlined. First, create a routes.js file within the server folder. The routes file is going to be pretty simple, and the only dependencies it requires will be the controllers we define:

```
var express = require('express'),
    router = express.Router(),
    home = require('../controllers/home'),
    image = require('../controllers/image');
module.exports = function(app) {
    router.get('/', home.index);
    router.get('/images/:image_id', image.index);
    router.post('/images', image.create);
    router.post('/images/:image_id/like', image.like);
    router.post('/images/:image_id/comment', image.comment);
    app.use(router);
};
```

Right off the bat, we declare a router variable and require each from the controllers folder to assign each application route (we haven't yet created these files but that's coming up next). Here, we are assigning each route to its corresponding function in the controllers. Then, we export a module that, when invoked by itself, will attach all these routes to the app instance.

The first parameter for a route is the string value of the route itself, which can contain variable values as subpaths. You can see with second `router.get`, we assign a route value of `/images/:image_id` that basically equates to `/image/ANYVALUE` in the browser address bar. When we write the `image.index` controller, you will see how to retrieve the value for `:image_id` and use it within the `controller` function itself.

The second parameter for a route is a callback function. You can completely omit the idea of using controllers and just define your callbacks as inline anonymous functions; however, as your routes grow, this file will get larger and larger, and the code will start to become a mess. It's always good practice to break your code up into as many small and manageable modules as possible to keep yourself sane!

The first two `router.get` routes are typical routes that would be called whenever a visitor points their browser to `yourdomain.com/routepath`—the browser sends a GET request to the server by default. The other three `router.post` routes are defined to handle when the browser posts a request to the server, typically done via a HTML form submission.

With all of our routes defined, let's now create the matching controllers. Within the controller's folder, create both the `home.js` and `image.js` files. The `home.js` file is very basic:

```
module.exports = {
    index: function(req, res) {
        res.send('The home:index controller');
    }
};
```

With this module, we are actually exporting an object that has a single function called `index`. The `function` signature for `index` is the signature that is required for every route using Express. The first parameter is a request object and the second parameter is a response object. Every detail specific to the request that the browser sent to the server will be available via the request object. In addition, the request object will be modified using all of the middleware that was declared earlier. You will use the response object to send a response back to the client—this may be a rendered HTML page, static asset, JSON data, an error, or whatever you determine. For now, our controllers just respond with simple text so you can see that they are all working.

Let's create an image controller that has a few more functions. Edit the /controllers/image.js file and insert the following code:

```
module.exports = {
    index: function(req, res) {
        res.send('The image:index controller ' +
                req.params.image_id);
    },
    create: function(req, res) {
        res.send('The image:create POST controller');
    },
    like: function(req, res) {
        res.send('The image:like POST controller');
    },
    comment: function(req, res) {
        res.send('The image:comment POST controller');
    }
};
```

Here, we defined the index function, just like we did in the home controller, except that we will also display image_id, which is set in the route when this controller function is executed. The params property was added to the request object via the urlencoded feature, which is part of the body parser module!

Note that neither controller currently requires any dependencies (there were no require declarations defined at the top of the file). This will change as we actually flesh out the controller functions and start to do things such as inserting records into our MongoDB database and using other third-party npm modules.

Now that your controllers are created and ready to be used, you just need to activate your routes. To do this, we will insert one last line of code into our configure.js file, right above the return app; line:

**routes(app);**

Don't forget to uncomment the routes = require('./routes') line at the top of the file as well. What we're doing here is using the routes module we defined and executing the initialize function, which will actually wire up our routes via our app object. We will need to comment out the redundant code that we just moved to routes, which is still present in server.js, as you can see in the following code snippet:

As a recap of each of the files you have created so far, here are the uninterrupted files listed so you can view the full code:

First, we need to boot up with `server.js`:

```
var express = require('express'),
    config = require('./server/configure'),
    app = express();
app.set('port', process.env.PORT || 3300);
app.set('views', __dirname + '/views');
app = config(app);

// app.get('/', function(req, res){
//    res.send('Hello World');
// });

var server = app.listen(app.get('port'), function() {
    console.log('Server up: http://localhost:' + app.get('port'));
});
```

Next, we will configure the server with `server/configure.js`:

```
var path = require('path'),
    routes = require('./routes'),
    exphbs = require('express-handlebars'),
    express = require('express'),
    bodyParser = require('body-parser'),
    cookieParser = require('cookie-parser'),
    morgan = require('morgan'),
    methodOverride = require('method-override'),
    errorHandler = require('errorhandler');

module.exports = function(app) {
app.use(morgan('dev'));
  app.use(bodyParser({
        uploadDir:path.join(__dirname, 'public/upload/temp')
})));
  app.use(methodOverride());
  app.use(cookieParser('some-secret-value-here'));
  routes(app);
  app.use('/public/', express.static(path.join(__dirname,
        '../public')));
```

```
    if ('development' === app.get('env')) {
       app.use(errorHandler());
    }
       return app;
   };
```

Then, we have our routes defined in `server/routes.js`:

```
   var express = require('express'),
       router = express.Router(),
       home = require('../controllers/home'),
       image = require('../controllers/image');
   module.exports = function(app) {
       router.get('/', home.index);
       router.get('/images/:image_id', image.index);
       router.post('/images', image.create);
       router.post('/images/:image_id/like', image.like);
       router.post('/images/:image_id/comment', image.comment);
       app.use(router);
   };
```

Finally, we will define our controllers with `controllers/home.js`:

```
   module.exports = {
       index: function(req, res) {
           res.send('The home:index controller');
       }
   };
```

Furthermore, we will also define our controllers with `controllers/image.js`:

```
   module.exports = {
       index: function(req, res) {
           res.send('The image:index controller ' +
                   req.params.image_id);
       },
       create: function(req, res) {
           res.send('The image:create POST controller');
       },
       like: function(req, res) {
           res.send('The image:like POST controller');
       },
       comment: function(req, res) {
           res.send('The image:comment POST controller');
       }
   };
```

Let's fire up the server one last time and check if it's all working.

Execute the `server.js` node, and this time point your browser to `http://localhost:3300`. Now, you should be seeing some responses in the browser. Go to `http://localhost:3300/images/testing123`. You should see **The image:index controller testing123** on the screen!

# Custom middleware

There will undoubtedly come a time when you want to write your own custom middleware in addition to the existing middleware provided by Connect or any other third party. Before you write your own custom middleware in Node, make it a habit to search through `https://www.npmjs.org/` first, as there's a fairly big chance someone else has already done the work.

Writing your own custom middleware is pretty simple. You simply need to write a function that accepts four parameters: `err`, `req`, `res`, and `next`.

- The first parameter is an error object, and if there were any stack errors prior to your middleware running, that error will be passed to your middleware so that you can handle it accordingly.

- You are already familiar with the `req` and `res` parameters, having written your routes.

- The fourth parameter is actually a reference to a callback. This next parameter is how the middleware stack is able to behave like a stack—each executing and ensuring that the next middleware in the pipeline is returned and called via `next`. Here is a super basic example of a custom middleware:

```
app.use(function(err, req, res, next) {
    // do whatever you want here, alter req, alter res, throw err,
    etc.
    return next();
});
```

The only important thing to keep in mind when writing your own custom middleware is that you have the correct parameters and that you return `next()`. The rest is completely up to you!

# Handlebars as view engines

By default, Express can and will happily render static HTML documents and serve them back to the client. However, unless you're building a purely static, content-driven site, which is doubtful, you're more than likely going to want to render your HTML dynamically. That is, you want to generate portions of the HTML on the fly as pages are requested, perhaps using loops, conditional statements, data-driven content, and so on. In order to render dynamic HTML pages, you need to use a rendering engine.

This is where Handlebars comes in. The rendering engine is given its name because of the syntax it uses to display data, namely double pairs of braces, {{ and }}. Using Handlebars, you can have sections of your HTML pages that are determined at runtime based on data passed to it. For example:

```
<div>
    <p>Hello there {{ name }}!  Todays date is {{ timestamp }}</p>
</div>
```

The actual HTML that would wind up on a visitor's browser would be:

```
<div>
    <p>Hello there Jason!  Todays date is Sun Apr 13</p>
</div>
```

The first thing we want to take care of in our `configure` module is to register Handlebars as the default view rendering engine. In the `configure.js` file, above the `return(app);` line, you should insert the following code:

```
app.engine('handlebars', exphbs.create({
    defaultLayout: 'main',
    layoutsDir: app.get('views') + '/layouts',
    partialsDir: [app.get('views') + '/partials']
}).engine);
app.set('view engine', 'handlebars');
```

First, using the Express `app` object that was passed into the `configure` function, we define our rendering engine of choice by calling the engine function of `app`. The first parameter to the `engine` function is the file extension that the rendering engine should look for, namely `handlebars`.

The second parameter builds the engine by calling the express-hbs module's create function. This create function takes an options object as a parameter, and this options object defines a number of constants for our server. Most importantly, we will define which layout is our default layout and also where our layouts will be stored. If you recall, in server.js, we used app.set to set a views property of our app that pointed to the current working directory + /views. This setting is used when we configure the options for our rendering engine as well. You'll notice that the partialsDir property uses an array (with a single item) and a single string value for layoutsDir. Both of these methods are interchangeable, and I just wanted to demonstrate that you could have more than one partials directory, and it could just be an array of string values.

With that set, our server now knows that any time we try to render a HTML page that has a file extension of handlebars, it will use the Handlebars engine to perform the rendering. This means that we need to be sure to use Handlebars-specific syntax in our dynamic HTML pages.

We will be learning more about Handlebars and how to write dynamic HTML pages in the next chapter.

> Using .handlebars as a file extension was purely a personal choice. Some people prefer .hbs, and if you want, you can use anything you like. Just make sure that the first parameter to the app.engine() function and the second parameter in the app.set('view engine') function are identical.
>
> To learn more about the many template engines available for use with Node, check out this list on the official Joyent GitHub wiki at https://github.com/joyent/node/wiki/modules#templating.

# Summary

In this chapter, we learned about the Express web framework for Node and wrote a basic web server using Express that will act as the foundation for the image uploading website that we will build throughout the remainder of the book.

The web server you wrote handles requests to specific routes, uses controllers to handle the logic for those routes, and supports all of the standard requirements a typical web server should.

In the next chapter, we will cover using the Handlebars template engine to write each of the dynamic HTML pages that the website needs. In addition, we will update the image and home controllers to include the necessary logic to properly render those HTML pages.

# 5
# Templating with Handlebars

In this chapter, we will be exploring the following topics:

- The Handlebars templating framework
- The steps to develop the templates necessary to build the presentation layer of our application

Before we start exploring the capabilities of Handlebars, we need to have an idea of what a templating framework generally does.

## Templating engines

As we already know, a Model View Controller (MVC) application framework divides the application-specific code into models, views, and controllers. Controllers are supposed to be handling the task of binding the appropriate data to its relevant views to generate the output for an incoming web application request. So, views are supposed to be independent of the data and only contain code relevant to the presentation of the data, which will be mostly HTML. Apart from HTML, views will need to contain presentation logic, which will be conditions written on the data passed to them via controllers. Then, the main task that templating frameworks do in this case is that they make this process of embedding presentational logic simpler and readable. Also, they attempt to segregate the views into more understandable subcomponents.

# Server-side and client-side templating

Templating solutions can be generally classified into two as client-side and server-side templating solutions. The web applications we build usually follow a server-side or client-side templating approach or even a hybrid of both.

## Client-side templating

Imagine a case where the web application, after loading the page, makes an API call via AJAX and gets a JSON response in return. How will it render the data it received into its corresponding HTML? Client-side templates are required in this case to keep our JavaScript code neat and clean, or else we will end up putting too much unreadable HTML code as strings inside the JavaScript code. Client-side templating frameworks allow us to dump the templates corresponding to the components of a page in the markup inside specific tags and render them via JavaScript code whenever necessary. The common disadvantage of following a client-side approach is the impact it has on the initial render time of this page.

Another important advantage of using client-side templating is that it helps to offload the templating effort from the server to the client. This helps to reduce the computational load on your server to a great extent, as the templating logic is executed only in the browser via JavaScript.

## Server-side templating

Server-side templating is where we will render the markup via calling the corresponding views before sending the HTML response back to the web browser. This is what we are going to explore in this chapter via Handlebars.

Many different rendering engines are available, which can be used with Node and Express. The most popular among them are Jade, EJS, and Handlebars. The particular engine we will explore in this book is Handlebars.js.

# Views

A view is what we refer to as a HTML page. They are called views because of the MVC design pattern. As we already discussed, a model is the data that is going to be displayed on a page, the view is the page itself, and the controller is the brain that communicates between the model and the view.

Our particular application is going to need two views. The first view is the home page, and the second view is the image page.

The HTML in the following section relies heavily on Bootstrap, a popular HTML framework created by Twitter, which provides a standard set of user interface elements. These include buttons, fonts, layout grids, color schemes, and a whole lot more. Using Bootstrap allows us to not only present our application with a nice clean UI, but also build it so that it is responsive and will look correct on any device that is viewing it. You can learn more about Bootstrap by visiting http://getbootstrap.com.

Let's start by creating the home page view. Create a new file within the `views` folder, name it `index.handlebars`, and insert the following HTML code:

```
<div class="panel panel-primary">
    <div class="panel-heading">
        <h3 class="panel-title">
            Upload an Image
        </h3>
    </div>
```

The reason we named our file `index.handlebars` is a purely personal choice, but it is also based on common naming conventions on the Web. Typically, a HTML page that acts as the root file for any website is named `index.whatever` (`.php`, `.aspx`, `.html`, and so on). Again, this is just common convention and not something you need to specifically adhere to.

Create a basic HTML form and set `method` to `post` and `action` to `/images`. Be sure to set the `enctype` attribute of the form, since we will be uploading files as well as submitting data via form fields:

```
<form method="post" action="/images" enctype="multipart/form-
data">
    <div class="panel-body form-horizontal">
        <div class="form-group col-md-12">
            <label class="col-sm-2 control-label"
            for="file">Browse:</label>
```

Here, we have included a standard HTML input field for the file to be uploaded:

```
            <div class="col-md-10">
                <input class="form-control" type="file"
                name="file" id="file">
            </div>
        </div>
        <div class="form-group col-md-12">
```

```
<label class="col-md-2 control-label"
  for="title">Title:</label>
<div class="col-md-10">
```

Another standard HTML input field for the title of the file can be whatever the user wants, as shown in the following code:

```
      <input class="form-control" type="text"
        name="title">
    </div>
  </div>
  <div class="form-group col-md-12">
    <label class="col-md-2 control-label"
      for="description">Description:</label>
    <div class="col-md-10">
```

And a standard HTML `textarea` input field to allow for a description is as follows:

```
      <textarea class="form-control"
        name="description" rows="2"></textarea>
    </div>
  </div>
  <div class="form-group col-md-12">
    <div class="col-md-12 text-right">
```

A standard HTML button is provided that will submit the form to the server. Using Bootstrap classes, we provide `btn` and `btn-success` to make this look like a Bootstrap-style button with the default color for success (green):

```
      <button type="submit" id="login-btn"
        class="btn btn-success" type="button">
        <i class="fa fa-cloud-upload ">
        </i> Upload Image</button>
      </div>
    </div>
  </div>
</form>
</div>
```

After the upload form section, we will display a list of the newest images uploaded to the website. Please refer to the `each` block in the code snippet that follows. It is a keyword supported by Handlebars to loop over the data provided to the template in case of reusable HTML blocks. We will discuss this in detail in the following code:

```
<div class="panel panel-default">
  <div class="panel-heading">
    <h3 class="panel-title">
```

```
            Newest Images
        </h3>
    </div>
    <div class="panel-body">
        {{#each images}}
            <div class="col-md-4 text-center" style="padding-bottom:
            1em;"><a href="/images/{{ uniqueId }}"><img
            src="/public/upload/{{filename}}" alt="{{title}}"
            style="width: 175px; height: 175px;"  class="img-
            thumbnail"></a></div>
        {{/each}}
    </div>
</div>
```

There are two important sections in the main home page HTML code. The first is the form we define, which will be the main way users will upload images to the website. As we will be accepting image files as well as the details of the image (title, description, and so on), we need to ensure that the form is set up to accept multipart data. We also set the form action to point to the /images route we defined earlier in our `routes` and `image` controller modules. When a user completes the form and clicks on the **Submit** button, the form will send a POST request to http://localhost:3300/images, and our router will catch that and forward it to our `image` controller. From there, the `image` controller will handle the processing of the data and will save it to the database, saving the image file to the filesystem, and redirecting to the image details page. We will actually be writing this logic in the next chapter. For now, nothing will actually happen if you submit the form.

Below the main image uploading form on the home page, we also have a section that performs a Handlebars loop using `each` and iterates through an image collection, displaying each image as a thumbnail and the link to the image page. The `images` collection will be populated from our `home` controller. It's important to take note here that when you are inside an {{#each}} loop in a Handlebars template, your context changes. That is, the path you use to access data inside `each` is now based on each item in the collection. Here, our object, which will be bound to the view, will have an image collection, and each item in the image collection will have a property for `uniqueid`, `filename`, and `title`. With the home page view out of the way, let's set up the view for the image page.

Create another file in the `views` folder and name it `image.handlebars`. This file is going to have a bit more functionality, so I'm going to break it down into chunks so that you can review each section. First, insert the following block of code:

```
<div class="panel panel-primary">
    <div class="panel-heading">
        <h2 class="panel-title">{{ image.title }}</h2>
```

```
        </div>
        <div class="panel-body">
            <p>{{ image.description }}</p>
            <div class="col-md-12 text-center">
                <img src="/public/upload/{{image.filename}}"
                  class="img-thumbnail">
            </div>
        </div>
        <div class="panel-footer">
            <div class="row">
                <div class="col-md-8">
                    <button class="btn btn-success" id="btn-like"
                      data-id="{{ image.uniqueId }}"><i class="fa fa-
                      heart">   Like</i></button>
                    <strong class="likes-count">{{ image.likes }}
                    </strong>   -   <i class="fa fa-eye">
                    </i> <strong>{{ image.views }}</strong>
                      -   Posted: <em class="text-muted">{{
                    timeago image.timestamp }}</em>
                </div>
            </div>
        </div>
    </div>
</div>
```

This block of code defines the bulk of the content that will be displayed on the page for a specific image. The `viewModel` for this page is going to consist of an image object that has various properties defined that you see being used throughout the code; properties such as title, description, filename, likes, views, and the timestamp of when the image upload was performed.

You may have noticed a slightly different piece of syntax in the code specific to the `{{ timeago image.timestamp }}` timestamp. That is actually a Handlebars helper. It is a custom function we will write shortly, which will perform some special string formatting—specifically, converting a timestamp string to how long it was sometime ago (that is, 2 days ago, 12 hours ago, 15 minutes ago, and so on).

We want to allow users to post comments to images, so let's include a simple form for that:

```
<div class="panel panel-default">
    <div class="panel-heading">
        <div class="row">
            <div class="col-md-8">
                <strong class="panel-title">Comments</strong>
            </div>
```

```
<div class="col-md-4 text-right">
    <button class="btn btn-default btn-sm" id="btn-
    comment" data-id="{{ image.uniqueId }}">
    <i class="fa fa-comments-o"> Post
    Comment...</i></button>
</div>
</div>
</div>
<div class="panel-body">
    <blockquote id="post-comment">
        <div class="row">
```

The following is another standard HTML form with the method and action set. This form allows a user to enter, via standard HTML input fields, his/her name, e-mail address, and comments. Another **Submit** button is provided to save the comment:

```
<form method="post" action="/images/{{
image.uniqueId }}/comment">
    <div class="form-group col-sm-12">
        <label class="col-sm-2 control-label"
         for="name">Name:</label>
        <div class="col-sm-10">
            <input class="form-control"
             type="text" name="name">
        </div>
    </div>
    <div class="form-group col-sm-12">
        <label class="col-sm-2 control-label"
         for="email">Email:</label>
        <div class="col-sm-10">
            <input class="form-control"
             type="text" name="email">
        </div>
    </div>
    <div class="form-group col-sm-12">
        <label class="col-sm-2 control-label"
         for="comment">Comment:</label>
        <div class="col-sm-10">
            <textarea class="form-control"
             name="comment" rows="2"></textarea>
        </div>
    </div>
    <div class="form-group col-sm-12">
        <div class="col-sm-12 text-right">
```

```
                              <button type="submit" id="comment-btn"
                               class="btn btn-success" type="button">
                               <i class="fa fa-comment"></i>
                               Post</button>
                          </div>
                      </div>
                  </form>
              </div>
          </blockquote>
```

The form action for comments is set to /images/{{ image.uniqueid }}/comment.
Again, if you recall from the routes we set up, we specifically defined a route to
handle this.

Finally, we want to display any comments that have been submitted for this image.
Our viewModel includes a collection of comments in addition to the image details, so
we can simply iterate over that collection by using the Handlebars #each block helper:

```
          <ul class="media-list">
              {{#each comments}}
              <li class="media">
                  <a class="pull-left" href="#">
                      <img class="media-object img-circle"
                      src="http://www.gravatar.com/avatar/
                      {{gravatar}}?d=monsterid&s=45">
                  </a>
                  <div class="media-body">
                      {{ comment }}
                      <br/><strong class="media-heading">{{ name
                      }}</strong> <small class="text-muted">{{
                      timeago timestamp }}</small>
                  </div>
              </li>
              {{/each}}
          </ul>
      </div>
  </div>
```

Much like the loop we performed on the home page to display a collection of images,
here we simply iterate through every comment in the comments collection and
display the comment and string-formatted timestamp (again using our timeago
global helper). We also use Gravatar to display universal avatar images for users
who have commented (assuming they have provided their e-mail addresses).

Gravatar is a service provided by `https://wordpress.com/` that allows a user's personal profile image to be provided via his/her e-mail address. Many popular web services rely on Gravatar as a quick and easy way to display a user's personal profile image, without requiring the additional functionality to support such a feature. You can learn more about Gravatar at `http://gravatar.com`.

# Layouts

So far we've created two specific views for our website, one for the home page and one for the details of an image. However, there's no consistent UI wrapping both of these pages together. We have no consistent navigation or logo. There's no common footer with standard copyright or additional information.

Usually, with any website that you create, you're going to want to have some form of a standard layout or master template that every page will use. This layout typically includes the website logo and title, main navigation, sidebar (if any), and the footer. It would be bad practice to include the HTML code for the layout in every single page on the website because if you wanted to make even the smallest change to the main layout, you would have to edit every single page as a result. Fortunately, Handlebars helps lessen the work of utilizing a layout file.

Let's create a layout file for our app by creating a new file named `main.handlebars` within the `views/layouts` folder and inserting the following HTML code:

```
<!DOCTYPE HTML>
<html lang="en">
    <head>
        <title>imgPloadr.io</title>
        <link
         href="//netdna.bootstrapcdn.com/bootstrap/3.1.1/css/
         bootstrap.min.css" rel="stylesheet">
        <link href="//netdna.bootstrapcdn.com/font-awesome/
         4.0.3/css/font-awesome.min.css" rel="stylesheet">
        <link rel="stylesheet" type="text/css"
         href="/public/css/styles.css">
    </head>
    <body>
        <div class="page-header">
            <div class="container">
                <div class="col-md-6">
                    <h1><a href="/">imgPloadr.io</a></h1>
                </div>
```

```
            </div>
        </div>
        <div class="container">
            <div class="row">
                <div class="col-sm-8">
                    {{{ body }}}
                </div>
                <div class="col-sm-4">
                    {{> stats this }}

                    {{> popular this }}

                    {{> comments this }}
                </div>
            </div>
        </div>
        <div style="border-top: solid 1px #eee; padding-top:
        1em;">
            <div class="container">
                <div class="row">
                    <div class="col-sm-12 text-center">
                        <p class="text-muted">imgPloadr.io |
                        &copy; Copyright 2014, All Rights
                        Reserved</p>
                        <p class="text-center">
                            <i class="fa fa-twitter-square fa-2x
                            text-primary"></i>
                            <i class="fa fa-facebook-square fa-2x
                            text-primary"></i>
                        </p>
                    </div>
                </div>
            </div>
        </div>
        <script src="//ajax.googleapis.com/ajax/libs/jquery/
        1.11.0/jquery.min.js"></script>
        <script type="text/javascript"
        src="/public/js/scripts.js"></script>
    </body>
</html>
```

Most of the preceding code is just HTML, and a lot of it uses Bootstrap for the actual physical layout of the page as well as a few other UI-related elements. The most important part is the highlighted section in the middle with {{{ body }}} and the few lines below that, as they pertain to the use of Handlebars.

{{{ body }}} is a reserved word in Handlebars that is used specifically with layouts. What we are basically saying is that any page we render that uses our default layout file will have its content inserted into the area where {{{ body }}} is defined. If you recall from the configure module we created earlier, we defined our default layout file when we set up Handlebars as our rendering engine. The slightly odd use of {{{ and }}} around the body is due to the fact that Handlebars escapes HTML by default when using {{ and }}. Since our views contain mostly HTML, we want this to stay intact so that we use {{{ and }}} instead.

The other three lines that use {{ > ... }} render Handlebars partials, which are like the shared HTML code blocks that we will cover next.

# Partial views

So far we've created a view, which acts as the bulk of the HTML for a specific page, and a layout, which acts as the wrapper for the consistent parts of the website on every page. Next, let's take a look at creating partials, which are really just small views that we can reuse and inject inside our layouts or views.

Partials are a terrific way to create reusable components in a website and reduce code duplication. Consider the comments in our application. We have an HTML form defined that a user uses to submit a comment, but what if we wanted to allow users to post comments from a number of different areas throughout the website? This type of scenario is a great candidate for moving our comment form out to its own partial and then just including that partial anywhere we want to display the comment form.

For this app, we're using partials specifically for the sidebar in the main layout. With every view's viewModel, we will include a JavaScript object called sidebar that will contain the data specifically for the stats, popular images, and recent comments found within the sidebar partial.

Let's create the HTML for each of the partials. First, create a file named stats.handlebars within the views/partials/ path and include the following HTML code:

```
<div class="panel panel-default">
    <div class="panel-heading">
        <h3 class="panel-title">
            Stats
        </h3>
    </div>
    <div class="panel-body">
        <div class="row">
            <div class="col-md-2 text-left">Images:</div>
```

```
                <div class="col-md-10 text-right">{{
                    sidebar.stats.images }}</div>
            </div>
            <div class="row">
                <div class="col-md-2 text-left">Comments:</div>
                <div class="col-md-10 text-right">{{
                    sidebar.stats.comments }}</div>
            </div>
            <div class="row">
                <div class="col-md-2 text-left">Views:</div>
                <div class="col-md-10 text-right">{{
                    sidebar.stats.views }}</div>
            </div>
            <div class="row">
                <div class="col-md-2 text-left">Likes:</div>
                <div class="col-md-10 text-right">{{
                    sidebar.stats.likes }}</div>
            </div>
        </div>
    </div>
```

Next, create `views/partials/popular.handlebars` and insert the following HTML code into it:

```
<div class="panel panel-default">
    <div class="panel-heading">
        <h3 class="panel-title">
            Most Popular
        </h3>
    </div>
    <div class="panel-body">
        {{#each sidebar.popular}}
            <div class="col-md-4 text-center" style="padding-
            bottom: .5em;">
                <a href="/images/{{uniqueId}}"><img
                src="/public/upload/{{filename}}"
                style="width: 75px; height: 75px;"
                class="img-thumbnail"></a>
            </div>
        {{/each}}
    </div>
</div>
```

Finally, create `views/partials/comments.handlebars` and insert the following HTML code into it:

```
<div class="panel panel-default">
    <div class="panel-heading">
        <h3 class="panel-title">
            Latest Comments
        </h3>
    </div>
    <div class="panel-body">
        <ul class="media-list">
            {{#each sidebar.comments}}
            <li class="media">
                <a class="pull-left" href="/images/{{
                  image.uniqueId }}">
                    <img class="media-object" width="45"
                      height="45" src="/public/upload/
                      {{ image.filename }}">
                </a>
                <div class="media-body">
                    {{comment}}<br/>
                    <strong class="media-heading">
                    {{name}}</strong> <small class="text-muted">
                    {{timeago timestamp }}</small>
                </div>
            </li>
            {{/each}}
        </ul>
    </div>
</div>
```

# The basics of Handlebars

Handlebars is a really simple and easy-to-use templating framework. Let's go through and explore the basic syntax of writing a Handlebars template.

## Binding an object to the template

Let's assume the following JavaScript object is passed to a Handlebars template:

```
var model = {
  name: 'World'
};
```

The template file itself will contain the following markup:

```
<div>
  Hello {{ name }}!
</div>
```

This file will render to a browser in the following way:

```
Hello World!
```

# Embedding presentation logic

Of course, there's a lot more that you can do than just this! Handlebars also supports conditional statements:

```
var model = {
  name: 'World',
  description: 'This will only appear because its set.'
};

<div>
   Hello {{ name }}!<br/><br/>
  {{#if description}}
     <p>{{description}}</p>
  {{/if}}
</div>
```

Using an if block helper, as shown in the preceding code, you can check for true conditionals and only display HTML and/or data if the condition is true. Alternatively, you can use the unless helper to do the opposite, and display HTML only if a condition is false:

```
var model = {
  name: 'World'
};

<div>
   Hello {{ name }}!<br/><br/>
  {{#unless description}}
     <p>NOTE: no description found.</p>
  {{/if}}
</div>
```

You can use both if and else as well as unless the same way you would use conditional if/else in other programming languages.

# Handlebars helpers

Handlebars supports the idea of helpers, which are special custom functions you can write to perform some special logic from within the template during runtime. This will encourage developers to migrate the common presentation logic present in views into helpers and reuse them, thereby adding much more readability to the views. A great example of a helper would be the date string formatter we've been using. Helpers can be registered globally and made available to every template file, or they can be defined per view and passed to the template on an as-needed basis as part of the `viewModel`.

## Global helpers

First, let's create a global helper that will be available to every Handlebars template we render. The global helper that we will create will be used to format a timestamp so that it is worded according to how long ago the event occurred. We will use this throughout our application for things such as comments and image timestamps.

The first thing we need to do is update our `server/configure.js` module, where we originally configured Handlebars as our rendering engine. We are going to add a section to define our helpers:

```
app.engine('handlebars', exphbs.create({
    defaultLayout: 'main',
    layoutsDir: app.get('views') + '/layouts',
    partialsDir: [app.get('views') + '/partials'],
    helpers: {
        timeago: function(timestamp) {
            return moment(timestamp).startOf('minute').fromNow();
        }
    }
}).engine);
```

As you can see from the additional code we added (highlighted in the preceding code), we defined the `helpers` property of the configuration options within `create()`. Inside the `helpers` property, we can define any number of functions we want. In this case, we defined a simple `timeago` function that actually uses another npm module called `moment`. The `moment` module is a great library for performing numerous different types of date string formatting. As we are using a new module, we need to be sure to perform `require()` at the top of our `configure` module:

```
var path = require('path'),
    routes = require('./routes'),
    exphbs = require('express3-handlebars'),
    bodyParser = require('body-parser'),
    cookieParser = require('cookie-parser'),
    morgan = require('morgan'),
    methodOverride = require('method-override'),
    errorHandler = require('errorhandler'),
    moment = require('moment');
```

As well as actually install it via npm:

```
$ npm install moment --save
```

## View-specific helpers

While defining helpers globally is nice because they are available to every view that's rendered, sometimes you might only need to define a helper for use within a single view. In this case, you can include the helper with the model itself when calling `res.render()`, as shown in the following code:

```
var viewModel = {
  name: 'Jason',
helpers: {
    timeago: function(timestamp) {
  return 'a long time ago!';
        }
}
};
res.render('index', viewModel);
```

Not only are we defining a custom helper that can be used specifically from this view in its model object, but in this particular instance, we are overriding the existing `timeago` global helper with a slightly different version that is perfectly valid.

# Rendering the views

Let's take a minute to do a quick recap and see what we've done up to this point. So far, we have:

- Created `index.handlebars` and `image.handlebars` — the views for the two main pages of the application

- Created `layouts/main.handelbars` — the main layout file for every page in the application

- Created `partials/comments.handlebars`, `popular.handlebars`, and `stats.handlebars`

- Created a global `timeago` Handlebars helper

So far, so good; however, none of these views actually do anything, receive any `viewModels`, or even appear when you run the application! Let's make a few quick minor modifications to our controllers to get our views to render properly.

Open `/controllers/home.js` so that you can edit the `home` controller module. Update the contents of that file so that it looks identical to the following block of code:

```
module.exports = {
    index: function(req, res) {
        res.render('index');
    }
};
```

Instead of performing `res.send`, which just sends a simple response, we are calling `res.render` and passing in the name of the template file we want to render as the only parameter (for now). Using the defaults that were defined in our `configure` module, the `index` file will be loaded from our `views` folder. Again, also using the defaults, we configured the default layout of `main` that will be applied to this view in our `configure` module.

Let's update the `image` controller to do the same thing as well. Edit `/controllers/image.js` and change the `index` function so that it looks identical to the following block of code:

```
index: function(req, res) {
    res.render('image');
},
```

And that's it! Let's fire up the server, open the app in our browser, and see how it looks:

```
$ npm start
$ open http://localhost:3300
$ open http://localhost:3300/images/1
```

Success! Hopefully, you see something that closely resembles the following screenshot of the home page:

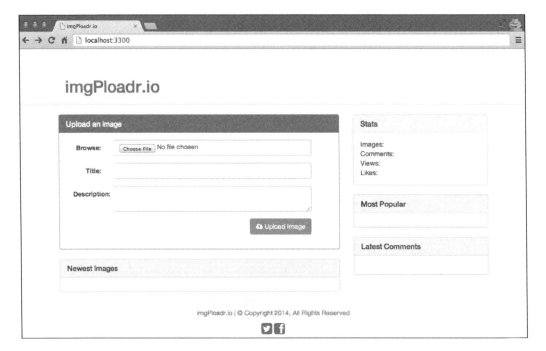

Additionally, if you provide a random URL to a specific image, for example
`http://localhost:3300/images/1`, you should see the following screenshot:

The preceding command uses `npm start` to start the application. Please note that this command will work only if you have the application entry point file configured in the `package.json` file. If this is not working, then you have to set the main attribute in the `package.json` and set it to the `server.js` file. Also, as an alternative, you can manually invoke the `server.js` file by using `node server.js`.

# Summary

In this chapter, the Handlebars template-rendering engine was introduced, following which we reviewed the syntax used when creating dynamic HTML pages. We created a main layout for our app as well as the home page and image page views. We included partial views for the sidebar in the layout and created a global Handlebars helper to display custom formatted dates.

Even though none of the views are currently displaying any data (because we aren't passing models to the views yet), you can see that things are starting to come along nicely! In the next chapter, we will wire up the actual logic in the controllers for each page and build up the Model objects so that we start seeing some actual content on our screens.

# 6

# Controllers and View Models

Up until this point, the controllers we wrote for our application have been extremely basic. They were started with a simple task of sending text responses to the client. In the previous chapter, we updated the controllers so that they render an HTML view and send the HTML code to the client, instead of a simple text response. The primary job of a controller is to act as the entity, which holds the logic that makes all of the necessary decisions to properly render a response to the client. In our case, this means retrieving and/or generating the data necessary for a page to appear complete.

In this chapter, we will:

- Modify the controllers so that they generate a data model and pass it to a view
- Include logic to support uploading and saving image files
- Update the controllers to actually render dynamic HTML
- Include helpers for the partials that generate the website statistics
- Iterate on the UI to include improved usability via jQuery

## Controllers

A controller can be defined as the entity that will be responsible for manipulating models and initiating the view render process with the data received from the corresponding models. In the code we have developed so far, we can see that the express router instance is used to tie functions to a corresponding route. These functions are nothing but controllers. For every route that we create in our router, two parameters are necessary:

- The first parameter is the string for the route itself, which is
  `/images/:image_id`

- The second parameter is a controller function that will be executed when that route is accessed

For any route that has to do with images, we rely on the `images` controller. Likewise, any route that has to do with the home page relies on the `home` controller, and so on and so forth.

The steps we will take to define our controllers in our app are purely organizational and based on personal preference. We created our controllers as modules so that our router wasn't a big, long convoluted mess of spaghetti code. We could have just as easily kept all of the logic contained in our controllers as functions directly within the routes themselves, but this would have been an organizational mess and made for very hard-to-read code to maintain later.

As our sample app is fairly small, we only have two controllers currently: `home` and `image`. It is the responsibility of these controllers to build the appropriate view models for our HTML pages and render the actual pages as well. Any logic that is required to execute per page and build the view model will be done so via our controllers.

# View models

Given a single HTML view in our app, we need to be able to attach data to that page so that the template that is being rendered can be included in such a way that the dynamic areas of the page are replaced with real content. To do this, we need to generate a view model. During the render, the template engine will parse the template itself and look for special syntax that indicates that specific sections should be replaced at runtime with values from the view model itself. We have seen examples of this while we explored the Handlebars template framework in the previous chapter. Think of this as a fancy runtime `find` and `replace` of your HTML templates—finding variables and replacing them with values stored in the view model sent to the template. It is important to note that this process happens at the server and the result is only sent as the response to the HTTP request that our application receives.

A view model is typically just a single JavaScript object that can be passed to the template. The template contains all of the necessary logic we need to properly render the page. It is the task of the templating engine to produce the corresponding HTML by processing the templates with the associated models. The view model for a page will typically contain all of the data necessary to render the content-specific portions of that page. Using our application as an example, the view model for a specific image's page might contain the title of the image, its description, and the information necessary to display the image and various stats such as the number of likes, views, and a collection of comments. A view model can be as simple or as complex as you like.

The term view model is used here to refer to the data form of model, which will be tied to the template while rendering the HTML via any templating framework.

# Updating the home controller

If you take a look at our current `home` controller (`controllers/home.js`), you can see that the `index` function barely has any code in it whatsoever:

```
res.render('index');
```

The first thing we want to do is build a basic view model using sample data so that we can see our view model at work. Replace that single `res.render` call with the following updated code:

```
var viewModel = {
    images: [
        {
            uniqueId:       1,
            title:          'Sample Image 1',
            description:    '',
            filename:       'sample1.jpg',
            views:          0,
            likes:          0,
            timestamp:      Date.now
        }, {
            uniqueId:       2,
            title:          'Sample Image 2',
            description:    '',
            filename:       'sample2.jpg',
            views:          0,
            likes:          0,
            timestamp:      Date.now
        }, {
            uniqueId:       3,
            title:          'Sample Image 3',
            description:    '',
            filename:       'sample3.jpg',
            views:          0,
            likes:          0,
            timestamp:      Date.now
        }, {
```

```
            uniqueId:        4,
            title:           'Sample Image 4',
            description:      '',
            filename:        'sample4.jpg',
            views:           0,
            likes:           0,
            timestamp:       Date.now
        }
    ]
};
```

```
res.render('index', viewModel);
```

In this code, we built a basic JavaScript collection of objects:

- The variable we declare is called `viewModel`, but the name of this variable doesn't actually matter and can be whatever you want. The `viewModel` variable is an object that contains a single property called `images`, which is itself an array.

- The `images` array contains four sample images, each with a few basic properties— we came up with the most obvious properties while deciding what kind of information we want per image. Each image in the collection has a `uniqueId`, `title`, `description`, `filename`, `views`, and `likes` count, and a `timestamp` property.

Once we have set up our `viewModel`, we simply pass it as the second parameter to the `res.render` call. Doing this while rendering a view makes the data in it available to the view itself. Now, if you recall from some of the template code we wrote for the home `index.handlebars` view, we had a `{{#each images}}` loop that iterated through each image in the `images` collection of the view model passed to the template. Taking another look at our view model we created, we see that it only has a single property named `images`. The HTML code inside the Handlebars loop will then specifically reference the `uniqueId`, `filename`, and `title` properties for each image in the `images` array.

Save the changes to the `home` controller, launch your app again, and point your browser to `http://localhost:3300`. You should see the four images that now appear on the homepage in the **Newest Images** section (although, as you can see in the following screenshot, the images are still broken, as we didn't actually create any image files):

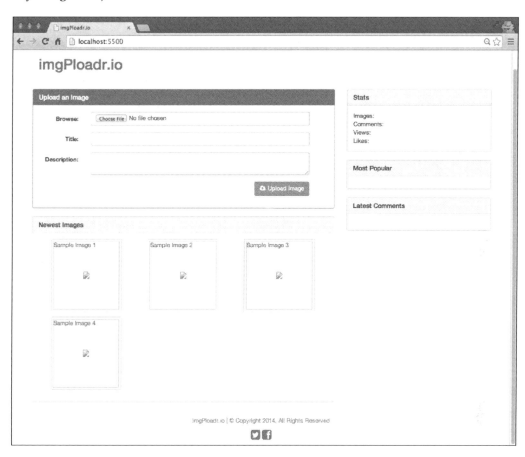

The homepage has a fairly simple controller and view model, and you might have noticed that the sidebar is still completely empty. We'll cover the sidebar a little later in this chapter.

# Updating the image controller

Let's create the controller and view model for the image page. The controller for the image will be a little more complex, as we'll write the logic to handle uploading and saving of the image files via the form on the homepage.

# Displaying an image

The `index` function in the `image` controller will look almost identical to the `index` function from the `home` controller. The only difference is that instead of generating an array of images, we will build a view model for a single image. However, the view model for this image will have a little more information than the one from the homepage, since we are building a page that renders a more detailed view of an image (versus the thumbnail collection on the homepage). The most noteworthy inclusion is that of a `comments` array for the image.

Taking another look at the original `index` function in our `controllers/image.js` file, we can see the simple existing `res.render` line of code:

```
res.render('image');
```

We want to replace this line with a view model and an updated `res.render` statement using the following code:

```
var viewModel = {
    image: {
        uniqueId:       1,
        title:          'Sample Image 1',
        description:    'This is a sample.',
        filename:       'sample1.jpg',
        views:          0,
        likes:          0,
        timestamp:      Date.nowDate.now()
    },
    comments: [
        {
            image_id:    1,
            email:       'test@testing.com',
            name:        'Test Tester',
```

```
            gravatar:    'http://lorempixel.com/75/75/animals/1',
            comment:     'This is a test comment...',
            timestamp:   Date.now()
        },{
            image_id:    1,
            email:       'test@testing.com',
            name:        'Test Tester',
            gravatar:    'http://lorempixel.com/75/75/animals/2',
            comment:     'Another followup comment!',
            timestamp:   Date.now()
        }
    ]
};
```

```
res.render('image', viewModel);
```

Here we declare a new `viewModel` variable again, this time with an `image` property
that contains the properties for the single image. In addition to the `image` property,
there is also a `comments` property, which is an array of comment objects. You can
see that each comment has various properties specific to a comment for each image.
This JavaScript object is actually a pretty good preview of what our real data will
wind up looking like once we include logic to connect our app to MongoDB!

After we build our sample `image` object and its collection of comments, we pass
that along to our `res.render` call, thus sending this new `viewModel` directly to
our image's Handlebars template. Again, if you review the HTML code in the
`image.handlebars` file, you can see where each property of the `viewModel` is
being displayed.

Again, let's run the application and make sure our image page is appearing properly:

```
$ node server.js
```

Once the app is running and you've launched it in your browser, click on any of the images that are listed in the **Newest Images** section of the homepage. This should take you to an individual image page where you will see something like the page shown in the following screenshot:

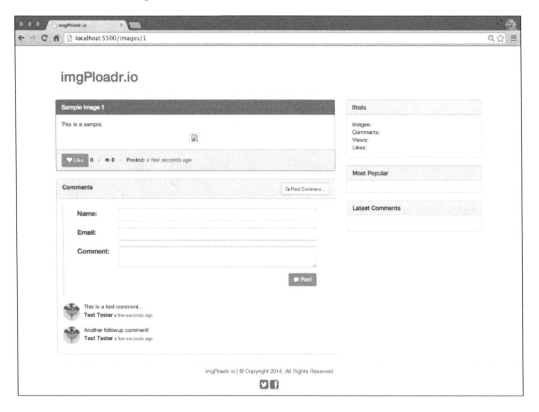

Notice that `title`, `description`, `likes` and `views`, and `timestamp` are all now appearing on the page. In addition, you can see a few comments listed below the image as well!

# Uploading an image

The next feature we need to implement in our `image` controller is the logic to handle when a user submits an image via the **Image Upload** form on the homepage. Even though the form is on the homepage of our app, we decided to house the logic to handle uploading within our `image` controller because logically, this makes the most sense (since this feature has primarily to do with images and not the homepage per se). This was purely a personal decision, and you can house the logic wherever you please.

You should note that the HTML for the form on the homepage has its action set to /images and its method is post. This perfectly matches the route we set up previously, where we listen for a post to the /images route and call the image controller's create function.

The create function in our image controller will have a few key responsibilities:

- It should generate a unique filename for the image, which will also act as an identifier
- It should save the uploaded file to the filesystem and ensure that it is an image file
- It should redirect to the image/image_id route once its task is complete to display the actual image

As we are going to be working with the filesystem in this function, we are going to need to include a few modules from the Node.js core set of modules, specifically the filesystem (fs) and the path (path) modules.

Before we begin with adding the necessary code for the upload image section, we need a small fix to be applied on the configuration of the application. If you look at the configure.js file, which we created in the beginning, you should see the lines specific to configuring the upload directory using the bodyParser module:

```
app.use(bodyParser({
uploadDir:path.join(__dirname, 'public/upload/temp')
}));
```

Here, the issue is that bodyParser supports only JSON and URL encoded form submissions and not multipart form submissions that we need in the case of our file upload. So we need to add an extra module in the configure file to support the file uploads, namely multer. Add it as a dependency to our application using the following command:

```
npm install multer --save
```

Now, go to the configure file and require it via

```
multer = require('multer');
```

You can place this below the initial require calls in the file. Then, find the following bodyParser configuration line:

```
app.use(bodyParser({
        uploadDir:path.join(__dirname, 'public/upload/temp')
}));
```

Replace the preceding line with the following line of code:

```
app.use(multer({ dest: path.join(__dirname,
                 'public/upload/temp') }));
```

Now, our upload actions will work fine, as expected.

Let's begin by first editing the `controllers/image.js` file and inserting the two new `require` statements at the very top of the file:

```
var fs = require('fs'),
    path = require('path');
```

Next, take the `create` function's original code:

```
res.send('The image:create POST controller');
res.redirect('/images/1');
```

Replace this original code with the following code:

```
var saveImage = function() {
    // to do...
};
saveImage();
```

Here, we created a function called `saveImage`, and we executed it immediately after we declared it. This might look a little odd, but the reason for this will become clear when we implement database calls in the following chapter. The main reason is that we are going to call `saveImage` repeatedly to ensure that the unique identifier we generated is in fact unique and doesn't already exist in the database (as a previously saved image's identifier).

Let's review a breakdown of the code that will be inserted in the `saveImage` function (replacing the `// to do...` comment). I will cover each line of code for this function and then give you the entire block of code at the end:

```
var possible = 'abcdefghijklmnopqrstuvwxyz0123456789',
    imgUrl = '';
```

We need to generate a random six-digit alphanumeric string to represent a unique identifier for an image. This identifier will work similar to other websites that provide tiny URLs for unique links (that is, `bit.ly`). To do this, we first provide a string of possible characters that can be used while generating the random string:

```
for(var i=0; i < 6; i+=1) {
    imgUrl += possible.charAt(Math.floor(Math.random() *
                             possible.length));
}
```

Then, loop six times and randomly pull out a single character from our string of possible characters, appending it in each cycle. By the end of this `for` loop, we should have a string that consists of six random letters and/or numbers, for example `a8bd73`:

```
var tempPath = req.files.file.path,
    ext = path.extname(req.files.file.name).toLowerCase(),
    targetPath = path.resolve('./public/upload/' + imgUrl + ext);
```

Here, we declare three variables; where our uploaded files will be stored temporarily, the file extension of the file that was uploaded (that is `.png`, `.jpg`, and so on), and a destination where the uploaded image should ultimately reside. For both the latter variables, we use the `Path` node module, which works great while dealing with file names and paths and getting information from a file (such as a file extension). Next, we move the image from its temporary upload path to its final destination:

```
if (ext === '.png' || ext === '.jpg' || ext === '.jpeg' || ext ===
    '.gif') {
    fs.rename(tempPath, targetPath, function(err) {
        if (err) throw err;

        res.redirect('/images/'+ imgUrl);
    });
} else {
    fs.unlink(tempPath, function () {
        if (err) throw err;

        res.json(500, {error: 'Only image files are allowed.'});
    });
}
```

This code performs some validation. Specifically, it conducts checks to make sure that the uploaded file extension matches a list of allowable extensions—namely, known image file types. If a valid image file was uploaded, it is moved from the `temp` folder via the filesystem's `rename` function. Notice how the filesystem (`fs`) `rename` function takes three parameters: the original file, the new file, and a callback function.

The callback function is executed once the rename is complete. If the node didn't work this way (always relying on callback functions), it's quite likely your code will execute immediately following the execution of the `rename` function and try to work against a file that doesn't exist yet (that is, the `rename` function didn't even finish doing its work). By using a callback function, we are effectively telling the node that once the rename of the file is finished and the file is ready and where it should be, then execute the following code.

The else condition that follows handles the situation when the uploaded file was invalid (that is, not an image), so we call the unlink function of the fs module, which will delete the original file (from the temp directory it was uploaded to) and then send a simple JSON 500 with an error message.

Here is the complete saveImage function (again, the following code will replace // to do... from earlier):

```
var possible = 'abcdefghijklmnopqrstuvwxyz0123456789',
    imgUrl = '';

for(var i=0; i < 6; i+=1) {
    imgUrl += possible.charAt(Math.floor(Math.random() *
                            possible.length));
}

var tempPath = req.files.file.path,
    ext = path.extname(req.files.file.name).toLowerCase(),
    targetPath = path.resolve('./public/upload/' + imgUrl + ext);

if (ext === '.png' || ext === '.jpg' || ext === '.jpeg' || ext ===
    '.gif') {
    fs.rename(tempPath, targetPath, function(err) {
        if (err) throw err;

        res.redirect('/images/' + imgUrl);
    });
} else {
    fs.unlink(tempPath, function () {
        if (err) throw err;

        res.json(500, {error: 'Only image files are allowed.'});
    });
}
```

With this code in place, we can now successfully upload an image file via the form on the homepage. Give it a try by launching the app and opening it in a browser. Once there, click on the **Browse** button in the main form, and select an image file from your computer. If successful, the image file should exist within the public/upload folder of your project with a new random filename.

Ensure that you have the `public/upload` folders created in your project, or you will get runtime errors when you attempt to write files to a location that doesn't exist. Write permissions might need to be set on the folder depending on your OS and security access.

After the upload form completes and the `create` controller function does its work, it will redirect to the individual image page for the image that was uploaded.

# Helpers for reusable code

So far, each of the pages that we have rendered display their `viewModel` data perfectly, but that pesky sidebar still remains blank. We're going to fix this by creating a few modules for the sidebar content by implementing them as helper modules. These helper modules will be used repeatedly by various parts of our application and don't necessarily belong to the `controller` folder or the `server` folder. So, we'll just create a new home called `helpers` and store these modules there.

 As we are just loading temporary fixture data into our view models, the data we set up in the helpers as well as the controllers will all be replaced with actual live data in the next chapter once we implement MongoDB.

# The sidebar module

First, we will create a module for the entire sidebar. This module will be responsible for calling multiple other modules to populate `viewModel` for each section of the sidebar. As we are going to be populating each page's own `viewModel` with data specifically for the sidebar, the sidebar module's function will accept that original `viewModel` as a parameter. This is so that we can append data to the existing `viewModel` for each page.

Here, we will be appending a `sidebar` property (which is a JavaScript object) that contains properties for each of the sections of the sidebar.

To get started, first create a file named `helpers/sidebar.js` and insert the following code:

```
var Stats = require('./stats'),
    Images = require('./images'),
    Comments = require('./comments');
```

```
module.exports = function(viewModel, callback){
    viewModel.sidebar = {
        stats: Stats(),
        popular: Images.popular(),
        comments: Comments.newest()
    };

    callback(viewModel);
};
```

In the preceding code, you can see that we first required a module for each section of the sidebar. The existing `viewModel` for any given page that displays the sidebar is the first parameter of the function. We add a `sidebar` property to `viewModel` and set values for each property by calling the module for each section of the sidebar. Finally, we execute a callback that was passed in as the second parameter to the `sidebar` module. This callback is an anonymous function that we will use to execute the rendering of the HTML page.

Let's update the `home` and `image` controllers to include a call to the `sidebar` module as well as defer rendering the HTML template for each page to the callback for the `sidebar` module.

Edit `controllers/home.js` and take the following line of code:

```
res.render('index', viewModel);
```

Replace it with this new block of code:

```
sidebar(viewModel, function(viewModel) {
    res.render('index', viewModel);
});
```

Make the exact same changes to the `controllers/image.js` file replacing `index` with `image`:

```
sidebar(viewModel,function(viewModel){
res.render('image', viewModel);
});
```

Again, notice how we execute the `sidebar` module and pass the existing `viewModel` as the first parameter and a basic anonymous function as a callback for the second parameter. What this is doing is waiting to render the HTML for the view until after the sidebar has completed populating `viewModel`. This is because of the asynchronous nature of Node.js. Suppose we wrote the code in the following way instead:

```
sidebar(viewModel);
res.render('index', viewModel);
```

Here, it's quite likely that the `res.render` statement will execute before `sidebar` has even finished doing any work. This is going to become very important once we introduce MongoDB in the next chapter.

Additionally, as we are now using the `sidebar` module in each controller, be sure to `require` it at the top of both controllers by including the following code:

```
var sidebar = require('../helpers/sidebar');
```

Now that our `sidebar` module is complete, and it's being called from both controllers, let's complete the sidebar by creating each of the submodules that are required.

# The stats module

The `stats` module is going to display a few random pieces of statistics about our app. Specifically, it will show the count for the total number of `images`, `comments`, `views`, and `likes` for the entire website.

Create the `helpers/stats.js` file and insert the following code:

```
module.exports = function() {
    var stats = {
        images:     0,
        comments:   0,
        views:      0,
        likes:      0
    };

    return stats;
};
```

This module is pretty basic and all it does is create a standard JavaScript object with a few properties for the various stats, each set initially to `0`.

# The images module

The `images` module is responsible for returning various collections of images. Initially, we will create a `popular` function that will be used to return a collection of the most popular images on the website. Initially, this collection will simply be an array of image objects with the sample fixture data present.

Create the `helpers/images.js` file and insert the following code:

```
module.exports = {
    popular: function() {
        var images = [
            {
                uniqueId:       1,
                title:          'Sample Image 1',
                description:    '',
                filename:       'sample1.jpg',
                views:          0,
                likes:          0,
                timestamp:      Date.now()
            }, {
                uniqueId:       2,
                title:          'Sample Image 2',
                description:    '',
                filename:       'sample2.jpg',
                views:          0,
                likes:          0,
                timestamp:      Date.now()
            }, {
                uniqueId:       3,
                title:          'Sample Image 3',
                description:    '',
                filename:       'sample3.jpg',
                views:          0,
                likes:          0,
                timestamp:      Date.now()
            }, {
                uniqueId:       4,
                title:          'Sample Image 4',
                description:    '',
                filename:       'sample4.jpg',
                views:          0,
                likes:          0,
                timestamp:      Date.now()
            }
        ];
        return images;
    }
};
```

# The comments module

Similar to the image's `helper` module, the `comments` module will return a collection of the newest comments posted to the site. The idea of particular interest is that each comment also has an image attached to it so that the actual image for each comment can be displayed as a thumbnail while displaying the list of comments (otherwise, we lose context when we see a random list of comments with no related image).

Create the `helpers/comments.js` file and insert the following code:

```
module.exports = {
    newest: function() {
        var comments = [
            {
                image_id:    1,
                email:       'test@testing.com',
                name:        'Test Tester',
                gravatar:    'http://lorempixel.com/75/75/animals/1',
                comment:     'This is a test comment...',
                timestamp:   Date.now(),
                image: {
                    uniqueId:       1,
                    title:          'Sample Image 1',
                    description:    '',
                    filename:       'sample1.jpg',
                    views:          0,
                    likes:          0,
                    timestamp:      Date.now
                }
            }, {
                image_id:    1,
                email:       'test@testing.com',
                name:        Test Tester',
                gravatar:    'http://lorempixel.com/75/75/animals/2',
                comment:     'Another followup comment!',
                timestamp:   Date.now(),
                image: {
                    uniqueId:       1,
                    title:          'Sample Image 1',
                    description:    '',
                    filename:       'sample1.jpg',
                    views:          0,
                    likes:          0,
                    timestamp:      Date.now
```

```
            }
        }
    ];

    return comments;
  }
};
```

Again, this is just a basic JavaScript array of objects with a few properties for each comment, one of which is an actual image and its properties (the `image` property should look familiar since it's the same as one of the items in the images `helper` module).

# Testing the sidebar implementation

Now that our `sidebar` module is complete along with its dependent submodules for the various stats, images, and comments, it's time to give our application another test run. Launch the node server and open the application in your browser.

You should now see the sidebar complete with content on both the homepage as well as the image landing page.

# Iterating on the UI

Now that we have our application working fairly well and we can actually interact with it, it's time to step back and take a look at some of the areas we might be able to improve.

One area is the **Post Comment** form on the image page. I don't think it's necessary that this form is always visible, but instead, it should be made available only when someone actually wants to post a comment.

Additionally, I'd love the **Like** button to not have to post a full form submission to the server and cause the entire page to reload (like the form on the homepage does when it uploads an image). We will use jQuery to submit an AJAX call to the server to handle the likes, and send and retrieve data in real time without ever reloading the page.

To make these tweaks, we're going to need to introduce a small amount of JavaScript on the page to add a little interactivity. To make things even easier, we'll use the popular jQuery JavaScript library to make creating interactive features a breeze.

jQuery has been around for a number of years and has been explosively popular in frontend development. Simply put, jQuery in JavaScript with training wheels. It allows you to manipulate the **Document Object Model (DOM)** — the HTML structure of any page — extremely easily; you will see this in the next section. You can learn more about jQuery at http://jquery.com.

You might not have noticed, but, in the HTML code that was provided for the main. handlebars layout file, jQuery has already been included as an external script tag (referencing jQuery hosted on a CDN). Additionally, a local scripts.js tag is also included, where we will put our custom jQuery JavaScript code for the changes we're going to make to the UI. When you look at the very bottom of main.handlebars, you can see the following code:

```
<script
src="//ajax.googleapis.com/ajax/libs/jquery/1.11.0/jquery.min.js"></
script>
<script type="text/javascript"
src="/public/js/scripts.js"></script>
```

The first script tag points to Google's code **Content Delivery Network (CDN)**, which means, we don't have to worry about hosting that file with our code. The second file, however, is our own file, so we will need to make sure that exists.

 CDN is a means of delivering a file from a globally distributed network of caching servers. What this means, generally speaking, is that, files that are very commonly downloaded by web visitors (such as jQuery, for example) can be loaded much quicker via a regionally closer download source as well as improved caching. If multiple websites use the same CDN URL to host jQuery, for example, it stands to reason that a visitor to your website might have already downloaded jQuery from visiting a previous unrelated website. Therefore, your website will load that much quicker!

Create the public/js/scripts.js file and insert the following code:

```
$(function(){
    // to do...
});
```

This is a standard code block that you'll see almost every time anyone uses jQuery. What this code does is execute an anonymous function within the $() jQuery wrapper, which is shorthand for writing the following code:

```
$(document).ready(function(){
    // to do...
});
```

This code basically just means that the callback function will wait until the page is fully loaded and ready before executing. This is important because we don't want to apply UI event handlers and/or effects to DOM elements that don't actually exist yet because the page is still loading. This is also another reason why the script tags in the main.handlebars layout file are the last lines of the page; so, they are the last to load ensuring that the document has already been fully downloaded and is ready to be manipulated.

First, let's address the **Post Comment** functionality. We want to hide the comment form by default, and then display it only when a user clicks on the **Post Comment** button below an image (to the right of the **Like** button). Insert the following code inside the callback function where the // to do... comment exists:

```
$('#post-comment').hide();
$('#btn-comment').on('click', function(event) {
    event.preventDefault();

    $('#post-comment').show();
});
```

The first line of code executes the hide function on the HTML div that has a post-comment ID. We then immediately apply an event handler to the HTML button with a btn-comment ID. The event handler we apply is for onClick because we want it to execute the anonymous function we provided whenever a user clicks on that button. That function simply prevents the default behavior (the default behavior for that particular element; in this case, a button) and then calls the show jQuery function, which reveals the post-comment div that was previously hidden. The event. preventDefault() part is important because if we didn't include that, the action of clicking on the button would do what a browser expects it to do and try to execute our custom JavaScript function at the same time. If we didn't include this, it's likely that our UI will behave in ways that are less than ideal. A good example is if you want to override the default behavior of a standard HTML link, you can assign an onClick event handler and do whatever you want. However, if you don't perform event.preventDefault(), the browser is going to send the user to the HREF for that link, regardless of what your code is trying to do.

Now let's add some code to handle the **Like** button functionality. We are going to add an event handler for the button, the same way we did for the **Post Comment** button, using jQuery's `.on` function. After the code that you added previously, insert this additional block of code inside the ready statement:

```
$('#btn-like').on('click', function(event) {
    event.preventDefault();

    var imgId = $(this).data('id');

    $.post('/images/' + imgId + '/like').done(function(data) {
        $('.likes-count').text(data.likes);
    });
});
```

The preceding code attaches an `onClick` event handler to the `btn-like` button. The event handler first retrieves the `data-id` attribute from the **Like** button itself (assigned via the `image.handlebars` HTML template code and `viewModel`) and then performs a jQuery AJAX post to the `/images/:image_id/like` route. Recall the following line from our Node `server/routes.js` file:

```
app.post('/images/:image_id/like', image.like);
```

Once that AJAX call is done, another anonymous callback function will be executed that will change the text of the HTML element with a `likes-count` class and replace it with the data that was returned from the AJAX call—in this case, the updated total count of likes (typically, it would be whatever it was previously plus one).

In order to test this functionality, we are going to need to implement some fixture data in our `like` function inside the `image` controller. Edit `controllers/image.js` and within the `like` function, replace the existing `res.send` function call with the following code:

```
like: function(req, res) {
    res.json({likes: 1});
},
```

All this code does is return JSON to the client with a simple object that contains a single `likes` property with a value of 1. In the next chapter, when we introduce MongoDB to the app, we'll update this code to actually increase the count of likes and return the true value for the liked image.

With all of those changes in place, you should be able to relaunch the node server and open the website in your browser. Click on any image on the homepage to view the image page and then click on the **Like** button to see it change from 0 to 1. Don't forget to check out the fancy new **Post Comment** button too—clicking on this should reveal the comment form!

# Summary

At the beginning of this chapter, we had some basic HTML pages that appear in a browser via our application, but they contained no content and no logic whatsoever. We implemented the logic for each of our controllers and learned about the view model and how to populate pages with content.

In addition to displaying content on our pages via a view model, we also implemented the code to handle uploading and saving image files to the local filesystem.

We tweaked the UI slightly to include some subtle enhancements using jQuery by revealing the comment form and used AJAX to track likes instead of relying on a full page postback.

Now that the groundwork has been laid for our view models and controllers, let's tie it all together using MongoDB and start working with real data. In the next chapter, we will update the controllers once again, this time implementing the logic to read from and save data to our MongoDB server.

# 7
# Persisting Data with MongoDB

With almost any application written for the Web nowadays, a highly interactive application is of limited value if the interaction between its users isn't permanently saved. You have to integrate your application with a proper database to solve this issue. Imagine a case where all of the data for your application (registered users, order transactions, and social interactions) was stored within the temporary memory of the server the application is running on. The moment that server is turned off or rebooted, all of your application data will be lost. Relying on a database to store this data permanently is crucial to any dynamic application.

In this chapter, the following topics will be covered:

- Connecting to MongoDB
- An introduction to Mongoose
- Schemas and models
- Adding CRUD to our controllers

In the previous chapter, we wrote and accounted for the actual logic of our application. The next step in building our application is to connect it to a database so that our user's interactions and data can be permanently saved and retrieved. Technically, we can get around this by storing data in the memory, but the moment our web server restarts or crashes, all of that data will be lost. Without connecting our application to a database server to persist data, every input interacted by a visitor will be obsolete. Without some kind of database server to store our data, most of the websites we interact with on a daily basis wouldn't even exist.

Here is a general breakdown of how our data is going to be persisted for every visitor interaction in our app:

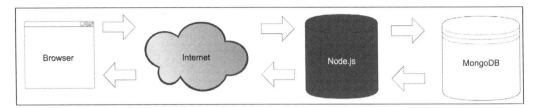

Consider the preceding diagram, which reflects the typical lifecycle of a web application request:

1. A visitor submits a request to view a page on our application via their web browser.

2. Node.js server receives this request and queries a MongoDB server for any data.

3. MongoDB server returns the queried data back to our Node.js server.

4. The Node.js server takes that data, builds it into the view model, and then sends the rendered HTML page back to the browser.

5. The web browser receives the response from our Node.js server and renders the HTML.

6. This cycle repeats typically for every interaction by every visitor.

For the purposes of this book, we are using MongoDB as our primary data store— but the reality is that we can use anything to store data: MySQL, PostgreSQL, MS SQL, the filesystem, and so on.

# Using MongoDB with Node.js

Before we officially implement MongoDB into our actual application, let's first take a look at some basic examples of connecting to a MongoDB server from within Node.js.

Create a new project folder to store some sample code to experiment with. I'll call my folder mongotest. Inside this folder, create a new file called test.js. In this file, we will play around with some code to test how to connect to MongoDB and how to insert and retrieve some data. The first thing we need to do in order to connect to a MongoDB server from node.js is to require a mongodb module.

To get started, change directories into the new `mongotest` folder and install the `mongodb` module using npm:

```
$ cd mongotest
$ npm install mongodb
```

 Don't be confused by the module's name. The `mongodb` npm module isn't MongoDB itself, but rather a third-party npm module that facilitates communicating to a MongoDB server from within Node.js. Also, because this is just a sample project to experiment with, we don't require the `--save` flag with `npm install` since we aren't maintaining a `package.json` file.

# Connecting to MongoDB

Now that the `mongodb` module is installed, we can use it in our experimentation file. Boot up your editor and create a file named `test.js`. Insert the following block of code into it:

```
var MongoClient = require('mongodb').MongoClient;

MongoClient.connect('mongodb://localhost:27017/mongotest',
function(err, db) {
    console.log('Connected to MongoDB!');

    db.close();
});
```

Executing the preceding code should log **Connected to MongoDB!** to your screen.

The first thing you'll notice is that we require the `mongodb` module, but we specifically use the `MongoClient` component of the module. This component is the actual interface we use to actively open a connection to a MongoDB server. Using `MongoClient`, we pass the `mongodb://localhost:27017/mongotest` string URL to our local server as the first parameter. Notice that the path in the URL points to the server and then the name of the database itself.

Remember to make sure you have your local MongoDB server instance running in another terminal for the duration of this chapter. To do so, open a command-line terminal window and execute `$ mongod`. Your server should launch and log information to the screen ending with `[initandlisten] waiting for connections on port 27017`.

You might find that when you run your application, you receive a stack trace error with something like the following code:

```
events.js:72

thrower; // Unhandled 'error' event
        ^
Error: failed to connect to [localhost:27017]
```

If this happens, you should realize that it failed to connect to localhost on port 27017 — which is the port that our local mongod server runs under.

Once we have an active connection to our database server, it's as if we are running the Mongo shell command. The MongoClient callback function returns a database connection object (that we named db in our code, but could have been named anything), which is almost exactly the same object we work with in the Mongo shell when we execute use <databasename>. Knowing this, at this point, we can use the db object to do anything we can do via the mongo shell. The syntax is slightly different, but the idea is generally the same.

# Inserting a document

Let's test out our new db object by inserting a record into a collection:

```
var MongoClient = require('mongodb').MongoClient;

MongoClient.connect('mongodb://localhost:27017/mongotest',
function(err, db) {
console.log('Connected to MongoDB!');

// using the db connection object, save the collection 'testing'
to a separate variable:
var collection = db.collection('testing');

  // insert a new item using the collection's insert function:
collection.insert({'title': 'Snowcrash'}, function(err, docs) {

        // on successful insertion, log to the screen the new
        // collection's details:
        console.log(docs.length + ' record inserted.');
        console.log(docs[0].title + ' - ' + docs[0]._id);

        // finally close the connection:
      db.close();
    });
});
```

In the preceding code, we establish a connection to the database and execute a callback once the connection is complete. That callback receives two parameters, the second of which is the db object itself. Using the db object, we can get a collection we want to work with. In this case, we save that collection as a variable so that we can more easily work with it throughout the rest of our code. Using the collection variable, we execute a simple insert command and pass in the JSON object we want to insert into the database as the first parameter.

The callback function that executes after insert accepts two parameters, the second of which is an array of documents affected by the command; in this case, an array of documents that we inserted. Once insert is complete and we are inside the callback function, we log some data. You can see that the length of the docs.ops array is 1 as we only inserted a single document. Furthermore, you can see that the single document in the array is the document we inserted, although now it has an extra _id field since MongoDB handles that automatically.

# Retrieving a document

Let's prove our code a little bit more by adding the findOne function call to look up the document we just inserted. Change the code in test.js to match the following example:

```
var MongoClient = require('mongodb').MongoClient;

MongoClient.connect('mongodb://localhost:27017/mongotest',
function(err, db) {
    console.log('Connected to MongoDB!');

    var collection = db.collection('testing');
    collection.insert({
        'title': 'Snowcrash'
    }, function(err, docs) {
        console.log(docs.ops.length + ' record inserted.');
        console.log(docs[0]._id + ' - ' + docs[0].title);

        collection.findOne({
            title: 'Snowcrash'
        }, function(err, doc) {
            console.log(doc._id + ' - ' + doc.title);
            db.close();
        });
    });
});
```

In this code, we insert a record in exactly the same way as before; only this time, we perform `findOne` on `title`. The `findOne` function accepts a JSON object to match against (this can be as precise or loose as you want) as its first parameter. The callback function that executes after `findOne` will contain the single document that was found as its second parameter. If we executed a `find` operation, we would have received an array of matching documents based on the search criteria.

The output of the last mentioned code should be:

```
$ node test.js
Connected to MongoDB!
1 record inserted.
538bc3c1a39448868f7013b4 - Snowcrash
538bc3c1a39448868f7013b4 - Snowcrash
```

In your output, you might notice that the `_id` parameter being reported on `insert` doesn't match the one from `findOne`. This is likely the result of running the code multiple times, which results in multiple records with the same title being inserted. The `findOne` function will return the first document found in no particular order, so chances are the document returned might not be the last one inserted.

Now that you have a basic understanding of how to easily connect and communicate with a MongoDB server from Node.js. Let's take a look at how we can work with MongoDB in a way that's a little less raw.

# Introducing Mongoose

While working directly with the `mongodb` module is great, it's also a bit raw and lacks any sense of the developer friendliness that we've come to expect working with frameworks such as Express in Node.js. Mongoose is a great third-party framework that makes working with MongoDB a breeze. Mongoose is an elegant `mongodb` object modeling for Node.js.

What that basically means is that Mongoose gives us the power to organize our database by using schemas (also known as model definitions) and provide powerful features to our models such as validation, virtual properties, and more. Mongoose is a great tool as it makes working with collections and documents in MongoDB feel much more elegant. The original `mongodb` module is a dependency of Mongoose, so you can think of Mongoose as being a wrapper on top of `mongodb` much like Express is a wrapper on top of Node.js—both abstract away a lot of the *raw* feeling and give you easier tools to work with directly.

It's important to note that Mongoose is still MongoDB, so everything you're familiar with and used to will work pretty much the same way; only the syntax will change slightly. This means that the queries, inserts, and updates that we know and love from MongoDB work perfectly fine with Mongoose.

The first thing we need to do is install Mongoose so that it's available to use within our `mongotest` project:

```
$ npm install mongoose
```

After installation, let's take a look at some of the features that Mongoose has to offer and what we'll take advantage of to make our lives easier when developing apps that rely heavily on a MongoDB database.

# Schemas

In Mongoose, schemas are what we use to define our models. Think of them as a blueprint that all models you create throughout the app will derive from. Using schemas, you can define much more than the simple blueprint of a MongoDB model. You can also take advantage of the built-in validation that Mongoose provides by default, add static methods, virtual properties, and more.

The first thing we do while defining a schema for a model is build a list of every field we think we will need for a particular document. The fields are defined by type, and the standard data types you would expect are available as well as a few others:

- **String**: This type stores a string value.
- **Number**: This type stores a number value, with restrictions.
- **Date**: This type holds a date and time object.
- **Buffer**:
- **Boolean**: This type is used to store a Boolean (true/ false) value.
- **Mixed**: This is basically an unstructured object that can contain anything. Consider this when storing JSON type data or data that is arbitrary and can literally be any JSON representation. It doesn't need to be predefined.
- **ObjectID**: This is typically used when you want to store the ObjectID of another document in a field, for example, when defining a relationship.
- **Array**: This is a collection of other schemas (models).

Here is an example of a basic Mongoose schema definition:

```
var mongoose = require('mongoose'),
    Schema = mongoose.Schema;

var Account = new Schema({
username: { type: String },
date_created: { type: Date, default: Date.now },
visits: { type: Number, default: 0 },
active: { type: Boolean, default: false }
});
```

Here, we define our schema for an `Accounts` collection. The first thing we do is require Mongoose and then define a schema object using `mongoose.Schema` in our module. We define a schema by creating a new `Schema` instance with a constructor object that defines the schema. Each field in the definition is a basic JavaScript object with type and then an optional default value.

# Models

A model in Mongoose is a class that can be instantiated (defined by a schema). Using schemas, we define models and then use them as a regular JavaScript object. The benefit is that the model object has the added bonus of being backed by Mongoose, so it also includes features such as saving, finding, creating, and removing. Let's take a look at defining a model using a schema and then instantiating a model and working with it. Add another file called `model.js` to your experimentation folder, `mongotest/model.js`, and include the following block in it:

```
var mongoose = require('mongoose'),
    Schema = mongoose.Schema;

mongoose.connect('mongodb://localhost:27017/mongotest');
mongoose.connection.on('open', function() {
console.log('Mongoose connected.');
});

var Account = new Schema({
username: { type: String },
date_created: { type: Date, default: Date.now },
visits: { type: Number, default: 0 },
active: { type: Boolean, default: false }
});
```

```
var AccountModel = mongoose.model('Account', Account);
var newUser = new AccountModel({  username: 'randomUser'
});
console.log(newUser.username);
console.log(newUser.date_created);
console.log(newUser.visits);
console.log(newUser.active);
```

Running the preceding code should result in something similar to the following:

```
$ node model.js
randomUser
Mon Jun 02 2014 13:23:28 GMT-0400 (EDT)
0
false
```

Creating a new model is great when you're working with new documents and you want a way to create a new instance, to populate its values, and then to save it to the database:

```
var AccountModel = mongoose.model('Account', Account);
var newUser = new AccountModel({  username: 'randomUser' });
newUser.save();
```

Calling .save on a mongoose model will trigger a command to MongoDB that will perform the necessary insert or update statements to update the server. When you switch over to your mongo shell, you can see the new user was indeed saved to the database:

```
>use mongotest
switched to db mongotest
>db.accounts.find()
{ "username" : "randomUser", "_id" :
ObjectId("538cb4cafa7c430000070f66"), "active" : false, "visits" : 0,
"date_created" : ISODate("2014-06-02T17:30:50.330Z"), "__v" : 0 }
```

Note that without calling .save() on the model, the changes to the model won't actually be persisted to the database. Working with Mongoose models in your Node code is just that—code. You have to execute MongoDB functions on a model for any actual communication to occur with the database server.

You can use `AccountModel` to perform a `find` operation and return an array of `AccountModel` objects based on some search criteria that retrieve results from the MongoDB database:

```
// assuming our collection has the following 4 records:
// { username: 'randomUser1', age: 21 }
// { username: 'randomUser2', age: 25 }
// { username: 'randomUser3', age: 18 }
// { username: 'randomUser4', age: 32 }

AccountModel.find({ age: { $gt : 18, $lt : 30} }, function(err,
accounts){
console.log(accounts.length);      // => 2
console.log(accounts[0].username);     // => randomUser1
mongoose.connection.close();
});
```

Here, we use the standard MongoDB commands `$gt` and `$lt` for the value of age when passing in our query parameter to find documents (that is, find any document where the age is above 18 and below 30). The callback function that executes after `find` references an `accounts` array, which is a collection of `AccountModel` objects returned from the query to MongoDB. As a general means of good housekeeping, we close the connection to the MongoDB server after we are finished.

# Built-in validation

One of the core concepts of Mongoose is that it enforces a schema on top of a schema-less design such as MongoDB. In doing so, we gain a number of new features, including built-in validation. By default, every schema type has a built-in required validator available. Furthermore, numbers have both `min` and `max` validators and strings have enumeration and matching validators. Custom validators can also be defined via your schemas. Let's take a brief look at some validation added to our example schema from earlier:

```
var Account = new Schema({
username: { type: String, required: true },
date_created: { type: Date, default: Date.now },
visits: { type: Number, default: 0 },
active: { type: Boolean, default: false },
age: { type: Number, required: true, min: 13, max: 120 }
});
```

The validation we added to our schema is that the username parameter is now required, and we included a new field called age, which is a number that must be between 13 and 120 (years). If either value doesn't match the validation requirements (that is username is blank or age is less than 13 or greater than 120), an error will be thrown.

Validation will fire automatically whenever a model's .save() function is called; however, you can also manually validate by calling a model's .validate() function with a callback to handle the response. Building on the example, add the following code, which will create a new mongoose model from the schema defined:

```
var AccountModel = mongoose.model('Account', Account);
var newUser = new AccountModel({ username: 'randomUser', age: 11 });
newUser.validate(function(err) {
console.log(err);
});
// the same error would occur if we executed:
// newUser.save();
```

Running the preceding code should log the following error to the screen:

```
{ message: 'Validation failed',
name: 'ValidationError',
errors:
{ age:
{ message: 'Path 'age' (11) is less than minimum allowed value
(13).',
name: 'ValidatorError',
path: 'age',
type: 'min',
value: 11 } } }
```

You can see that the error object that is returned from validate is pretty useful and provides a lot of information that can help when validating your model and returning helpful error messages back to the user.

Validation is a very good example of why it's so important to always accept an error object as the first parameter to any callback function in Node. It's equally important that you check the error object and handle it appropriately.

# Static methods

Schemas are flexible enough so that you can easily add your own custom static methods to them, which then become available to all of your models that are defined by that schema. Static methods are great for adding helper utilities and functions that you know you're going to want to use with most of your models. Let's take our simple age query from earlier and refactor it so that it's a static method and a little more flexible:

```
var Account = new Schema({
username: { type: String },
date_created: { type: Date, default: Date.now },
visits: { type: Number, default: 0 },
active: { type: Boolean, default: false },
age: { type: Number, required: true, min: 13, max: 120 }
});

Account.statics.findByAgeRange = function(min, max, callback) {
this.find({ age: { $gt : min, $lte : max} }, callback);
};

var AccountModel = mongoose.model('Account', Account);

AccountModel.findByAgeRange(18, 30, function(err, accounts){
console.log(accounts.length);     // => 2
});
```

Static methods are pretty easy to implement and will make your models much more powerful once you start taking full advantage of them!

# Virtual properties

Virtual properties are exactly what they sound like—fake properties that don't actually exist in your MongoDB documents, but you can fake them by combining other real properties. The most obvious example of a virtual property would be a field for fullname, when only firstname and lastname are actual fields in the MongoDB collection. For fullname, you simply want to say, return the model's first and last name combined as a single string and label it fullname:

```
// assuming the Account schema has firstname and lastname defined:

Account.virtual('fullname')
.get(function() {
return this.firstname + ' ' + this.lastname;
```

```
    })
  .set(function(fullname) {
  var parts = fullname.split(' ');
  this.firstname = parts[0];
  this.lastname = parts[1];
    });
```

We call the `.get()` and `.set()` functions. It's not required to provide both, although it's fairly common.

In this example, our `get()` function simply performs basic string concatenation and returns a new value. Our `.set()` function performs the reverse—splitting a string on a space and assigning the models `firstname` and `lastname` field values with each result. You can see that the `.set()` implementation is a little flakey if someone attempts to set a model's `fullname` with a value of say, Dr. Kenneth Noisewater.

It's important to note that virtual properties are not persisted to MongoDB since they are not real fields in the document or collection.

There's a lot more you can do with Mongoose, and we only just barely scratched the surface. Fortunately, it has a fairly in-depth guide you can refer to at the following link:

```
http://mongoosejs.com/docs/guide.html
```

Definitely spend some time reviewing the Mongoose documentation so that you are familiar with all of the powerful tools and options available.

That concludes our introduction to Mongoose's models, schemas, and validation. Next up, let's dive back into our main application and write the schemas and models that we will be using to replace our existing sample `viewModels` as well as connecting with Mongoose.

# Connecting with Mongoose

The act of connecting to a MongoDB server with Mongoose is almost identical to the method we used earlier when we used the `mongodb` module.

First, we need to ensure that Mongoose is installed. At this point, we are going to be using Mongoose in our main app, so we want to install it in the main project directory and also update the `package.json` file. Using your command-line terminal program, change locations to your `projects` folder, and install Mongoose via `npm`, making sure to use the `--save` flag so that the `package.json` file is updated:

```
$ cd ~/projects/imgPloadr
$ npm install mongoose --save
```

With Mongoose installed and the `package.json` file updated for the project, we're ready to open a connection to our MongoDB server. For our app, we are going to open a connection to the MongoDB server once the app itself boots up and maintains an open connection to the database server for the duration of the app's lifetime. Let's edit the `server.js` file to include the connection code we need. First, include Mongoose in the app by requiring it at the very top of the file:

```
var express = require('express'),
config = require('./server/configure'),
app = express(),
mongoose = require('mongoose');
```

Then, insert the following code right after the `app = config(app);` line:

```
mongoose.connect('mongodb://localhost/imgPloadr');
mongoose.connection.on('open', function() {
console.log('Mongoose connected.');
});
```

That's it! Those few simple lines of code are all it takes to open a connection to a MongoDB server, and our app is ready to start communicating with the database. The only parameter we pass to the `connect` function of Mongoose is a URL string to our locally running MongoDB server and a path to the collection we want to use. Then, we add an event listener to the `open` event of the `mongoose.connection` object and, when that fires, we simply log an output message that the database server has connected.

# Defining the schemas and models

For the purposes of the application we are building, we're only going to have two different unique schemas and associated models: an `Image` model and a `Comment` model. If we were to take this application to production and really build it out with all of the necessary features, we could expect to have many more models as well.

First, create a new directory labeled `models` in your project and we will store the Node.js modules for each of our models here. Create three files named `image.js`, `comment.js`, and `index.js` in this directory. Let's take a look at the `Image` model first. Copy the following block of code into the `models/image.js` file:

```
var mongoose = require('mongoose'),
    Schema = mongoose.Schema,
path = require('path');

var ImageSchema = new Schema({
```

```
title:              { type: String },
description:        { type: String },
filename:           { type: String },
views:              { type: Number, 'default': 0 },
likes:              { type: Number, 'default': 0 },
timestamp:          { type: Date, 'default': Date.now }
});

ImageSchema.virtual('uniqueId')
.get(function() {
return this.filename.replace(path.extname(this.filename), '');
    });

module.exports = mongoose.model('Image', ImageSchema);
```

First, we define our `ImageSchema` with the various fields that we are going to want to store in MongoDB for each of the images. We created a `virtual` property of `uniqueId`, which is just the filename with the file extension removed. As we want our `Image` model to be available throughout the rest of our app, we export it using `module.exports`. Note that we are exporting the model not the schema (as the schema itself is fairly useless to us). Let's set up a similar model for comments. Copy the following block of code into the `models/comment.js` file:

```
var mongoose = require('mongoose'),
    Schema = mongoose.Schema,
ObjectId = Schema.ObjectId;

var CommentSchema = new Schema({
image_id:   { type: ObjectId },
email:      { type: String },
name:       { type: String },
gravatar:   { type: String },
comment:    { type: String },
timestamp:  { type: Date, 'default': Date.now }
});

CommentSchema.virtual('image').set(function(image){
this._image = image;
    }).get(function() {

return this._image;
    });

module.exports = mongoose.model('Comment', CommentSchema);
```

There are a few important things to take note of with `this` model. First, we have a field labeled `image_id`, which has an `ObjectId` type. We're going to use this field to store the relationship between `comment` and `image` that it was posted to. The `ObjectId` that gets stored in this field is the `_id` of the related image document from MongoDB.

We also define `virtual` on the `comment` schema labeled `image`, which we provide a getter and setter for. The `image` virtual property will be how we attach the related image when we retrieve comments later in our controllers. For every comment, we are going to iterate through and look up its associated image and attach that `image` object as a property of the comment.

**Handling the name of collections**

You name your models using singular terms, and Mongoose will recognize this and create your collections using a pluralized model name. So, a model defined as `Image` will have a collection in MongoDB named `images`. Mongoose tries to be smart about this; however, a model defined as `Person` will have a corresponding collection named `people` and so on. (And yes, octopus will result in octopi!)

# The models index file

There's one last file in the `models` folder that we haven't yet touched on in our project. The `index.js` file within any folder in Node.js acts as an `index` file for the modules within it. This is by convention, so you don't have to adhere to this if you don't want to.

Since our `models` folder will contain a number of different files, each a unique module for one of our models, it would be nice if we could just include all of our models in a single `require` statement. Using the `index.js` file, we can do so pretty easily too. Copy the following block of code into the `models/index.js` file:

```
module.exports = {
    'Image': require('./image'),
    'Comment': require('./comment')
};
```

The `index.js` file inside the `models` directory simply defines a JavaScript object that consists of a name-value pair for each module in our directory. We manually maintain this object, but this is the simplest implementation of the concept. Now, thanks to this basic file, we can perform `require('./models')` anywhere in our application and know that we have a dictionary of each of our models via that module. To reference a specific model in that module, we simply refer to the specific model as a property of the module. If we only wanted to require a specific model somewhere in our app instead, we can perform `require('./models/image')` just as easily! You will see more of this a little later and it will become much more clear.

Because our two models are so closely related, we are typically always going to require the `models` dictionary using `require('./models')` throughout our application.

# Adding CRUD to the controllers

CRUD stands for Create, Read, Update, and Delete. Now that our schemas are defined and our models are ready, we need to start using them throughout our application by updating our controllers with various CRUD methods, where necessary. Up until this point, our controllers have consisted of only fixture, or fake, data so we can prove that our controllers are working and our view models were wired up to our templates. The next logical step in our development is to populate our view models with data directly from MongoDB. It would be even better if we could just pass our Mongoose models right to our templates as the `viewModel` itself.

## The home controller

If you recall from the *Updating the home controller* section of *Chapter 6, Controllers and View Models*, we originally created `viewModel` in our home controller, which consisted of an array of JavaScript objects that were just placeholder fixture data:

```
var viewModel = {
images: [
        {
uniqueId:       1,
title:          'Sample Image 1',
description:    '',
filename:       'sample1.jpg',
views:          0,
likes:          0,
timestamp:      Date.now()
        }, {
uniqueId:       2,
```

```
title:           'Sample Image 2',
description:      '',
filename:        'sample2.jpg',
views:           0,
likes:           0,
timestamp:       Date.now()
        }, {
uniqueId:        3,
title:           'Sample Image 3',
description:      '',
filename:        'sample3.jpg',
views:           0,
likes:           0,
timestamp:       Date.now()
        }, {
uniqueId:        4,
title:           'Sample Image 4',
description:      '',
filename:        'sample4.jpg',
views:           0,
likes:           0,
timestamp:       Date.now()
        }
    ]
};
```

We are going to replace that `viewModel` with a very stripped down version that we will then populate with real data from our Mongoose models:

```
var viewModel = {
images: []
};
```

Before we can populate that `viewModel` with real data, we need to first make sure our home controller can use our models. To do so, we must require the `models` module. Include this at the very top of the `controllers/home.js` file:

```
var sidebar = require('../helpers/sidebar'),
    ImageModel = require('../models').Image;
```

We could have required the full `models` module and have had access to both the `Comment` model and the `Image` model; however, for the homepage, we really only need to use the `Image` model. Now our `mongoose` model for `Image` is available to our home controller, we can perform a `find` operation to retrieve a list of the newest images to display on the homepage. Replace the existing `sidebar()` call in your home controller with this updated version of the code:

```
ImageModel.find({}, {}, { sort: { timestamp: -1 }},
function(err, images) {
if (err) { throw err; }

viewModel.images = images;
sidebar(viewModel, function(viewModel) {
res.render('index', viewModel);
        });
    });
```

Using `ImageModel`, we execute a MongoDB `find` query, but we provide no specifics for the actual query (a blank JavaScript object), which means it will return every document. The second parameter is also a blank JavaScript object, which means we aren't specifying how to map the results, so the full schema will be returned. The third parameter is an `options` object where we can specify things such as the sort field and order. In this particular query, we are retrieving every single image in the images collection sorted by timestamp in descending order (ascending order would have had a value of 1 instead of -1).

The callback function that executes after a successful `find` query to the MongoDB database server will return both an `error` object and an `images` array of matching models; in our case, every image in the database. Using the array that's returned from the query, we simply attach it to our `viewModel` via its `images` property. Then, we call our `sidebar` function exactly as we did previously.

At this point, we are no longer populating `viewModel` with fixture data but instead populating it with exactly what is returned from the database when we perform a basic `find` query using our Mongoose `Image` model. The homepage for the application is officially data driven. Here is a recap of the entire `controllers/home.js` file:

```
var sidebar = require('../helpers/sidebar'),
ImageModel = require('../models').Image;

module.exports = {
index: function(req, res) {

var viewModel = {
```

```
images: []
       };

ImageModel.find({}, {}, { sort: { timestamp: -1 }},
function(err, images) {
if (err) { throw err; }

viewModel.images = images;
sidebar(viewModel, function(viewModel) {
res.render('index', viewModel);
              });
          });
    }
};
```

If you were to run the app and open it in a browser, you wouldn't actually see anything on the homepage. That's because we haven't actually inserted any data yet. That's coming up next. However, note that the page itself still works and you didn't get any errors. This is because MongoDB is simply returning an empty array from the `find` on `ImageModel`, which the Handlebars homepage template is handling fine because it's performing an `each` operation against an empty array so it's displaying zero images on the homepage.

# The image controller

The `image` controller is by far the biggest component of our application. It contains most, if not all, of the logic that's powering our app. This includes displaying all of the details for an image, handling the uploading of images, and handling likes and comments. There's a lot to cover in this controller, so let's break it down by each section.

## Index – retrieving an image model

The primary responsibility of the `index` function in our `image` controller is to retrieve the details for a single specific image and display that via its `viewModel`. In addition to the details for the actual image, the comments for an image are also displayed on the page in the form of a list. Whenever an image is viewed, we also need to update the views count for the image and increment it by one.

Begin by editing the `controllers/image.js` file and updating the list of required modules at the top to include our `models` module:

```
var fs = require('fs'),
path = require('path'),
sidebar = require('../helpers/sidebar'),
Models = require('../models');
```

We also want to strip `viewModel` down to its most basic form, exactly as we did in the home controller. Replace the existing `viewModel` object variable with this new, lighter version:

```
var viewModel = {
image: {},
comments: []
};
```

After defining blank `viewModel`, let's include a `find` call on the `Image` model so that we can look up an image specifically by its `filename`:

```
Models.Image.findOne({ filename: { $regex: req.params.image_id }
    },
function(err, image) {
if (err) { throw err; }
if (image) {
            // to do...
        } else {
res.redirect('/');
        }
    });
```

In the preceding code, we are using the `Models` module's `Image` model and performing `findOne`, which is identical to `find`, except it will only ever return a single document (matching or not) instead of an array as `find` returns. By convention, we use a singular variable name in our callback's second parameter versus a plural, just so we as developers can easily tell we are working with a single object or an array/collection of objects.

The `query` object we provide as the first parameter matches the `filename` field of an image document using MongoDB's `regex` filter and compares this to `req.params.image_id`, which is the value of the parameter in the URL as defined in our `routes` file. The URL for an image page will always be `http://localhost:3300/images/abcdefg`, where `abcdefg` will be the value of `req.params.image_id`. If you recall, we are randomly generating this value in the `create` function when an image is uploaded.

After checking to make sure our `err` object isn't null, we then check to make sure our `image` object is also not null. If it's not null, that means a model was returned from MongoDB; so, we found our image and we're good to go. If an `image` model wasn't returned because we tried searching for an image by a filename that doesn't exist, we simply redirect the user back to the homepage.

Let's now populate our `viewModel` by inserting the following lines into the area where we have the `// to do...` placeholder comment:

```
image.views = image.views + 1;
viewModel.image = image;
image.save();
```

We attach the `image` model that was returned from `findOne` to our `viewModel`. `image` property, but not before incrementing the `views` property of that model by 1 (so that we represent our actual plus one view as we load the page). Since we modified the model (by incrementing its views count), we need to ensure that it's saved back to MongoDB so we call the model's `save` function.

Now that `viewModel` has been updated with the `image` model and the views count has been incremented and saved, we next need to retrieve a list of comments associated with the image. Let's include a little bit more code to query the `Comment` model and find any comments that belong to the image. Insert the following block of code immediately after `image.save();` from earlier:

```
Models.Comment.find({ image_id: image._id}, {}, { sort: {
'timestamp': 1 }},
function(err, comments){
if (err) { throw err; }

viewModel.comments = comments;

sidebar(viewModel, function(viewModel) {
res.render('image', viewModel);
        });
    }
);
```

Using `find` on our `Comment` model, we can pass in an object that contains our query as the first parameter; in this case, we are specifying that we want all comments where the `image_id` field is equal to the `_id` property of the main `image` model we attached to our `viewModel` earlier.

That code might look a little odd, so let's elaborate. Remember that the `image` object that is returned from the original `Models.Image.findOne()` call is available throughout the entire scope of that callback function. No matter how deep we get nesting callback functions, we will always have access to that original `image` model. Therefore, we can access it and its properties inside the callback function that fires when our `Model.Comment.find()` has executed.

Once inside the find callback of Comment, we attach the comments array that was returned to our viewModel and then call our sidebar function exactly as we did before when we first opened the controller and started editing this index function.

As a review, here is the entire index function inside the controllers/image.js file after it's been completely updated:

```
index: function(req, res) {
  // declare our empty viewModel variable object:
var viewModel = {
image: {},
comments: []
   };

  // find the image by searching the filename matching the url
parameter:
Models.Image.findOne({ filename: { $regex: req.params.image_id }
},
function(err, image) {
if (err) { throw err; }
if (image) {
  // if the image was found, increment its views counter
image.views = image.views + 1;
    // save the image object to the viewModel:
viewModel.image = image;
    // save the model (since it has been updated):
image.save();

    // find any comments with the same image_id as the image:
Models.Comment.find({ image_id: image._id},{},{ sort: {
                  'timestamp': 1 }},
function(err, comments){
    // save the comments collection to the viewModel:
viewModel.comments = comments;
    // build the sidebar sending along the viewModel:
sidebar(viewModel, function(viewModel) {
    // render the page view with its viewModel:
res.render('image', viewModel);
                  });
              }
          );
        } else {
    // if no image was found, simply go back to the homepage:
res.redirect('/');
          }
      });
  },
```

Let's quickly recall all of the `index` controller's responsibilities and tasks:

- Create a new empty `viewModel` object
- Create the `findOne imagefindOneimage` model where the filename is a regex match to the URL `image_id` parameter
- Increment the found views of `image` by one
- Attach the found `image` model to `viewModel`
- Save the `image` model since its `views` have been updated
- Find all comments with the `image_id` property equal to the `_id` of the original `image` model
- Attach the array of found `comments` to `viewModel`
- Render the page using `sidebar`, passing in the `viewModel` and callback function

## Create – inserting an image model

We already have the functionality in place in our `create` function to handle randomly naming and uploading an image file. Now we need to save that information to MongoDB for the uploaded image.

Let's update the original `saveImage` function inside `controllers/images.js:create` and include the functionality to tie it into the database.

Our goal with the `saveImage` function is two-fold. First, we want to make sure that we never save an image to the database with the same randomly generated filename as an already existing image. Second, we want to ensure that we only insert the image into the database after it has been successfully uploaded, renamed, and saved to the filesystem. We are going to make two modifications to the existing code to achieve this.

The first modification is to wrap the bulk of the logic with `find` against the randomly generated filename, and if any documents are returned from MongoDB as a match, we need to start the process over to repeat this as many times as necessary until we achieve a truly unique filename. The code to perform the search is as follows:

```
Models.Image.find({ filename: imgUrl }, function(err, images) {
if (images.length> 0) {
saveImage();
    } else {
        // do all the existing work...
    }
});
```

If an `images` array that is returned from `find` has a length greater than zero, it means at least one image was found to have the same filename as was generated with our random `for` loop. If that's the case, we want to call `saveImage` again, which will repeat the whole process (randomly generate a new name and perform a `find` on the database for that new name). We do this by previously defining the `saveImage` function as a variable so that within the `saveImage` function itself, we can execute it again by calling the original variable as the function.

 A function that calls itself is called a recursive function.

Assuming no images were returned from `find`, it means we have generated a truly unique filename for our image and we are safe to rename the file and upload it to the server as well as save a record to the database.

Originally, the last step of the `create` function was to redirect the visitor to the image's page within the callback that fired when the filesystem rename was finished. This is where we're going to want to create a new Mongoose `image` model. We should redirect only when the database server has finished saving the image (again relying on a callback function). Consider the following line in the original function:

```
res.redirect('/images/' + imgUrl);
```

Replace this with this new block of code:

```
var newImg = new Models.Image({
title: req.body.title,
description: req.body.description,
filename: imgUrl + ext
});
newImg.save(function(err, image) {
console.log('Successfully inserted image: ' + image.filename);
res.redirect('/images/' + image.uniqueId);
});
```

Here, we create a brand new `Image` model and pass in the default values via its constructor. The `title` and `description` fields get set right from the values passed in via the HTML form using `req.body` and the form field names (`.title`, `title`, and `.description`). The `filename` parameter is what we build the same way we did originally when we set its destination for renaming it, except we don't include the path and directory names, just the randomly generated filename and the image's original extension.

We call the model's `.save()` function (just as we did earlier when we updated the image's `views` property in the `index` controller function). The `save` function accepts a second parameter in its callback, which will be the updated version of itself. Once the save is completed, and the image has been inserted into the MongoDB database, we then redirect to the image's page. The reason the callback returns the updated version of itself is because MongoDB will automatically include additional information such as `_id`.

As a review and sanity check, here is the complete code for the `saveImage` function in `controllers/image.js:create`, with the new lines of code clearly highlighted:

```
var saveImage = function() {
var possible = 'abcdefghijklmnopqrstuvwxyz0123456789',
imgUrl = '';
for(var i=0; i< 6; i+=1) {
imgUrl += possible.charAt(Math.floor(Math.random() *
                          possible.length));
    }
/* Start new code: */
  // search for an image with the same filename by performing a find:
Models.Image.find({ filename: imgUrl }, function(err, images) {
if (images.length> 0) {
  // if a matching image was found, try again (start over):
saveImage();
        } else {
/* end new code:*/
var tempPath = req.files.file.path,
ext = path.extname(req.files.file.name).toLowerCase(),
targetPath = path.resolve('./public/upload/' + imgUrl + ext);

if (ext === '.png' || ext === '.jpg' || ext === '.jpeg' || ext ===
    '.gif') {
fs.rename(tempPath, targetPath, function(err) {
if (err) { throw err; }

/* Start new code: */
  // create a new Image model, populate its details:
var newImg = new Models.Image({
title: req.body.title,
filename: imgUrl + ext,
description: req.body.description
                });
```

```
    // and save the new Image
newImg.save(function(err, image) {
res.redirect('/images/' + image.uniqueId);
                    });
/* End new code: */
                });
            } else {
fs.unlink(tempPath, function () {
if (err) { throw err; }

res.json(500, {error: 'Only image files are allowed.'});
                });
            }
/* Start new code: */
}
    });
/* End new code: */
};

    saveImage();
```

Don't forget to initially execute `saveImage()` right after the function is defined; otherwise, nothing will happen!

# Testing everything out so far

At this point, we have most of the key functionalities wrapped with MongoDB integration, and our app should really feel like it's coming together. Let's give it a test run and make sure all of our endpoints are working so far. Launch the app and open it in a browser:

**$ node server.js**

**Server up: http://localhost:3300**

**Mongoose connected.**

Open up a browser, point it to `http://localhost:3300`, and you should see your application up and running, as shown in the following screenshot:

Go ahead and use the form on the homepage to search for an image file on your computer and select it. Provide an input for **Title** and **Description** and click on the **Upload** button. You should be taken directly to the image page with the details for your uploaded image displayed:

Go back to the homepage, and you should now see your new image displayed under the **Newest Images** section:

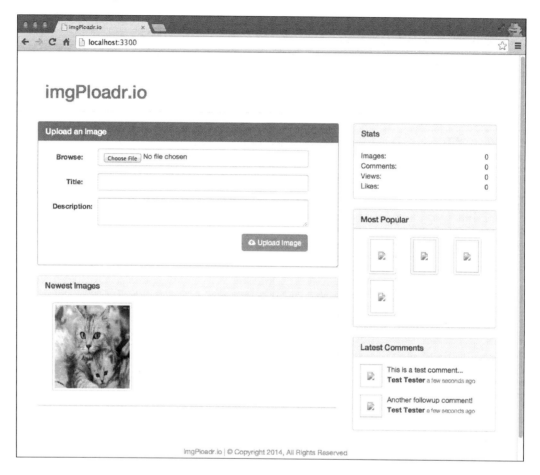

# The Like button and updating an image model

Next, let's add support for the **Like** button. Remember that our **Like** button works a little differently. It uses AJAX with jQuery so that data can be sent and received in real time without reloading the entire page. The experience for the user is seamless and enjoyable, as they don't lose their scroll place on the page or experience any other jarring UI-related issues.

The endpoint that the **Like** button hits is /images/:image_id/like, so we are going to use the value in the URL for image_id to find and retrieve the image in MongoDB, increment its likes value by 1, and then return the new total number of likes for the image (so that the UI can update with the new value).

Currently, the `like` function in `controllers/image.js` only does a simple JSON response with a hardcoded value of 1:

```
res.json({likes: 1});
```

Let's replace that original code with new code that will use the Mongoose `Image` model to find an image with a filename that matches the `image_id` passed in via the URL:

```
Models.Image.findOne({ filename: { $regex: req.params.image_id }
},
function(err, image) {
if (!err && image) {
image.likes = image.likes + 1;
image.save(function(err) {
if (err) {
res.json(err);
    } else {
res.json({ likes: image.likes });
    }
  });
 }
});
```

Assuming the callback function receives a valid `image` model response from the query, we'll then increment its `likes` property, and since the model is then modified, we need to execute its `save` function. Inside the `save` function's callback, we send a JSON response back to the browser with the real current value of the image's likes.

Sometimes, we will use shorthand in JavaScript and write something similar to the following:

**`if (!err && image)`**

In the `if` statement in the preceding example, we are saying, "if the `err` object is `false` (that is `null`) and the `image` object is `true` (that is not `null`), then we're good to go!"

With this code in place, you can run the app again and test out the **Like** button by viewing the image that you uploaded earlier and simply clicking on **Like**. If it worked, the counter next to the button should increase by one. Refresh the page, and the likes count should remain as the new value.

# Comment – inserting a comment model

Inserting comments will work almost exactly the same way as the likes for an image. The only difference is that we are creating a new `comment` model instead of updating an `image` model. The original code we had in our `comment` function was:

```
res.send('The image:comment POST controller');
```

Let's replace this with some code that will find the image by `image_id` in the URL again, but this time instead of updating its likes, we are going to create a new comment and assign the comment's `image_id` value with the `_id` of the image we are currently viewing (this is to attach a relationship to the comment so that it actually belongs to an image). Replace the entire `comment` function in `controllers/image.js` with the following block of code:

```
Models.Image.findOne({ filename: { $regex: req.params.image_id }
},
function(err, image) {
if (!err && image) {
var newComment = new Models.Comment(req.body);
newComment.gravatar = md5(newComment.email);
newComment.image_id = image._id;
newComment.save(function(err, comment) {
if (err) { throw err; }

res.redirect('/images/' + image.uniqueId + '#' + comment._id);
        });
    } else {
res.redirect('/');
    }
});
```

Here, you can see that we are using the same code from the `like` function to query MongoDB and find the image with the matching filename from the URL.

Assuming a valid image is returned as a match, we create a new `comment` object called `newComment` and actually pass the entire HTML form body into the constructor. This is a bit of a cheat as it's a coincidence (not accidental) that our HTML form uses form fields that have the same name and structure as that of a `comment` model. If you were to perform the `console.log` operation on the `req.body` object, you would see something like the following:

```
{
name: 'Jason Krol',
email: 'jason@kroltech.com',
comment: 'This is what a comment looks like?!'
}
```

That's identical to what we would have built manually anyway, so we just take a shortcut and pass the whole thing in as it is! After that, we update a few more properties on the `newComment` model. First, we manually set a `gravatar` property, which is where we will store the MD5 hash value of the commenter's e-mail address so that we can retrieve their Gravatar profile picture. Gravatar is a universal avatar service that stores profile pictures based on a user's e-mail address. However, the unique ID they use for each profile is an MD5 hash value, which is why we have to store that value.

As we are relying on the third-party MD5 module, we need to ensure that it's installed in our project and saved to our `package.json` file as a dependency. From your project's root folder, execute the following command:

```
$ npm install MD5 --save
```

In addition, we need to require the module in the `controllers/image.js` file at the very top, along with the other modules we are requiring:

```
var fs = require('fs'),
path = require('path'),
sidebar = require('../helpers/sidebar'),
    Models = require('../models'),
md5 = require('MD5');
```

Finally, we set the `image_id` property of `newComment` to the `_id` property of the image we found at the beginning of the function. Then, we call the `comment` model's `.save()` function and redirect the user back to the image page. For convenience, we append a bookmark to the new comment's `_id` to the URL so that when the page loads it will automatically scroll down to the users' comments that have just been posted.

With that functionality in place, go ahead and fire up the app and open it in your browser. Visit the image page for any images you've uploaded and post a comment. Once the comment posts and the page reloads, you should see something like the following screenshot under an image:

We could have chosen to handle comments using jQuery and AJAX the same way we handled the **Like** button. However, this introduces a bit more complexity because if we were to do that, we would have needed a slightly more sophisticated way to display that inserted comment to the screen. This would have involved relying heavily on jQuery to do some advanced DOM manipulation to display the comment after it was posted using AJAX.

In a later chapter, when we review Single-Page Applications, we will take a brief look at some JavaScript frameworks that perform this kind of functionality and a lot of other advanced features!

That concludes the code and functionality for the image controller.

# Wrapping it up

Let's do a quick recap of all of the changes we've made to this controller:

- We updated the index function to retrieve an image from MongoDB and populate viewModel with the details of the image model. We also found all the comments related to that image and attached an array of those to viewModel as well.

- We tweaked the create function to insert a new image model into the database once it has been successfully renamed and saved to the filesystem.

- The like function was updated to actually increment the value of an image's likes property and save that value to the database as well as return the new value via a JSON response.

- Comments are now inserted for a particular image via the comment function. Not only is a comment model inserted into the database, but its corresponding image is also found and the image model's _id value is attached to the comment to solidify a relationship.

# Helpers

The last piece of the puzzle and last area we need to tie into MongoDB is the sidebar. To do this, we are going to need to update each of the helpers we previously created. Most of the helpers that we write code for will be using the concepts and functionality that we've already covered in this chapter. However, there is the addition of one new concept that I want to focus on before we take a look at the code.

# Introducing the async module

As JavaScript by its very nature is asynchronous, there undoubtedly comes a time when we need a way to handle executing a number of different asynchronous functions at the same time. The big issue here is that if we tried to perform three different queries on a MongoDB server for example, how will we know when all three are finished before we move on and do work with the results? Up until this point, we've simply been relying on a single callback function, which works great for a single call. How can we assign a single callback function to multiple asynchronous calls? The answer is we can't—not directly anyway. You can use a lot of nested callbacks to achieve this, but that is generally considered bad practice and will significantly reduce the readability of your code. We can use a third-party module, however, that was designed very specifically for this exact need.

`async` is a powerful node module that can be downloaded and installed via `npm`, which provides a number of extremely useful utility functions all designed to help when working with a series of asynchronous functions. Two functions that we are going to work with in this chapter are `series` and `parallel`. The `series` function allows us to execute asynchronous functions sequentially, each waiting until the previous function finishes before executing a single callback function at the end. The `parallel` function allows us to do the opposite—execute a number of asynchronous functions simultaneously, waiting until they all complete executing a single callback function when the last function is finished. How does a single callback function handle the responses of a number of different asynchronous functions, you ask? By accepting an array of the responses of each function as a parameter!

Since we are going to be using `async` for our project, let's install it via `npm` and make sure our `package.json` file is updated as well. Within the root of your `project` folder, execute the following from the command line:

```
$ npm install --save async
```

# The comments helper

Let's take a look at the first use of `async` in one of our helpers—the `comments` helper. Originally, `helpers/comments.js` was a module that had a `newest` function that returned an array of fixture data with some sample comments. We are going to completely remove this code and instead query MongoDB for the `newest` comments and return those as an array. Start by clearing the `comment` helper module and start from scratch (note that we included a new `callback` parameter to the `newest` function):

```
var models = require('../models'),
    async = require('async');
```

```
module.exports = {
newest: function(callback) {
        // to do...
     }
};
```

Notice that we added the additional `require` statements at the top of the file for our `models` and `async`. Within the `newest` function, let's replace the `// to do...` comment with code to query MongoDB and find the five most recent comments:

```
models.Comment.find({}, {}, { limit: 5, sort: { 'timestamp': -1 }
},
function(err, comments){
        // to do - attach an image to each comment...
    });
```

Notice that the first parameter in the `find` query is an empty JavaScript object, meaning we will retrieve every comment in the database. For the third parameter, however, we're using `limit` and `sort` so that we limit the number of records returned to five, and we sort the query by `timestamp` in descending order.

Now that we have an array of comments, ideally, we'd like the image that each comment belongs to to be returned as well. Typically, this would be accomplished by using an `aggregate` query in MongoDB to join different collections together (such as a `JOIN` in SQL). We will see `aggregate` in more detail in the next chapter. For the purposes of our code, we're going to instead query MongoDB separately for each comment and retrieve the image associated with the comment's `image_id` value.

First, let's define a function that will query MongoDB and retrieve and attach an `image` model to a `comment` model:

```
var attachImage = function(comment, next) {
models.Image.findOne({ _id : comment.image_id},
function(err, image) {
if (err) throw err;
comment.image = image;
next(err);
        });
};
```

This function will accept a `comment` model as the first parameter and a callback function as the second parameter (named `next`). The `next` callback as the second parameter is important because it's the key to how `async` is able to function. Imagine that the `next` callback acts as a chain link. Since the same function is going to be called for every item in a collection, there needs to be a way to daisy-chain the calls together. This is performed via the callback.

Basically, every time the callback is called for an item in the array, it performs its work and then executes the same callback with the next item in the array, and so on and so forth, which is why we named the callback function parameter next.

Another important element to point out with this function is that when we attach the image model to the comment's image property, we are using the virtual property we set up earlier in the main comment's schema. If you recall, when we set the image property, we are actually setting the private _image property. Likewise, when we get the image property, we are actually retrieving the private _image property.

After we have defined the attachImage function, we need to use the each function of async to apply that function to every item in the comments collection:

```
async.each(comments, attachImage,
function(err) {
if (err) throw err;
callback(err, comments);
    });
```

The each function of async will loop through every item in the collection in the first parameter, and send each item as a parameter to a callback function in the second parameter. The third parameter is the final callback function that is executed once the entire series is finished with the collection. In this case, every comment in the comment's array will be passed individually to the attachImage function. When the entire collection has been iterated through, the final callback will execute, which basically fires the very first callback function that was passed into the newest function as its only parameter. Boy, that was a mouthful! Let's try to break this down a little further so it makes a bit more sense:

- The newest function of the comment helper module accepts a single parameter named callback—this is the function that will be called once all of the work is finished in this entire function.

- The first thing the newest function does is find the latest five comments and returns them as an array to an anonymously defined inline function.

- First, we define a function and store it in a variable named attachImage.

- The attachImage function accepts two parameters, an individual comment model, and a callback function that we named next.

- The attachImage function will query MongoDB to find an image with an _id value that is the same as the image_id property of the comment that was passed into it as the first parameter.

- Once that image is found, it is attached to the comment via its image property and then the next callback function is executed.

- We use `async.each` to loop through every comment in the `comments` array that was passed as the first parameter to `each`.

- Pass the `attachImage` function as the second parameter, which is the function that will be called for every comment in the comment's array.

- Finally, define an inline anonymous function that will be executed once the last item in the comments collection has been iterated on. This inline function itself only accepts an error object as its parameter. Assuming every iteration of the `comments` collection was successful, this function will be executed with no error. Inside this function, we execute the original function named `callback` that was the only parameter to the `newest` function, and `callback` is called with the newly updated comment's array as its second parameter.

OK, the hardest part is over! You survived a crash course on the `async` module and came out, hopefully, unscathed! Just to be safe, here is the code for the `helpers/comments.js` module file in its entirety:

```
var models = require('../models'),
async = require('async');

module.exports = {
newest: function(callback) {
models.Comment.find({}, {}, { limit: 5, sort: { 'timestamp': -1 } },
function(err, comments){
var attachImage = function(comment, next) {
models.Image.findOne({ _id : comment.image_id},
function(err, image) {
if (err) throw err;

comment.image = image;
next(err);
});
};

async.each(comments, attachImage,
function(err) {
if (err) throw err;
callback(err, comments);
});
});
}
};
```

**Callback, callback, callbacks everywhere!**

At this point, it's probably getting a little confusing with the number of callbacks we've been dealing with. A part of the problem is the terminology we've been using. Any function that is passed as a parameter and only executed after certain conditions are met, typically as the end result of the original function, is referred to as a callback. The popular convention with JavaScript is to label a callback function in a parameter literally with the variable name callback, so that it's obvious. This works great when you are reading code, but not so much when you are explaining code and referring to a function named callback that's also known as the callback!

# The sidebar helper

OK! So, of course, there's a catch right!? Well, kind of. Since we introduced async in our comments helper module, we now need to introduce it in our sidebar helper. This is because of the simple fact that our comments helper is now really asynchronous, so anything that uses our comments module needs to deal with that. As our sidebar module currently stands, it's just expecting the comments helper module to return an array and do it instantly; so, it's not expecting to have to wait around for the actual data. Because of this, if we ran our code as is, our comments sidebar would remain blank (because the sidebar would have rendered the page before the MongoDB calls were even finished thinking within the comments module). Let's fix this by updating our sidebar helper module to use async as well.

First, let's edit the helpers/sidebar.js file and replace its entire contents with this slightly modified version that uses async.parallel:

```
var Stats = require('./stats'),
    Images = require('./images'),
    Comments = require('./comments'),
async = require('async');

module.exports = function(viewModel, callback){
async.parallel([
function(next) {
next(null, Stats());
        },
function(next) {
next(null, Images.popular());
        },
function(next) {
Comments.newest(next);
```

```
            }
    ], function(err, results){
viewModel.sidebar = {
stats: results[0],
popular: results[1],
comments: results[2]
        };

callback(viewModel);
    });
};
```

The first thing we did was make sure `async` was included as a required module at the top of the file. Inside the primary `exports` function, we basically wrapped our existing code and integrated it into `async.parallel` so that we can easily tweak it a little later as we update each section of the `sidebar` helpers. Since we've so far only completed the `comments` helper module, that's the only one that's actually been changed. The other `Stats` and `Images.popular` calls are being forcibly used with `async.parallel` even though it doesn't quite make sense to do that right now. It will once those two sections become more asynchronous in the next sections.

The `parallel` function of `async` works in a similar way to its `each` function that we used earlier. The main difference is that `parallel` isn't performing the same function in a loop through a collection, but is instead performing a series of unique functions all at the same time. If you look closely, you can see that the first parameter to `parallel` is actually an array, and each item in the array is a unique function. Every function in the array accepts a `next` callback parameter function, which is executed at the conclusion of each of the functions. The second parameter in the `next` callback is the result of the work that was performed within the function itself. In the case of `Stats` and `Images.popular`, those two functions simply return values instantly with no asynchronous calls to anything else, so we just expect the results to be returned by executing them directly.

However, as you can see with the `Comments.newest` section, we are passing in the `next` callback function as a parameter because we want its execution to be deferred until the last second (until `Comments.newest` has completed all of its work). Once that `next` callback function is called, it is passed the results of all of its work.

The last parameter to the `parallel` function is an inline function that accepts a results array as its second parameter. This array is a collection of each of the results that were returned from each of the functions in the array in the first parameter. You can see that when we build `viewModel` now, we are referring to indexes in the `results` array. The index order is the order that the functions were defined in the original array. We know that the first function was to retrieve `Stats`, the second function to retrieve `Images.popular`, and the third function to retrieve `Comments.newest`. So, we can reliably assign `results[0]` to `viewModel.Stats` and so on. As a reference, here is what the `viewModel` definition originally looked like in the `sidebar` module:

```
viewModel.sidebar = {
stats: Stats(),
popular: Images.popular(),
comments: Comments.newest()
};
```

You can compare this with the updated version that uses `async`:

```
viewModel.sidebar = {
stats: results[0],
popular: results[1],
comments: results[2]
};
```

Now that the sidebar is set up to properly handle the helper modules that are (and eventually will be) asynchronous, we can run the application and test it to ensure that our sidebar is properly displaying the top five most recent comments on the website. Run the application and launch it in a browser. If you haven't already posted any comments to an image, do so now so that you can see those comments appearing in the sidebar along with a thumbnail of the image they belong to.

# Troubleshooting

At this point, we've covered and implemented a large number of changes to our application. It's understandable that something might be broken for you, so let's run through a quick checklist to make sure we haven't missed any trouble spots that might be preventing your app from running properly:

- Make sure you've installed all of the required modules for this chapter and that they are saved to your `package.json` file. This includes `mongoose`, `async`, and MD5.

- Make sure the appropriate dependency modules are being required at the top of each of the module files they are used in.

- Make sure you remember to launch `mongod` in another terminal instance whenever you run the application.

- When in doubt, pay attention to the stack trace output that node is giving you in your terminal when it fails, as it is typically pretty obvious what's wrong. It will also give you the filename and line number of the offending module.

- When all else fails, execute `console.log` everywhere!

Next up, let's update the `stats` helper module to use parallel as well so we can get some real stats for the application.

# The stats helper

The primary responsibility of the `stats` helper module is to gather some totals for our application. These `stats` are for things such as the total number of images uploaded, total number of comments, total views for all the images combined, and total likes for all the images combined. Your first inclination might be to assume that we are going to query MongoDB for all the images and loop through every image to track all of the views and totals. That's one way to do it, but it's pretty inefficient. Fortunately, MongoDB has some built-in functionalities, which makes generating these kinds of values a snap.

As we are going to be making a number of calls to MongoDB, we are going to rely on the `async.parallel` function again much like we did in the `sidebar` module. The original `helpers/stats.js` file was very bare bones, so let's completely replace that file with this new version, which uses `parallel`:

```
var models = require('../models'),
async = require('async');

module.exports = function(callback) {
async.parallel([
function(next) {
next(null, 0);
        },
function(next) {
next(null, 0);
        },
function(next) {
next(null, 0);
        },
function(next) {
next(null, 0);
        }
```

```
    ], function(err, results){
  callback(null, {
  images:    results[0],
  comments:  results[1],
  views:     results[2],
  likes:     results[3]
        });
     });
  };
```

This code does exactly what the module originally did; only it's a little more verbose! I'm pretty sure we don't want to just return 0 for all of our stats forever though, as that'd be pretty useless and unimpressive to say the least! Let's update the each function to properly query MongoDB and get some stats. Looking at the object returned in the callback in the last function, we can see that we already defined the order of the functions that are being executed in parallel. Let's start with images. Replace the next(null, 0); line in the first function with the following code snippet:

```
models.Image.count({}, next);
```

Easy! Just use MongoDB's count method to find the total number of documents in the images collection matching any criteria (the first parameter). Then, we just pass the next function as the callback because, coincidentally enough, the parameter signatures match. If we didn't want to use shorthand here, we could have written this the long way, as follows:

```
models.Image.count({}, function(err, total){
next(err, total);
});
```

However, who feels like typing all that when you don't have to! Let's do the same thing for the second function in the parallel array for total comments. Replace the next(null, 0); line in the second function with the following line of code:

```
models.Comment.count({}, next);
```

Again, this was a piece of cake!

Now, the next two functions are going to be a little different, but they are almost identical to each other. What we want to do with next is get the total views and likes for every image. We can't use MongoDB's count method because that only counts individual documents in a collection. We need to use MongoDB's aggregate functionality instead.

Using `aggregate`, we can perform a mathematical operation, such as `$sum`, to tally results for us. Replace the `next(null, 0);` line in the third function with the following code snippet:

```
models.Image.aggregate({ $group : {
    _id : '1',
viewsTotal : { $sum : '$views' }
}}, function(err, result) {
var viewsTotal = 0;
if (result.length> 0) {
viewsTotal += result[0].viewsTotal;
    }
next(null, viewsTotal);
});
```

Using MongoDB's `aggregate` function, we are telling MongoDB to group every document together and sum up all of their views into a single new field called `viewsTotal`. The resulting collection that is returned to the callback function is an array of documents with the `_id` and `viewsTotal` fields. In this case, the results array will only contain a single document with the grand total because we weren't that tricky with our `aggregate` functionality. If there aren't any images in the collection at all, we need to handle that and check accordingly. Finally, the `next` callback function is called with the actual value for `viewsTotal`.

Let's use the same exact functionality to total up the `likes` for all images. Replace the `next(null, 0);` line of code in the fourth and final function in parallel with the following code snippet:

```
models.Image.aggregate({ $group : {
    _id : '1',
likesTotal : { $sum : '$likes' }
}}, function (err, result) {

var likesTotal = 0;
if (result.length> 0) {
likesTotal += result[0].likesTotal;
    }
next(null, likesTotal);
});
```

Now that the `sidebar` helper module has been updated and is complete with the `async.parallel` functionality, let's make a minor tweak to our `sidebar` module to ensure we are calling the `Stats` module correctly so that it's properly asynchronous. The original line in `helpers/sidebar.js` was:

```
next(null, Stats());
```

Replace that line of code with this slightly different version:

```
Stats(next);
```

Last but not least, let's take care of the most popular helper module of the images sidebar.

# The popular images helper

Again, the original `helpers/images.js` file was mostly filled with fixture data and placeholder code that's fairly useless. Let's replace the entire file with this new version that's actually pretty tame in comparison to all of the other helper modules:

```
var models = require('../models');

module.exports = {
popular: function(callback) {
models.Image.find({}, {}, { limit: 9, sort: { likes: -1 }},
function(err, images) {
if (err) throw err;

callback(null, images);
        });
    }
};
```

At this point, this code should be pretty familiar to you. We just query MongoDB and find the top nine most liked images by sorting the images by total such as count in descending order and limiting the results to nine documents.

Let's edit the `helpers/sidebar.js` file again to include the updated call to the `Images.popular` function. Consider the original code:

```
next(null, Images.popular());
```

Replace this with the following slightly newer version:

```
Images.popular(callback);
```

And now the sidebar is completely finished and completely dynamic. No more fixture data or placeholder variables anywhere. Running the application should yield a fully functional website with all of the features we set out to implement working perfectly! Give it a spin and make sure it's working correctly.

# Iterating by adding an image removal capability

At this point, I think our application is pretty awesome, but there's something missing that's nagging me. During testing, I've been creating all kinds of new images and uploading them to the application but it's starting to get a bit cluttered and messy. It dawned on me that the most obvious thing that's missing is the ability to delete an image!

In reality, I left out this feature on purpose so that we could use this opportunity to incorporate a completely new functionality that touches almost every area of the application. This seemingly simple addition is actually going to require the following changes:

- Update `routes.js` to include a new route to handle `Delete` requests
- Update `controllers/image.js` to include a new function for the route

  This should not only remove the image from the database, but also delete the file and all related comments

- Update the `image.handlebars` HTML template to include a **Remove** button
- Update the `public/js/scripts.js` file with an AJAX handler for the **Remove** button

# Adding a route

The first thing we need to update in order to add this new functionality is the main `routes` list. Here, we will add a new endpoint that handles the `delete` function and points to a function within the `image` controller. Edit the `server/routes.js` file and insert the following new line of code:

```
router.delete('/images/:image_id', image.remove);
```

# Adding a controller handler

Now that we have added a new route, we need to create the controller function that it's using as its callback (`image.remove`). Edit `controllers/image.js` and add the following new function code after the existing `comment: function(req, res){}` operation (don't forget to add a trailing comma after the `comment` function since you are adding a new function):

```
remove: function(req, res) {
Models.Image.findOne({ filename: { $regex: req.params.image_id }
},
```

```
function(err, image) {
if (err) { throw err; }

fs.unlink(path.resolve('./public/upload/' + image.filename),
function(err) {
if (err) { throw err; }

Models.Comment.remove({ image_id: image._id},
function(err) {
image.remove(function(err) {
if (!err) {
res.json(true);
                              } else {
res.json(false);
                              }
                          });
                      });
                  });
              });
    }
```

This function performs four primary functions (and as such nests four layers deep with callbacks—we could have used the async's `series` method here to prevent the crazy amount of nesting). The first task is to find the image that we are attempting to remove. Once that image is found, the file associated with the image should be deleted. Next, find the comments associated with the image and remove them. Once they have been removed, the last step is to remove the image itself. Assuming all of that was a success, simply send a `true` Boolean JSON response back to the browser.

# Updating the Handlebars image page template

Now that we have a `route` and `controller` function to support deleting an image, we need a way for the UI to send the request. The most obvious solution is to add a **Delete** button somewhere on the page. Edit the `views/image.handlebars` file and, after the existing HTML, where we had the **Like** button, we are going to add new HTML for a **Delete** button:

```
<div class="col-md-8">
<button class="btnbtn-success" id="btn-like" ...
    // existing HTML for Like button and misc details
</div>
<div class="col-md-4 text-right">
<button class="btnbtn-danger" id="btn-delete" data-id="{{
image.uniqueId }}">
```

```
<i class="fafa-times"></i>
</button>
</div>
```

Here, we just include new `div` that's set to four columns using Bootstrap and are right aligned. The UI here is that the **Like** button and the stats are the leftmost portion of the row, and the **Delete** button (an X icon from Font Awesome) is all the way to the right of the same row (and red since we use Bootstrap's danger color class).

# Updating jQuery

Finally, we are going to tie it all together by implementing code similar to the **Like** button, where we send an AJAX `delete` method to the server with the URL and the image ID when the button is clicked on. To be safe, we display a standard JavaScript confirmation dialog to ensure the button wasn't clicked on by accident.

Assuming the server responds with a `true` value, we will turn the button green and change the icon to a checkmark with the word **Deleted!** in place. Edit `public/js/scripts.js` and insert the following block of code after the existing code (be sure to insert the new code inside the `$(function(){ ... })` jQuery function):

```
$('#btn-delete').on('click', function(event) {
event.preventDefault();
var $this = $(this);

var remove = confirm('Are you sure you want to delete this image?');
if (remove) {
var imgId = $(this).data('id');
$.ajax({
url: '/images/' + imgId,
type: 'DELETE'
      }).done(function(result) {
if (result) {
            $this.removeClass('btn-danger').addClass('btn-
            success');
            $this.find('i').removeClass('fa-
            times').addClass('fa-check');
            $this.append('<span> Deleted!</span>');
        }
     });
  }
});
```

Let's test this brand new functionality by launching the application, loading it up in a browser, finding an image we no longer want, and viewing its image page. The **Delete** button should now show up in place.

# Refactoring and improvements

At this point, the application that we've been building is pretty much complete! Before we iterate anymore on the project and continue to build it out and make it ready for production, we should probably consider some refactoring and/or general improvements. Some areas that I would personally take a look at to refactor and/or rewrite to improve the application's performance and overall sanity are as follows:

- I might rethink working directly with models so much within the controllers and instead create a utility that I can wrap a lot of that noise and rely on more basic CRUD calls to my models and only provide a callback to each. This is most visible in the `image` controller with `like`, `comment`, and `remove`.

- There is literally no validation in the project that we wrote and that's mostly for brevity. In reality, we should have included validation on any input fields a user interfaces with. Validation should be provided both on the frontend via jQuery or plain old vanilla JavaScript as well as on the backend with Node. The validation should protect users from submitting invalid and/or malicious code (that is XSS or Cross-Site Scripting).

- Right now, our application is open to the general public, which means any visitor that comes along can upload images as well as delete them! It would be fairly simple to include a user authentication process within our application. Passport.js is a great third-party module to integrate user authentication into Node.js applications.

- Instead of attaching images to comments for the purposes of the sidebar (the `newest` comments), we should consider creating a more robust aggregate query using MongoDB to retrieve a hybrid collection of comments that includes the image provided directly from MongoDB.

# Summary

This chapter was a monster but was also the last piece of the puzzle to complete our app and have a fully dynamic database-driven Node.js app that uses MongoDB. Congratulations on making it this far and sticking with it! You're well on your way to being a true full-stack JavaScript developer.

In the next chapter, we'll step away from our application for a bit as we take a look at working with REST APIs using Node.js.

# 8
# Creating a RESTful API

Now that your application is complete and ready for the world to see, you could start thinking of ways to make it more popular. What if you wanted to allow external systems with access rights to your data in a way that they could mass produce inserts to your website without the need for users to visit the actual website? One example that comes to mind almost immediately is how users of another website, say www.facebook.com, can upload an image to Facebook and have it automatically uploaded to your website as well.

The only way to make a scenario like this possible is by providing an API to your data and the code that gives external developers access to a suite of tools that will allow them to perform actions without the need to interact with the actual web pages.

In this chapter, we will review the following topics:

- Introducing RESTful APIs
- Installing a few basic tools
- Creating a basic API server and sample JSON data
- Responding to GET requests
- Updating data with POST and PUT
- Removing data with DELETE
- Consuming external APIs from Node.js

# What is an API?

An **Application Programming Interface (API)** is a set of tools that a system makes available so that unrelated systems or software have the ability to interact with each other. Typically, a developer uses an API when writing software that will interact with a closed, external, software system. The external software system provides an API as a standard set of tools that all developers can use. Many popular social networking sites provide developers access to APIs to build tools to support those sites. The most obvious examples are Facebook and Twitter. Both have a robust API that provides developers with the ability to build plugins and work with data directly, without them being granted full access as a general security precaution.

As you will see with this chapter, providing your own API is not only fairly simple, but it also empowers you to provide your users with access to your data. You also have the added peace of mind knowing that you are in complete control over what level of access you can grant, what sets of data you can make read-only, as well as what data can be inserted and updated.

# What is a RESTful API?

**Representational State Transfer (REST)** is a fancy way of saying CRUD over HTTP. What this means is, when you use a REST API, you have a uniform means to create, read, and update data using simple HTTP URLs with a standard set of HTTP verbs. The most basic form of a REST API will accept one of the HTTP verbs at a URL and return some kind of data as a response.

Typically, a REST API GET request will always return some kind of data, such as JSON, XML, HTML, or plain text. A POST or PUT request to a RESTful API URL will accept data to create or update. The URL for a RESTful API is known as an endpoint, and while working with these endpoints, it is typically said that you are consuming them. The standard HTTP verbs used while interfacing with REST APIs include:

- GET: This retrieves data
- POST: This submits data for a new record
- PUT: This submits data to update an existing record
- PATCH: This submits a date to update only specific parts of an existing record
- DELETE: This deletes a specific record

Typically, RESTful API endpoints are defined in a way that they mimic the data models and have semantic URLs that are somewhat representative of the data models. What this means is that to request a list of models, for example, you would access an API endpoint of `/models`. Likewise, to retrieve a specific model by its ID, you would include that in the endpoint URL via `/models/:Id`.

Some sample RESTful API endpoint URLs are as follows:

- `GET http://myapi.com/v1/accounts`: This returns a list of accounts
- `GET http://myapi.com/v1/accounts/1`: This returns a single account by `Id: 1`
- `POST http://myapi.com/v1/accounts`: This creates a new account (data submitted as a part of the request)
- `PUT http://myapi.com/v1/accounts/1`: This updates an existing account by `Id: 1` (data submitted as part of the request)
- `GET http://myapi.com/v1/accounts/1/orders`: This returns a list of orders for account `Id: 1`
- `GET http://myapi.com/v1/accounts/1/orders/21345`: This returns the details for a single order by `Order Id: 21345` for account `Id: 1`

It's not a requirement that the URL endpoints match this pattern; it's just common convention.

# Introducing Postman REST Client

Before we get started, there are a few tools that will make life much easier when you're working directly with APIs. The first of these tools is called Postman REST Client, and it's a Google Chrome application that can run right in your browser or as a standalone packaged application. Using this tool, you can easily make any kind of request to any endpoint you want. The tool provides many useful and powerful features that are very easy to use and, best of all, free!

# Installation instructions

Postman REST Client can be installed in two different ways, but both require Google Chrome to be installed and running on your system. The easiest way to install the application is by visiting the Chrome Web Store at `https://chrome.google.com/webstore/category/apps`.

Perform a search for `Postman REST Client` and multiple results will be returned. There is the regular Postman REST Client that runs as an application built into your browser, and then separate Postman REST Client (packaged app) that runs as a standalone application on your system in its own dedicated window. Go ahead and install your preference. If you install the application as the standalone packaged app, an icon to launch it will be added to your dock or taskbar. If you installed it as a regular browser app, you can launch it by opening a new tab in Google Chrome, going to Apps, and finding the Postman REST Client icon.

After you've installed and launched the app, you should be presented with an output similar to the following screenshot:

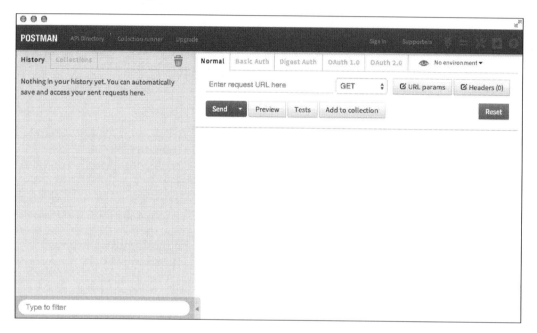

# A quick tour of Postman REST Client

Using Postman REST Client, we're able to submit REST API calls to any endpoint we want, as well as modify the type of request. Then, we can have complete access to the data that's returned from the API, as well as any errors that might have occurred. To test an API call, enter the URL to your favorite website in the **Enter request URL here** field and leave the dropdown next to it as GET. This will mimic a standard GET request that your browser performs anytime you visit a website. Click on the blue **Send** button. The request is made and the response is displayed at the bottom half of the screen.

In the following screenshot, I sent a simple GET request to http://kroltech.com and the HTML is returned as follows:

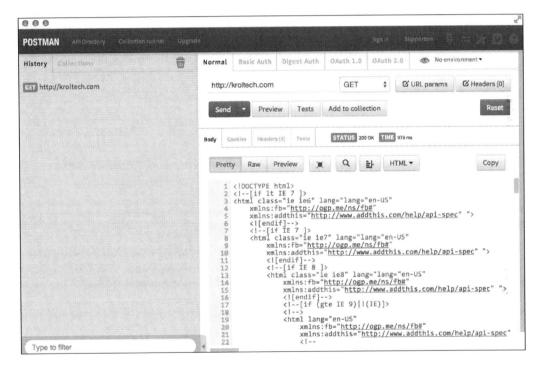

If we change this URL to that of the RSS feed URL for my website, you can see the XML returned:

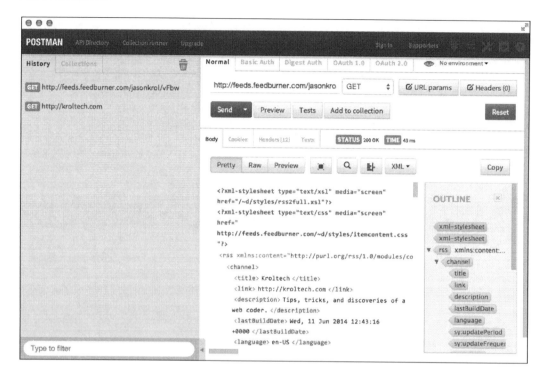

The XML view has a few more features as it exposes the sidebar to the right that gives you a glimpse at the tree structure of the XML data. Not only that, you can now see a history of the requests we've made so far along the left sidebar. This is great when we're performing more advanced POST or PUT requests and don't want to repeat the data setup for each request while testing an endpoint.

Here is a sample API endpoint I submitted a GET request to that returns the JSON data in its response:

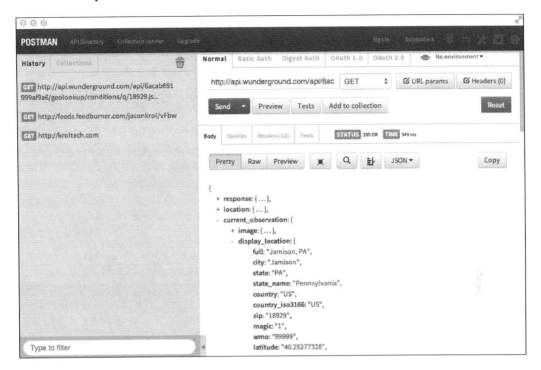

A really nice thing about making API calls to endpoints that return JSON using Postman Client is that it parses and displays the JSON in a very nicely formatted way, and each node in the data is expandable and collapsible.

The app is very intuitive, so make sure you spend some time playing around and experimenting with different types of calls to different URLs.

# Using the JSONView Chrome extension

There is one other tool I want to talk to you about (while extremely minor) that is actually a really big deal. The JSONView Chrome extension is a very small plugin that will instantly convert any JSON you view directly via the browser into a more usable JSON tree (exactly like Postman Client). Here is an example of pointing to a URL that returns JSON from Chrome before JSONView is installed:

Here is that same URL after JSONView has been installed:

You should install the JSONView Google Chrome extension the same way you installed Postman REST Client—access the Chrome Web Store and perform a search for JSONView.

Now that you have the tools to be able to easily work with and test API endpoints, let's take a look at writing your own and handling the different request types.

# Creating a basic API server

Let's create a super basic Node.js server using Express that we'll use to create our own API. Then, we can send tests to the API using Postman REST Client to see how it all works. In a new project workspace, first install the npm modules that we're going to need in order to get our server up and running:

```
$ npm init

$ npm install --save express body-parser underscore
```

Now that the `package.json` file for this project has been initialized and the modules installed, let's create a basic server file to bootstrap an Express server. Create a file named `server.js` and insert the following block of code:

```
var express = require('express'),
    bodyParser = require('body-parser'),
    _ = require('underscore'),
    json = require('./movies.json'),
    app = express();

app.set('port', process.env.PORT || 3500);

app.use(bodyParser.urlencoded());
app.use(bodyParser.json());

var router = new express.Router();
// TO DO: Setup endpoints ...
app.use('/', router);

var server = app.listen(app.get('port'), function() {
    console.log('Server up: http://localhost:' + app.get('port'));
});
```

Most of this should look familiar to you. In the `server.js` file, we are requiring the express, body-parser, and underscore modules. We're also requiring a file named `movies.json`, which we'll create next.

After our modules are required, we set up the standard configuration for an Express server with the minimum amount of configuration needed to support an API server. Notice that we didn't set up Handlebars as a view-rendering engine because we aren't going to be rendering any HTML with this server, just pure JSON responses.

# Creating sample JSON data

Let's create the sample `movies.json` file that will act as our temporary data store
(even though the API we build for the purpose of demonstration won't actually
persist data beyond the app's life cycle):

```json
[{
    "Id": "1",
    "Title": "Aliens",
    "Director": "James Cameron",
    "Year": "1986",
    "Rating": "8.5"
},
{

    "Id": "2",
    "Title": "Big Trouble in Little China",
    "Director": "John Carpenter",
    "Year": "1986",
    "Rating": "7.3"
},
{

    "Id": "3",
    "Title": "Killer Klowns from Outer Space",
    "Director": "Stephen Chiodo",
    "Year": "1988",
    "Rating": "6.0"
},
{

    "Id": "4",
    "Title": "Heat",
    "Director": "Michael Mann",
    "Year": "1995",
    "Rating": "8.3"
},
{

    "Id": "5",
    "Title": "The Raid: Redemption",
    "Director": "Gareth Evans",
    "Year": "2011",
    "Rating": "7.6"
}]
```

This is just a really simple JSON list of a few of my favorite movies. Feel free to populate it with whatever you like. Boot up the server to make sure you aren't getting any errors (note that we haven't set up any routes yet, so it won't actually do anything if you tried to load it via a browser):

```
$ node server.js
Server up: http://localhost:3500
```

# Responding to GET requests

Adding a simple GET request support is fairly simple, and you've seen this before already in the app we built. Here is some sample code that responds to a GET request and returns a simple JavaScript object as JSON. Insert the following code in the routes section where we have the // TO DO: Setup endpoints ... waiting comment:

```
router.get('/test', function(req, res) {
    var data = {
        name: 'Jason Krol',
        website: 'http://kroltech.com'
    };

    res.json(data);
});
```

Just like we set up viewModel in *Chapter 5, Templating with Handlebars*, we create a basic JavaScript object that we can then send directly as a JSON response using res.json instead of res.render. Let's tweak the function a little bit and change it so that it responds to a GET request against the root URL (that is /) route and returns the JSON data from our movies file. Add this new route after the /test route added previously:

```
router.get('/', function(req, res) {
    res.json(json);
});
```

 The res (response) object in Express has a few different methods to send data back to the browser. Each of these ultimately fall back on the base send method, which includes header information, statusCodes, and so on. res.json and res.jsonp will automatically format JavaScript objects into JSON and then send using res.send. res.render will render a template view as a string and then send it using res.send as well.

With that code in place, if we launch the `server.js` file, the server will be listening for a GET request to the / URL route and will respond with the JSON data of our movies collection. Let's first test it out using the Postman REST Client tool:

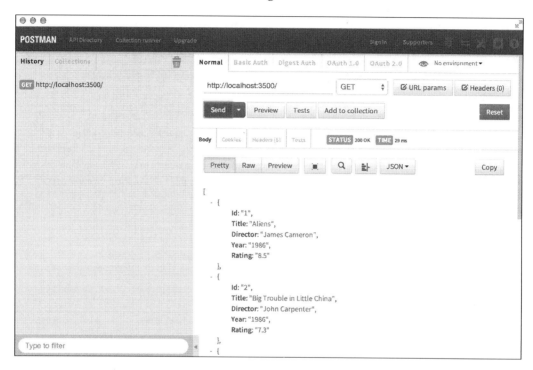

GET requests are nice because we could have just as easily pulled that same URL via our browser and received the same result:

However, we're going to use Postman for the remainder of our endpoint testing as it's a little more difficult to send POST and PUT requests using a browser.

# Receiving data – POST and PUT requests

When we want to allow those using our API to insert or update data, we need to accept a request from a different HTTP verb. When inserting new data, the POST verb is the preferred method to accept data and know it's for an insert. Let's take a look at code that accepts a POST request and data along with the request, inserts a record into our collection, and returns the updated JSON.

Insert the following block of code after the route you added previously for GET:

```
router.post('/', function(req, res) {
    // insert the new item into the collection (validate first)
    if(req.body.Id && req.body.Title && req.body.Director &&
        req.body.Year && req.body.Rating) {
        json.push(req.body);
        res.json(json);
    } else {
        res.json(500, { error: 'There was an error!' });
    }
});});
```

The first thing we do in the POST function is check to make sure the required fields were submitted along with the actual request. Assuming our data checks out and all the required fields are accounted for (in our case, every field), we insert the entire req. body object into the array *as is* using the array's push function. If any of the required fields aren't submitted with the request, we return a 500 error message instead. Let's submit a POST request this time to the same endpoint using the Postman REST Client. (Don't forget to make sure your API server is running with node server.js.):

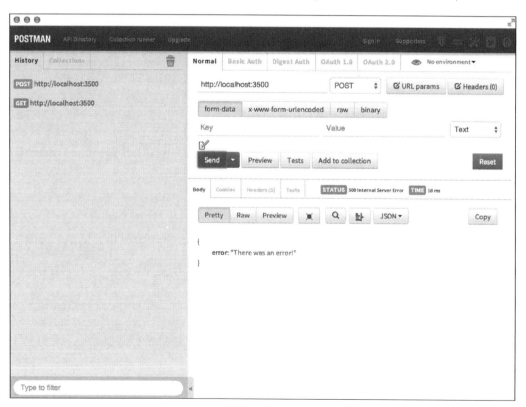

First, we submitted a POST request with no data, so you can clearly see the 500 error response that was returned:

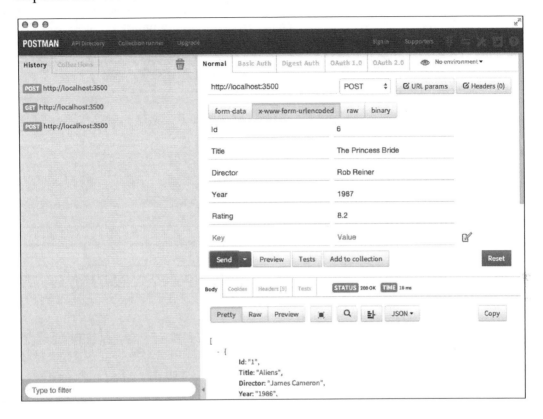

Next, we provided the actual data using the `x-www-form-urlencoded` option in Postman and provided each of the name/value pairs with some new custom data. You can see from the results that **STATUS** was **200**, which is a success and the updated JSON data was returned as a result. Reloading the main `GET` endpoint in a browser yields our original movies collection with the new one added.

`PUT` requests will work in almost exactly the same way except, traditionally, the `Id` property of the data is handled a little differently. In our example, we are going to require the `Id` attribute as a part of the URL and not accept it as a parameter in the data that's submitted (since it's usually not common for an `update` function to change the actual `Id` of the object it's updating). Insert the following code for the `PUT` route after the existing `POST` route you added earlier:

```
router.put('/:id', function(req, res) {
    // update the item in the collection
    if(req.params.id && req.body.Title && req.body.Director &&
        req.body.Year && req.body.Rating) {
        _.each(json, function(elem, index) {
            // find and update:
```

```
        if (elem.Id === req.params.id) {
            elem.Title = req.body.Title;
            elem.Director = req.body.Director;
            elem.Year = req.body.Year;
            elem.Rating = req.body.Rating;
        }
    });

    res.json(json);
} else {
    res.json(500, { error: 'There was an error!' });
}
});
```

This code again validates that the required fields are included with the data that was submitted along with the request. Then, it performs an _.each loop (using the underscore module) to look through the collection of movies and find the one whose Id parameter matches that of the Id included in the URL parameter. Assuming there's a match, the individual fields for that corresponding object are updated with the new values that were sent with the request. Once the loop is complete, the updated JSON data is sent back as the response. Similarly, in the POST request, if any of the required fields are missing, a simple 500 error message is returned. The following screenshot demonstrates a successful PUT request updating an existing record:

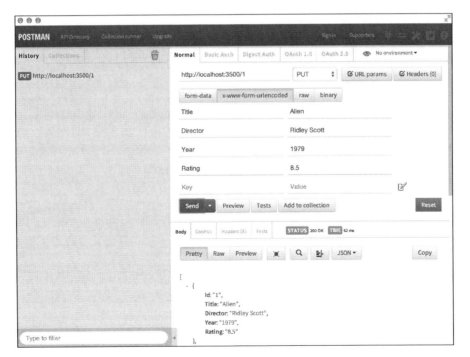

The response from Postman after including the value 1 in the URL as the Id parameter, which provides the individual fields to update as x-www-form-urlencoded values, and finally sending as PUT shows that the original item in our movies collection is now the original Alien (not Aliens its sequel, as we originally had).

# Removing data – DELETE

The final stop on our whirlwind tour of the different REST API HTTP verbs is DELETE. It should be no surprise that sending a DELETE request should do exactly what it sounds like. Let's add another route that accepts DELETE requests and deletes an item from our movies collection. Here is the code that takes care of the DELETE requests that should be placed after the existing block of code from the previous PUT:

```
router.delete('/:id', function(req, res) {
    var indexToDel = -1;
    _.each(json, function(elem, index) {
        if (elem.Id === req.params.id) {
            indexToDel = index;
        }
    });
    if (~indexToDel) {
        json.splice(indexToDel, 1);
    }
    res.json(json);
});
```

This code will loop through the collection of movies and find a matching item by comparing the values of Id. If a match is found, the array index for the matched item is held until the loop is finished. Using the array.splice function, we can remove an array item at a specific index. Once the data has been updated by removing the requested item, the JSON data is returned. Notice in the following screenshot that the updated JSON that's returned is in fact no longer displaying the original second item we deleted.

Note that ~ use in JavaScript! That's a little bit of JavaScript black magic! The tilde (~) in JavaScript will bit flip a value. In other words, take a value and return the negative of that value incremented by one, that is ~n === - (n+1). Typically, the tilde is used with functions that return -1 as a false response. By using ~ on -1, you are converting it to 0. If you were to perform a Boolean check on -1 in JavaScript, it would return true. You will see that ~ is used primarily with the indexOf function and jQuery's $.inArray(); both return -1 as a false response.

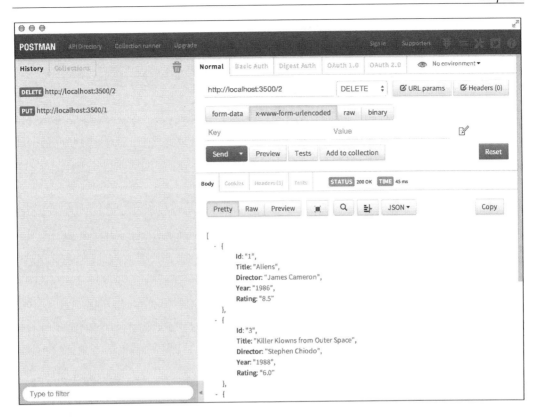

All of the endpoints defined in this chapter are extremely rudimentary, and most of these should never see the light of day in a production environment! Whenever you have an API that accepts anything other than GET requests, you need to be sure to enforce extremely strict validation and authentication rules. After all, you are basically giving your users direct access to your data.

# Consuming external APIs from Node.js

There will undoubtedly be a time when you want to consume an API directly from within your Node.js code. Perhaps your own API endpoint needs to first fetch data from some other unrelated third-party API before sending a response. Whatever the reason, the act of sending a request to an external API endpoint and receiving a response can be done fairly easily using a popular and well-known npm module called request. The request module was written by Mikeal Rogers and is currently the third most popular (and most relied upon) npm module after async and underscore.

Request is basically a super simple HTTP client, so everything you've been doing with Postman REST Client so far is basically what Request can do, only the resulting data is available to you in your Node code as well as the response status codes and/ or errors, if any.

# Consuming an API endpoint using request

Let's do a neat trick and actually consume our own endpoint as if it was some third-party external API. First, we need to ensure we have request installed and can include it in our app:

```
$ npm install --save request
```

Next, edit server.js and make sure you include request as a required module at the start of the file:

```
var express = require('express'),
    bodyParser = require('body-parser'),
    _ = require('underscore'),
    json = require('./movies.json'),
    app = express(),
    request = require('request');
```

Now, let's add a new endpoint after our existing routes, which will be an endpoint accessible in our server via a GET request to /external-api. This endpoint, however, will actually consume another endpoint on another server, but for the purposes of this example, the other server is actually the same server we're currently running!

The request module accepts an options object with a number of different parameters and settings, but for this particular example, we only care about a few. We're going to pass an object that has a setting for the method (GET, POST, PUT, and so on) and the URL of the endpoint we want to consume. After the request is made and a response is received, we want an inline callback function to execute.

Place the following block of code after your existing list of routes in server.js:

```
router.get('/external-api', function(req, res) {
    request({
        method: 'GET',
        uri: 'http://localhost:' + (process.env.PORT || 3500),
    }, function(error, response, body) {
        if (error) { throw error; }

        var movies = [];
        _.each(JSON.parse(body), function(elem, index) {
```

```
                    movies.push({
                        Title: elem.Title,
                        Rating: elem.Rating
                    });
                });
                res.json(_.sortBy(movies, 'Rating').reverse());
            });
        });
```

The `callback` function accepts three parameters: error, response, and body. The `response` object is like any other response that Express handles and has all of the various parameters as such. The third parameter, body, is what we're really interested in. That will contain the actual result of the request to the endpoint that we called. In this case, it is the JSON data from our main GET route we defined earlier that returns our own list of movies. It's important to note that the data returned from the request is returned as a string. We need to use JSON.parse to convert that string to actual usable JSON data.

We manipulate the data that came back from request to suit our needs. In this example, we took the master list of movies and just returned a new collection that consists of only the Title and Rating of each movie and then sorts the results by the top scores. Load this new endpoint by pointing your browser to http://localhost:3500/external-api, and you can see the new transformed JSON output to the screen.

Let's take a look at another example that's a little more real world. Let's say that we want to display a list of similar movies for each one in our collection, but we want to look up that data somewhere, such as on www.imdb.com. Here is the sample code that will send a GET request to IMDB's JSON API, specifically for the word aliens, and returns a list of related movies by the Title and Year. Go ahead and place this block of code after the previous route for external-api:

```
router.get('/imdb', function(req, res) {
    request({
        method: 'GET',
        uri: 'http://sg.media-
            imdb.com/suggests/a/aliens.json',
    }, function(err, response, body) {
        var data = body.substring(body.indexOf('(')+1);
        data = JSON.parse(data.substring(0,data.length-1));
        var related = [];
        _.each(data.d, function(movie, index) {
            related.push({
                Title: movie.l,
                Year: movie.y,
```

```
                    Poster: movie.i ? movie.i[0] : ''
                });
            });

            res.json(related);
        });
    });
```

If we take a look at this new endpoint in a browser, we can see the JSON data that's returned from our /imdb endpoint is actually itself retrieving and returning data from some other API endpoint:

```
localhost:3500/imdb
← → C ⌂   localhost:3500/imdb                                                        ☆ ≡
[                                                                          + - View source
  - {
        Title: "Aliens",
        Year: 1986,
        Poster: "http://ia.media-imdb.com/images/M/MV5BMTYzNzU5MzQ4OV5BM15BanBnXkFtZTcwMDcxNDq3OA@@._V1_.jpg"
    },
  - {
        Title: "Cowboys & Aliens",
        Year: 2011,
        Poster: "http://ia.media-imdb.com/images/M/MV5BMTM1MzkyNzQ3OV5BM15BanBnXkFtZTcwMDk1NTq2NQ@@._V1_.jpg"
    },
  - {
        Title: "AVPR: Aliens vs Predator - Requiem",
        Year: 2007,
        Poster: "http://ia.media-imdb.com/images/M/MV5BMTI5NDY2NDUwM15BM15BanBnXkFtZTYwNzQxMTA3._V1_.jpg"
    },
  - {
        Title: "Monsters vs. Aliens",
        Year: 2009,
        Poster: "http://ia.media-imdb.com/images/M/MV5BMTY0OTQ3MzE3MV5BM15BanBnXkFtZTcwMDQyMzMzMg@@._V1_.jpg"
    },
  - {
        Title: "Aliens in the Attic",
        Year: 2009,
        Poster: "http://ia.media-imdb.com/images/M/MV5BMTk3NTMzNTIxNV5BM15BanBnXkFtZTcwOTI4ODU1Mg@@._V1_.jpg"
    },
  - {
        Title: "Aliens of the Deep",
```

Note that the JSON endpoint I am using for IMDB isn't actually from their API, but rather what they use on their homepage when you type in the main search box. This would not really be the most appropriate way to use their data, but it's more of a hack to show this example. In reality, to use their API (like most other APIs), you would need to register and get an API key that you would use so that they can properly track how much data you are requesting on a daily or hourly basis. Most APIs will require you to use a private key with them for this reason.

# Summary

In this chapter, we took a brief look at how APIs work in general, the RESTful API approach to semantic URL paths and arguments, and created a bare bones API. We used Postman REST Client to interact with the API by consuming endpoints and testing the different types of request methods (GET, POST, PUT, and so on). You also learned how to consume an external API endpoint by using the third-party node module `request`.

In the next chapter, we will revisit our original application as we implement best practices by introducing testing in Node.js. We'll take a look at popular testing frameworks and write tests for the application to prove that our code works as expected.

# 9
# Testing Your Code

Up until this point, we've been pretty much flying by the seat of our pants when it comes to the code we've been writing! We've literally had no way of knowing whether the code worked until we tested it out in an actual browser.

In this chapter, we will cover the following topics:

- Running tests with the Mocha test framework
- Writing tests with the Chai assertion library
- Spies and stubs with Sinon and Proxyquire
- Writing your first test
- Testing our application

Tests are great for making sure your code functions properly, but they're also awesome for preventing new unexpected bugs from suddenly popping up because of an innocent little change you made to some unsuspecting code.

## The tools of the trade

Let's start by taking a look at the various tools and libraries we're going to be using to run and write our tests. There are three main concepts we need to cover before we can actually start writing real tests.

The first is a test runner or the framework we use to run our suite of tests.

Most of the frameworks follow **Test Driven Development** (TDD) and its process relies on the following steps:

1. It defines a unit test
2. Implements the unit
3. Executes the test and verifies that the test passes

The second concept is the assertion library itself—the language we use to write our tests. A special version of using assertion language, to design and build pieces of functionality incrementally guided by an expected behavior is **Behavior Driven Development (BDD)**.

For both TDD and BDD, we can use the Mocha testing framework; however, we will be writing assertions using a special assertion library called Chai.js

Finally, we'll take a look at the idea of spies and stubs, which are fake representatives of certain parts of our code that are relied on when we need to track function calls to ensure an expected behavior.

# Running tests with the Mocha framework

When writing tests for an application, you typically write them in batches that are module specific. These batches are referred to as suites or specs. Each suite typically contains a batch of tests organized in a way that almost mirrors the application itself. With Node, the idea is no different in that each suite of tests we write will be specific to an individual module. You'll require the module you want to test against, and write a collection of tests for each part of the module's functionality.

Since you'll have many different test files testing each and every component of your application, you'll want a way to quickly execute all of the tests. This is where the test runner comes in. The test runner that we've decided to use is called Mocha.

You can install Mocha globally like any other npm package:

```
$ npm install -g mocha
```

You might require security privileges while installing on Linux or OS X, which can done simply using sudo before npm.

Once installed, the Mocha command line tool is now available. Simply executing mocha from a command line will execute the test run with a few default options.

The test runner will look for a folder named test and any .js file within. In our case, we haven't actually set up any tests yet so executing mocha alone won't accomplish anything; instead, it will throw an error of cannot resolve path.

When the Mocha test runner does find .js files, it executes them like any other Node file except it looks for a few specific keywords within the file.

Here is some sample code for a typical test block:

```
var expect = require('chai').expect;
describe('The code', function() {
    beforeEach(function(){
        // optional preparation for each test
    });
    afterEach(function(){
        // optional cleanup after each test
    });

    it('should test something', function(){
        var something = 1;
        // here we "expect" some condition to declare our test
        // in this case, we expect the variable to exist
        // more on the assertion syntax a little later
        expect(something).to.exist;
    });
    it('should test something_else', function(){
        var something_else = false;
        // now we test a different variable against its value
        // and expect that value to equal false
        expect(something_else).to.equal(false);
    });
});
```

The first thing Mocha will scan the file for is a `describe` block. A `describe` block is a way to define a specific group of test cases in single line. You can have many `describe` blocks in a `test` file, and each `describe` block can have many specific tests. In addition, `describe` blocks can be nested as deep as you like to better organize your tests.

Once a `describe` block is found, a few other items are executed within it. A `beforeEach` and `afterEach` block is checked for to see whether there is any pretest work that needs to be executed before each test is executed. Likewise, any cleanup that needs to occur between tests can be taken care of within the `afterEach` block. Both of these blocks are optional and therefore not required. A good example of when you would want to use a `beforeEach` block is if you need to instantiate an object that you will be testing, you would want to create a new instance before every single test. This way, whatever changes a test might push to the object will be reset and will not inadvertently affect any other tests. Likewise, any changes you've made during a test to any other related objects can be reset during an `afterEach` block.

Within the `describe` block, defining individual tests is done with `it` statements. Within each `it` statement, it's generally considered good practice to include a single `expect` to assert the actual test (although you can include as many `expect` function calls as you like, its still only considered a single test because of the single `it`).

We're using the BDD style syntax when writing our suites, which allows our tests to read like user stories. With the preceding example, you can read the tests as `The code should test something` and `The code should test something_else`. In fact, if we ran the previous tests, we would see the following output:

```
The code
    should test something
    should test something_else


2 passing (5ms)
```

# Asserting tests with Chai.js

As you saw in the previous example, we used special blocks to define our test groups with Mocha but we used a separate language when defining our actual individual tests. These tests are called assertions and we chose to use the Chai.js library. This is purely a personal preference, as there are a number of different assertion libraries that exist. Each library does basically the same thing with slight variations on the syntax and style of actually writing the tests. Since Chai.js is project specific and based on a personal preference, we're going to install it as a project dependency (instead of globally). In addition, as our tests are not actually required for our application to run, we'll include Chai.js under the `devDependencies` list in our `package.json` file).

Performing `npm install` on the developer 's machine will yield all packages under normal dependencies as well as `devDependencies` from `package.json`. When the environment changes to production, we need to execute `npm install --prod` to specify the environment.

This will help `npm` to install packages under dependencies and not `devDependencies` from `package.json`.

In order to include Chai.js in our project as a `devDependency`, we will use the `--save-dev` flag instead of `--save` when performing the `npm` install:

```
$ npm install --save-dev chai
```

# Getting started with Chai

Chai itself has a few different flavors of API styles that can be used when writing tests. The BDD API, which is what we will use for the tests we write, uses expect and should. There's also the assert API, which is more of a TDD style. The benefit of using the BDD style with expect/should is that you can chain the assertion methods to improve readability of the tests.

 You can learn more about BDD as well as TDD by accessing the following Wikipedia page:

```
http://en.wikipedia.org/wiki/Behavior-driven_
development
```

Using the BDD assertion API with Chai.js provides a number of methods at our disposal such as to, be, is, and many more. They have no testing capability, but instead they improve the assertion readability. All the getters are listed at http://chaijs.com/api/bdd/.

All of these getters will follow an expect() statement and can be coupled with not, in case we want to flip the assertion negatively.

The preceding getters are combined with Chai assertion methods such as ok, equal, within, and so on, to determine a test's outcome. All those methods are listed at http://chaijs.com/api/assert/.

Let's start constructing simple assertions. Chai provides three different assertion styles expect, should, and assert. Consider some simple illustrations as follows:

```
var chai    = require('chai');
var expect  = chai.expect;
var should  = chai.should();
var assert  = chai.assert;
var animals = { pets: [ 'dog', 'cat', 'mouse' ] };
var foo     = 'bar';

expect(foo).to.be.a('string').and.equal('bar');
expect(animals).to.have.property('pets').with.length(4);
animals.should.have.property('pets').with.length(4);
assert.equal(foo, 'bar', 'Foo equal bar');
```

As you can see, the expect/should function is based on self-descriptive language chains. Both differ in a way of declaration, the expect function provides a starting point for a chain whereas the should interface extends a Object.prototype.

The `assert` interface provides simple but powerful TDD style assertions. Apart from the preceding example that yields a deep equality assertion, exception testing, and instance of are also available.

For a more in-depth learning, refer to the Chai documentation at `http://chaijs.com/api`.

# Spies and stubs with Sinon.js

Testing your code will prove to be extremely difficult if there isn't an easy way to `spy` on functions and know whenever they are called. Additionally, when one of your functions is called, it will be nice to know what arguments were passed to it and what was returned. A `spy` in testing is a special placeholder function that replaces an existing function when you want to check specifically if/when `it` was called. Spies track a number of properties for a function when it's called, and they can also pass through to the expected functionality of the original function. The Sinon.js library provides both `spy` and `stub` functionalities and is quite extensive. For a complete list of the different options available with this powerful framework, I strongly recommend you spend some time reading the documentation at `http://sinonjs.org/docs`.

Since we will be using Sinon.js with our tests, we should install it as another `devDependency` exactly the same way we did with Chai.js. In addition, we should also install the `sinon-chai` helper, which provides additional Chai assertion verbs specifically for use with Sinon:

```
$ npm install --save-dev sinon sinon-chai
```

The inclusion of `sinon-chai` allows us to write special assertions such as `to.be.calledWith`, which would otherwise not work with Chai alone.

Imagine you have a function that simply adds two numbers together and returns the sum:

```
var sum = function(a, b) {
    return a + b;
}
var doWork = function() {
    var x = 1,
        y = 2;
    console.log(sum(x,y));
}
```

When writing a test for the doWork function, we want to assert that the sum function was called. We don't necessarily care what the function does or whether it even works; we just want to make sure since doWork relies on sum that it's actually calling the function() function. In this scenario, the only way we could be sure is if we had a way to spy on the sum function and know if it was ever called. Using spy, we can do just that:

```
var sinon = require("sinon");
var sinonChai = require("sinon-chai");
chai.use(sinonChai);

describe('doWork', function() {
    var sum;

    it('should call sum', function() {
        sum = sinon.spy();
        doWork();
        expect(sum).to.be.calledWith(1,2);
    });
});
```

In the preceding scenario, the sum function is replaced with a spy function. So its actual functionalities will no longer exist. If we want to ensure that the sum function is not only spied on but still functions the way we expect, we need to attach .andCallThrough() after sinon.spy():

```
describe('doWork', function() {
    var sum;
    console.log = sinon.spy();

    it('should call sum', function() {
        sum = sinon.spy().andCallThrough();
        doWork();
        expect(sum).to.be.calledWith(1,2);
        expect(console.log).to.be.calledWith(3);
    });
});
```

Notice that by including andCallThrough on our sum spy, we're able to not only spy on it and assert that it was called but also spy on the console.log function and assert that it was called with the correct value returned by sum.

Where a `spy` is typically just a watcher to a function and only reports whether the function was called, a `stub` allows you to provide custom functionalities for a function on the fly during test execution. Test stubs are said to be preprogrammed behavioral functions that are used to test wrapped boilerplate code required as a module dependency in an application.

Think of `stub` as a super spy, where it reports the same things that a spy does, but also performs whatever specific tasks you want as well. Using the same example, let's stub the `sum` function to always return the same value:

```
it('should console.log sum response', function(){
    // replace the existing sum function with a new stub,
    // a generic function that does exactly what we specify
    // in this case always just return the number 2
    sum = sinon.stub(function(){
        return 2;
    });

    // lets replace the standard console.log function
    // with a spy
    console.log = sinon.spy();
    // call our doWork function (which itself uses console.log)
    doWork();
    // and if doWork executed the way its supposed to, console.log
    // should have been called and the parameter 2 passed to it
    expect(console.log).to.be.calledWith(2);
});
```

Stubbing a function is great when a function performs work that might yield unexpected results, and you just want to force the response for the purposes of your test. Stubbing is also handy when you're doing TDD and you're testing against a function that you haven't even written yet.

# Stubbing node modules with Proxyquire

Spies and stubs are great when writing tests against code within the same module, but when you need to spy on or stub a module required within another node module, things get a little trickier. Fortunately, there's a tool called Proxyquire that will allow you to stub modules that are required from your code.

Examine the following code sample:

```
// google.js
var request = require('request');

module.exports = function() {
    request('http://www.google.com', function (err, res, body) {
        log(body);
    });
}
```

You can see that we require the `request` module. The `request` module accepts two parameters, the second of which is a callback function. This is where things start to get tricky. How are we going to implement spies and/or stubs in this type of scenario? Furthermore, how can we prevent our tests from explicitly making a network call to fetch `google.com`? What if `google.com` is down (ha!) when we run our tests?

In order to be able to spy on the `request` module, we need a way to intercept actual `require` and attach our own stubbed version of `request` instead. The `request` module is actually a great example of a module that you would want to stub because `request` is used to make a network call, and that's something that you want to make sure your tests never actually do. You don't want your tests relying on an external resource like a network connection or being dependent on the data returned from a live request.

Using Proxyquire, we can actually set up our tests in a way that they'll intercept the `require` module and replace what gets executed with our own stub. Here's an example of a test file written against the module we created earlier:

```
var log = sinon.spy(),
    requestStub = sinon.stub().callsArgWith(1, null, null,
                                        'google.com'),
    google = proxyquire('../google', { 'request': requestStub });

describe('google module', function(){
    beforeEach(function() {
        google();
    });
    it('should request google.com', function() {
        expect(reqstub).to.be.called();
    });
    it('should log google body', function(){
```

```
        expect(callback).to.be.calledWith(null, null,
                                          'google.com');
    });
});
```

The first thing the test suite does is set up a `spy` and generic `stub` function that will be used as the `request` module. Then, we include our `google` module but we include it using `proxyquire` instead of a typical `require` module. Using `proxyquire`, we pass the path to the module the same way we would with `require`, except the second parameter is the module that would be required within that module and the `stub` function to use in its place.

Before each test, we execute the original `google` module and assert against our `stub` that it was in fact called. Additionally, we assert that the `log` spy was called with whatever data was returned from the `request` module. Since we are in control of that module, we can test, quite literally, that the string `google.com` was returned when a request was made to `http://google.com` (which we know for a fact is not true — not only that, but we know that a network call was never sent to `www.google.com` either).

We're using a special power of a stub that allows us to execute a particular parameter to the stubbed function assuming it was a callback function. Here, we're using `callsArgWith` and including the argument `index` (zero based) as the first parameter; in this case, 1. Of the two parameters that were passed to the request, the first (index 0) was the URL itself and the second (index 1) was the callback function. By using `callsArgWith`, we can execute the callback function and specifically provide its parameters; in this case, `null`, `null`, and a string.

Like Sinon.js and Chai.js, Proxyquire will also need to be included in our project as `devDependency`:

```
$ npm install --save-dev proxyquire
```

# Writing and running your first test

Up to this point, all of the test code we've seen has just been demos and examples and we haven't actually run any tests. Let's set up the basic structure of our application so that we can start writing real tests.

The first thing to do is set up the folder structure that will house all of our tests. Consider the following steps:

1.  Within the root of the application project folder, create a folder named `tests`.

2.  Within the `tests` folder, create three more folders for `controllers`, `models`, and `server`:

```
/(existing app root)
tests/
----/controllers/
----/models/
----/server/
```

# Writing a test helper

Before we start writing the tests for our application, there's a small amount of overhead we need to take care of to prepare for our tests. To take care of this overhead, we're going to write a `testhelper` file that will be included and run with every test file we execute via Mocha.

Create a file named `testhelper.js` within the `tests` folder and insert the following block of code:

```
var chai = require('chai'),
    sinon = require('sinon'),
    sinonChai = require('sinon-chai');

global.expect = chai.expect;
global.sinon = sinon;
chai.use(sinonChai);
```

This is code that we would typically need to include at the top of every one of our test files, but by including it in a single file we can instruct Mocha to automatically require this file for every test file that is run. The file itself just includes the `chai` and `sinon` modules and defines a few global variables as shortcuts for our test writing. Additionally, it instructs `chai` to use the `sinonChai` module so that our syntax is extended and we can write Sinon-specific Chai assertions.

The command to actually run our suite of tests is:

```
$ mocha -r tests/testhelper.js -R spec tests/**/*.test.js
```

Remember that we installed Mocha globally earlier so that we can execute the mocha command from anywhere.

Based on the path to our tests in the preceding command, it's assumed that the command will be executed from the root of the application project folder. The -r flag instructs Mocha to require the testhelper.js module. The -R flag is an option to define the style of the test reporting output. We chose to use the spec style, which lists our report in a nested indentation style with each describe and it statement along with a green checkmark for the passed tests. Finally, the last argument is the path to our test files; in this case, we provided wildcards so that all of our tests will be run.

Mocha has a few different reporting styles that you can choose from. These include dot (repeating dots for each test), list, progress (a percentage bar), JSON and spec. One of the more interesting, albeit somewhat useless, is the -R nyan reporting style.

Let's write a quick sample test to make sure our project is properly set up. Within the tests folder, create a new file named mocha.test.js and include the following code:

```
describe('Mocha', function() {
    describe('First Test', function() {
        it('should assert 1 equals 1', function() {
            expect(1).to.equal(1);
        });
    });
});
```

The preceding test is pretty straightforward and simply asserts that 1 is equal to 1. Save this file and run the Mocha test command again, and you should get the following output:

```
$ mocha -r tests/testhelper.js -R spec tests/mocha.test.js
Mocha
  First Test
    should assert 1 equals 1


1 passing (5ms)
```

You might find it tiresome and frustrating to remember and execute that long convoluted command for Mocha. Fortunately, there's a pretty easy solution. Edit the `package.json` file in the application and add the following section:

```
"scripts": {
    "start": "node server.js",
    "test": "mocha -r tests/testhelper.js -R spec
     tests/**/*.test.js"
},
```

By making this tweak in the `package.json` file, you can now simply execute `npm test` from a command line as a quick and easy shortcut. This is a standard convention with the `package.json` file so any developer will know to simply execute `npm test` as follows:

```
$ npm test

> chapter9@0.0.0 test /Users/jasonk/repos/nodebook/chapter9

> mocha -r tests/testhelper.js -R spec tests/**/*.test.js


Mocha
  First Test
    should assert 1 equals 1


1 passing (5ms)
```

Now that your project is set up to properly run and execute tests, let's start writing some real tests for the application.

# Testing the application

With all of that background information out of the way, let's focus on writing some real tests for the application we've built. In the following sections, we will write tests for the routes, servers, models, and controllers in our application.

## Testing the routes

Let's start things a little slow by taking a look at one of the most basic files in our application, the `routes.js` file. This file simply defines the number of routes that the application should respond to. This is going to be one of the easiest files to write tests for.

Since the `routes.js` file is in the `server` folder within our main application, let's put its corresponding test file in a similar location. Within the `tests/server` folder, create a file named `routes.test.js`. Since the `routes.test.js` file is going to be testing the functionalities of our `routes.js` file, we need it to require the same modules. Include the following code in `test/server/routes.test.js`:

```
var home = require('../../controllers/home'),
    image = require('../../controllers/image'),
    routes = require('../../server/routes');
```

Notice that the paths are different since we require modules from within our `test/server` folder, but we also require app-specific modules. Also, note that in addition to the modules that our original `routes.js` file requires, we also require the `routes` module itself. How else are we going to be able to test the functionalities of the module if it isn't included? Next, let's set up the structure of the test suite and create a few spies. Include this new block of code following the previous code within `tests/server/routes.test.js`:

```
describe('Routes', function(){
    var app = {
        get: sinon.spy(),
        post: sinon.spy(),
        delete: sinon.spy()
    };
    beforeEach(function(){
        routes.initialize(app);
    });

    // to do: write tests...
});
```

If you recall, the `routes` module's `initialize` function accepted a single parameter, an `app` object. In our tests, we defined `app` as a simple anonymous object with three functions such as `get`, `post`, and `delete`, each of which is a spy. We include a `beforeEach` block to execute the `initialize` function before every one of our test runs.

Now let's include some tests. First, we'll test that the GET endpoints are configured correctly. Immediately after the `// to do: write tests...` comment, place the following block of code:

```
describe('GETs', function() {
    it('should handle /', function(){
        expect(app.get).to.be.calledWith('/', home.index);
    });
```

```
    it('should handle /images/:image_id', function(){
        expect(app.get).to.be.calledWith('/images/:image_id',
        image.index);
    });
});
```

Then, test the POST endpoints:

```
describe('POSTs', function() {
    it('should handle /images', function(){
        expect(app.post).to.be.calledWith('/images',
                                    image.create);
    });
    it('should handle /images/:image_id/like', function(){
        expect(app.post)
            .to.be.calledWith('/images/:image_id/like',
                            image.like);
    });
    it('should handle /images/:image_id/comment', function(){
        expect(app.post)
            .to.be.calledWith('/images/:image_id/comment',
                            image.comment);
    });
});
```

Finally, test the DELETE endpoint:

```
describe('DELETEs', function() {
    it('should handle /images/:image_id', function(){
        expect(app.delete)
            .to.be.calledWith('/images/:image_id', image.remove);
    });
});
```

Each of these tests assert the same thing, that the app object's corresponding the get, post, or delete function was executed with the correct parameters for each route. We were able to test against the parameters because the app object we used was a spy.

If you run the mocha command to execute the suite of tests, you should see the following output:

```
$ npm test

Routes

    GETs

        should handle /
```

```
        should handle /images/:image_id
    POSTs
        should handle /images
        should handle /images/:image_id/like
        should handle /images/:image_id/comment
    DELETEs
        should handle /images/:image_id


  6 passing (14ms)
```

# Testing the server

Testing the `server.js` file will be slightly different than any of our other files. The file runs as the root of our application, so it doesn't export a module or any object that we can directly test. Since we launch our server using `server.js`, we need to emulate launching our server from our code. We'll create a function called `server`, which will require the `server.js` file using Proxyquire, and stub each of the modules that it requires itself. Executing the `server()` function will be exactly the same as executing node `server.js` from a command line. All of the code within the file will execute via that function, and then we can test against each of the calls that are made using stubs from within Proxyquire.

Create a file named `server.test.js` within the `tests/server/` folder and insert the following block of code:

```
var proxyquire, expressStub, configStub, mongooseStub, app,
    server = function() {
        proxyquire('../../server', {
            'express': expressStub,
            './server/configure': configStub,
            'mongoose': mongooseStub
        });
    };

describe('Server', function() {
    beforeEach(function(){
        proxyquire = require('proxyquire'),
        app = {
            set: sinon.spy(),
            get: sinon.stub().returns(3300),
            listen: sinon.spy()
        },
```

```
        expressStub = sinon.stub().returns(app),
        configStub = sinon.stub().returns(app),
        mongooseStub = {
            connect: sinon.spy(),
            connection: {
                on: sinon.spy()
            }
        };

        delete process.env.PORT;
    });

    // to do: write tests...
});
```

Before each test is run for our server, we reset the stubs for all of the major components of the server. These stubs include the app object itself, express, config, and mongoose. We're stubbing each of these modules since we want to spy on them (and we use a stub because some of them need to return objects that we'll work with in our file). Now that we have all of our spies in place and our app object scaffold set up, we can start testing the main functionalities of our code.

We need to check whether the following conditions pass:

- An application is created
- The views directory is set
- The port is set and can be configured and/or set to default
- The app itself is configured (config is called with it)
- Mongoose connects to a database URI string
- Finally, the app itself is launched

Replace the // to do: write tests... comment in the earlier code with the following block of code:

```
describe('Bootstrapping', function(){
    it('should create the app', function(){
        server();
        expect(expressStub).to.be.called;
    });
    it('should set the views', function(){
        server();
        expect(app.set.secondCall.args[0]).to.equal('views');
    });
```

```
    it('should configure the app', function(){
        server();
        expect(configStub).to.be.calledWith(app);
    });
    it('should connect with mongoose', function(){
        server();
expect(mongooseStub.connect).to.be.calledWith
(sinon.match.string);

    });
    it('should launch the app', function(){
        server();
        expect(app.get).to.be.calledWith('port');
        expect(app.listen).to.be.calledWith(3300,
                                        sinon.match.func);
    });
});
```

In the preceding group of tests, we are testing the bootstrapping of our server, which is all of the functionalities that initially run within `server.js`. The names of the tests are pretty self-explanatory. We're checking against the various methods of the `app` object, ensuring that they're called and/or the correct parameters were passed in. For the tests, we want to test that a specific type of parameter was called, not literally what the parameter value was; we use Sinon's match element, which allows our tests to be a little more generic. We wouldn't want to hard code the MongoDB URI string in our tests because that's just another place we would have to maintain—although you could very well do this if you wanted your test to be that strict (that is to assert that quite literally the exact URI string was passed).

In the second set of tests, we want to ensure that the port is set, that it defaults to 3300, and that it can be changed via the use of a node environment variable:

```
describe('Port', function(){
    it('should be set', function() {
        server();
        expect(app.set.firstCall.args[0]).to.equal('port');
    });
    it('should default to 3300', function() {
        server();
        expect(app.set.firstCall.args[1]).to.equal(3300);
    });
    it('should be configurable', function() {
        process.env.PORT = '5500';
        server();
        expect(app.set.firstCall.args[1]).to.equal('5500');
    });
});
```

With these tests in place, run the `npm test` command again and you should get the following output:

```
$ npm test

Server
    Bootstrapping
        should create the app (364ms)
        should set the views
        should configure the app
        should connect with mongoose
        should launch the app
    Port
        should be set
        should default to 3300
        should be configurable
```

# Testing a model

When testing our models, we want to include the `model` module itself and then write tests against it. The easiest solution here is that we create a test `model` object and then assert that the model has all of the fields that we expect, as well as any virtuals we might have created.

Create the `tests/models/image.test.js` file and insert the following code:

```
var ImageModel = require('../../models/image');

describe('Image Model', function() {
    var image;

    it('should have a mongoose schema', function(){
        expect(ImageModel.schema).to.be.defined;
    });

    beforeEach(function(){
        image = new ImageModel({
            title: 'Test',
            description: 'Testing',
            filename: 'testfile.jpg'
```

```
        });
    });

    // to do: write tests...
});
```

First, we include `ImageModel` using `require` (note the path for the `require` statement). The very first test we run is to make sure that `ImageModel` has a mongoose schema property. After this test, we define the `beforeEach` block that we'll rely on for the remainder of our tests. Before every test, we want to instantiate a new `ImageModel` object that we can test against. We do this in a `beforeEach` block so that we're sure we're dealing with a fresh object in every test and that it hasn't been tainted by any tests that were previously run. It's also important to note that the order of the first test and the `beforeEach` block doesn't actually matter, as the `beforeEach` block will run before every test in its parent `describe` function regardless of the order it was defined in.

Include the following suite of tests replacing the placeholder `// to do: write tests...` comment:

```
describe('Schema', function() {
    it('should have a title string', function(){
        expect(image.title).to.be.defined;
    });
    it('should have a description string', function(){
        expect(image.description).to.be.defined;
    });
    it('should have a filename string', function(){
        expect(image.filename).to.be.defined;
    });
    it('should have a views number default to 0', function(){
        expect(image.views).to.be.defined;
        expect(image.views).to.equal(0);
    });
    it('should have a likes number default to 0', function(){
        expect(image.likes).to.be.defined;
        expect(image.likes).to.equal(0);
    });
    it('should have a timestamp date', function(){
        expect(image.timestamp).to.be.defined;
    });
});
```

Here, we check to ensure that each property we expect an `ImageModel` instance to have is defined. For the properties that have default values set, we also check to ensure the default values are set as well.

Next, we test against the `virtuals` we expect `ImageModel` to have, and verify that they function the way they're supposed to:

```
describe('Virtuals', function(){
    describe('uniqueId', function(){
        it('should be defined', function(){
            expect(image.uniqueId).to.be.defined;
        });
        it('should get filename without extension', function(){
            expect(image.uniqueId).to.equal('testfile');
        });
    });
});
```

When testing the `uniqueId` virtual, it should return the `image` model's filename without the extension. As the `beforeEach` defined our `image` model with a filename of `testfile.jpg`, we can assert with our test that the `uniqueId` returned is equal to `testfile` (the filename without the extension).

Running the tests for our model should output the following results:

```
$ npm test
Image Model
    should have a mongoose schema
  Schema
      should have a title string
      should have a description string
      should have a filename string
      should have a views number default to 0
      should have a likes number default to 0
      should have a timestamp date
  Virtuals
    uniqueId
        should be defined
        should get filename without extension
```

# Testing a controller

Last but not least, let's take a look at the `image` controller, and specifically test for the main `index` function. Because the `index` function does a lot of work and performs a number of different tasks, the test file will make extensive use of stubs and spies. The first thing we need to do before any tests is declare a number of global variables for our tests as well as set up all of our stubs, spies, and placeholder objects for use with Proxyquire. Then, we require the actual image controller using Proxyquire. Create a file named `tests/controllers/image.test.js` and insert the following code:

```
var proxyquire = require('proxyquire'),
    callback = sinon.spy(),
    sidebarStub = sinon.stub(),
    fsStub = {},
    pathStub = {},
    md5Stub = {},
    ModelsStub = {
        Image: {
            findOne: sinon.spy()
        },
        Comment: {
            find: sinon.spy()
        }
    },
    image = proxyquire('../../controllers/image', {
        '../helpers/sidebar': sidebarStub,
        '../models': ModelsStub,
        'fs': fsStub,
        'path': pathStub,
        'md5': md5Stub
    }),
    res = {},
    req = {},
    testImage = {};
```

With this code, we define a number of global variables as spies, stubs, or empty placeholder JavaScript objects. Once our stubs are prepared, we call `proxyquire` to include our `image` controller (ensuring that the required modules within the image controller are actually replaced with our various stubs and spies). Now that all of our globals, stubs, and spies are prepared, let's include some tests.

Include the following code after the previous block of code:

```
describe('Image Controller', function(){
    beforeEach(function() {
        res = {
            render: sinon.spy(),
            json: sinon.spy(),
            redirect: sinon.spy()
        };
        req.params = {
            image_id: 'testing'
        };
        testImage = {
            _id: 1,
            title: 'Test Image',
            views: 0,
            likes: 0,
            save: sinon.spy()
        };
    });
    // to do: write tests...
});
```

Once again, we build up some setup using a `beforeEach` block for our tests. This sets spies on each of the `res` object's functions including render, JSON and redirect (each of these are used throughout the `image` controller). We fake the query string parameter by setting the `req.params` object with an `image_id` property. Finally, we create a test `image` object that will be used by our fake mongoose `image` model stub to emulate a database object being returned from MongoDB:

```
describe('Index', function(){
    it('should be defined', function(){
        expect(image.index).to.be.defined;
    });
    it('should call Models.Image.findOne', function(){
        ModelsStub.Image.findOne = sinon.spy();
        image.index(req, res);
        expect(ModelsStub.Image.findOne).to.be.called;
    });
    it('should find Image by parameter id', function(){
        ModelsStub.Image.findOne = sinon.spy();
        image.index(req, res);
        expect(ModelsStub.Image.findOne).to.be.calledWith(
            { filename: { $regex: 'testing' } },
            sinon.match.func);
```

```
    });
    // to do: write more tests...
  });
```

The first test we run is to ensure that the index function actually exists. Within the index function, the very first action that occurs is that the image model is found via the Models.Image.findOne function. In order to test that function, we need to first set it as spy. The reason we do this here and not in beforeEach is because we might want the findOne method to behave slightly differently in each test, so we don't want to set a strict rule to be applied for all the tests.

In order to emulate that a GET call was posted to our server and our image index controller function was hit, we can just fire the function manually. We do this using image.index(req, res) and pass in our fake request and response objects (defined earlier as globals and stubbed in the beforeEach function).

Since ModelsStub.Image.findOne is a spy, we can test that it was called, and then separately test that it was called specifically with the parameters we expect it to be called with. In the case of findOne, where the second parameter is a callback function, we don't care or want to test the very specific function that was included, only ensure that an actual function was included. To do this, we can use Sinon's matcher API and specify that a func, or function, was included as the second parameter.

This last set of tests tests the code that executes when an image is found and returned from the findOne function:

```
describe('with found image model', function() {
    beforeEach(function(){
        ModelsStub.Image.findOne =
            sinon.stub().callsArgWith(1,null,testImage);
    });
    it('should incremement views by 1 and save', function(){
        image.index(req, res);
        expect(testImage.views).to.equal(1);
        expect(testImage.save).to.be.called;
    });
    it('should find related comments', function(){
        image.index(req, res);
        expect(ModelsStub.Comment.find).to.be.calledWith(
            {image_id: 1},
            {},
            { sort: { 'timestamp': 1 }},
            sinon.match.func
        );
    });
```

```
it('should execute sidebar', function(){
    ModelsStub.Comment.find =
        sinon.stub().callsArgWith(3, null, [1,2,3]);
    image.index(req, res);
    expect(sidebarStub).to.be.calledWith(
        {image: testImage, comments: [1,2,3]},
        sinon.match.func);
});
it('should render image template with image and comments',
function(){
    ModelsStub.Comment.find =
        sinon.stub().callsArgWith(3, null, [1,2,3]);
    sidebarStub.callsArgWith(1, {image: testImage, comments:
    [1,2,3]});
    image.index(req, res);
    expect(res.render).to.be.calledWith('image', {image:
    testImage, comments: [1,2,3]});
});
});
```

The first thing to notice here is that findOne is no longer a spy in these tests, but a stub that will manually fire the callback function that's provided as its second parameter. The callback function that's fired will include our test image model. With this stub, we are emulating that the database call was in fact made via findOne and that a valid image model was returned. Then, we can test the remainder of the code that executes within that main callback. We perform a similar setup with the Comment.find call as well.

When the sidebarStub gets executed, we use the callsArgWith Sinon function—which fires the callback function that was originally included as a parameter. Within that callback function, we include fake viewModel as a parameter.

Once sidebarStub does its job, we expect res.render to have been called, and we specify the exact parameters we expect it to have been called with.

Running the tests for the image controller should yield the following output:

```
$ npm test
Image Controller
    Index
        should be defined
        should call Models.Image.findOne
        should find Image by parameter id
    with found image model
```

```
should incremement views by 1 and save

should find related comments

should execute sidebar

should render image template with image and comments
```

# Spy and stub everything!

When in doubt, the safest thing you can do when writing your tests is spy on everything and stub everything else. There are always going to be times that you'll want a function to execute naturally; in that case, leave it alone. Ultimately, you never want your tests to be dependent on any other system — that includes database servers, other network servers, other APIs, and so on. You only want to test that your own code works, nothing more. If your code is expected to make a call to an API, spy on the actual call and just assert that your code attempted to make the call. Likewise, fake the response from the server via a stub and ensure that your code handles the response properly.

The easiest way to check for dependencies in your code is to stop any other services from running (your local node app, and so on), as well as, possibly even, disabling your network connection. If your tests timeout or fail somewhere unexpectedly, it's likely because you missed a function you needed to spy on or stub along the way.

Don't get stuck going down a rabbit hole when writing your tests. It's easy to get carried away and start testing functionalities that should safely be assumed to be working. An example of this is writing tests to ensure a third-party module is performing correctly. If it's not a module you wrote, don't test it. Don't worry about writing tests to prove the module does what it says it should.

To learn more about TDD specifically when writing JavaScript, I would highly recommend Christian Johansen's beast of a book *Test-Driven JavaScript Development*. This book is huge and speaks of the sheer volume of information related to TDD. In some circles, TDD truly is a way of life and it will define the style with which you write your code.

# Summary

This has definitely been a crash course on testing, but the groundwork has been laid and I hope that you have a solid understanding of the tool chain that you can use to write your own tests. Trust this powerhouse suite of tools and you'll be writing bulletproof code in no time!

The ultimate goal with writing tests is to have 100 percent complete code coverage and have unit tests exist for every line of code you write. From here, the true test is to switch to TDD, which dictates that you write tests before any code exists at all. Obviously, tests against nonexistent code will fail, so then you'll need to write the least amount of code to get it to pass, and repeat!

In the next chapter, we'll take a look at a number of cloud-based hosting options available to get your application up and running online.

# 10
# Deploying with Cloud-Based Services

Inevitably, you'll want the application you've been building to be online and available to the world—whether you want to host your application online during its development process or when it's complete and ready for production. There are a number of different hosting options currently available for Node.js and MongoDB-based apps, and in this chapter, we'll take a look at deploying to a few different popular services.

In this chapter, we will cover:

- Cloud versus traditional web hosting
- Introduction to Git source control
- Deploying an application with Nodejitsu
- Deploying an application with Heroku
- Deploying an application with Amazon Web Services
- Deploying an application with Microsoft Azure
- A brief look at Digital Ocean

# Cloud versus traditional hosting

If you had any previous experience with website hosting in the past, which I'll refer to as traditional hosting, you're probably pretty familiar with the process of using FTP to upload your web files to your hosting provider. With traditional web hosting, service providers typically offer shared space to every user, each configured with their own public folder that houses the web files. In a scenario like this, every customer hosts the same kind of website, and their files are all stored and served from a single web server.

Traditional web hosting is fairly inexpensive because a single web server can host literally hundreds, if not thousands, of individual websites. Scaling is typically a problem with traditional hosting because if your website demanded more power, it would need to be moved to another server (with more hardware) and could experience potential downtime during this move. As a side effect, if a website on the same server as your own is being particularly demanding of the hardware, every site on that server could suffer.

With cloud-based hosting, every instance of a website or service is hosted on its own **Virtual Private Server (VPS)**. When a customer uploads a copy of their website, that website is running in its own isolated environment, and the environment is specifically designed to run only that website. Virtual private servers are instances of a server, typically all running simultaneously on the same hardware. Because of their isolated nature, VPS scales very well because settings simply need to be changed for hardware allocation and the server restarts. If your VPS is hosted on the same hardware as others, and they are experiencing high-volume spikes, your website will not suffer because of the isolated nature of the VPS.

# Infrastructure as a Service versus Platform as a Service

The beauty of the cloud is that the level and amount of service one can obtain varies greatly. From something as simple as a basic hosting plan to run your web application, you can use any number of services that are considered a **Platform as a Service (PaaS)**. This is a service that provides a platform for you to host and run your web application. Increasing in scale and complexity, you can turn to an **Infrastructure as a Service (IaaS)** provider, which offers an entire cloud-based data center at your disposal.

You can learn more about the differences between IaaS, PaaS, and **Software as a Service (SaaS)** by reading this detailed article at `http://www.rackspace.com/knowledge_center/whitepaper/understanding-the-cloud-computing-stack-saas-paas-iaas`.

Cloud-based hosting costs can vary greatly because of the simple fact that they are so scalable. Your costs could fluctuate throughout a single month dramatically depending directly on your need for power (that is more demanding times of the month and/or big social media hits such as HackerNews or Reddit). On the flip side, if you require very little power for a server, often you can get cloud hosting for free!

 Traditional web hosting service providers include GoDaddy, Dreamhost, 1&1, HostGator, and Network Solutions. Popular cloud-based hosting options include Nodejitsu (PaaS), Heroku (PaaS), Amazon Web Services (IaaS), Microsoft Azure (IaaS), and Digital Ocean.

# An introduction to Git

With traditional hosting providers, the standard method for connecting to your server and uploading your files was to use **File Transfer Protocol (FTP)**. You would connect using any standard FTP software and push a copy of your files to the server and those changes would be reflected instantly online when accessing your website URL. With cloud-based hosting providers, the standard typically is to use the Git source control. Git is a source control technology that allows you to track changes and history with your project source code as well as provide an easy-use means of collaboration with multiple developers. The most popular Git online code repository provider currently is `www.github.com`.

We are going to use Git in order to track our application project source code as well as the method of pushing our code up to the various cloud-hosting providers. When you push code using Git, you are effectively transferring all or only the changed version of your code to an online repository (for example, Git as well as `www.github.com` are relatively easy to get into but can seem intimidating and complex). If you're unfamiliar with Git and/or `https://GitHub.com`, I would strongly suggest taking a moment to get acquainted by checking out the following guides:

- `https://help.github.com/articles/set-up-git`
- `https://gist.github.com/andrewpmiller/9668225`

The guides will take you through the following concepts:

- Downloading and installing Git
- Registering an account at https://github.com
- Authenticating your machine with https://github.com and creating your first repository
- Committing your project source code to the repository

Once you have your project source code configured as a local Git repository and all of the code committed to the master branch, proceed to the following sections.

# Deploying your application

Now that you have your project set up as a local GitHub repository, its time to take that code and get it online! The following sections will each cover the process of deploying your application to a few different popular cloud-based hosting providers.

Feel free to explore and experiment with each as most have free or relatively inexpensive plans. Each provider has its strengths and weaknesses, so I'll leave it up to you to decide which to stick with for your particular needs. The services that we cover aren't presented in any particular order.

 Note that for the purposes of this chapter, I will consistently name my app imgploadr; however, your app name needs to be different and unique. Wherever I include imgploadr in this chapter, you should replace it with your own app's unique name.

## Nodejitsu

To get started with Nodejitsu, first visit www.nodejitsu.com and register for a free account. After providing your e-mail address, username, and password, you will be presented with a pricing plan page where you can configure your service. If you just want to create the free account and experiment, simply click on the **No Thanks** button and the registration process is complete. Then, simply click on the **Login** button in the upper right corner to log in and proceed to your **Apps** dashboard:

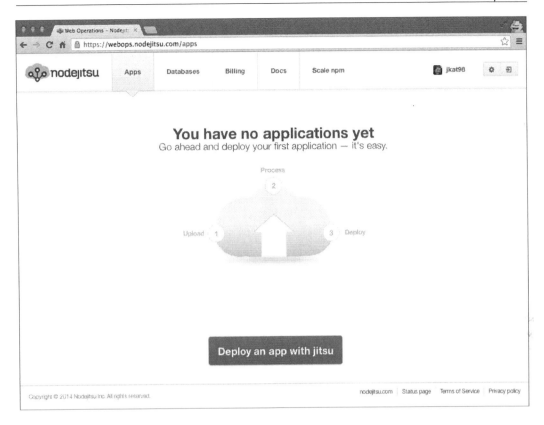

Deploying your app to Nodejitsu is going to require a new command-line interface tool, specifically, the `jitsu` CLI. Clicking on the big blue **Deploy an app with jitsu** button will take you to the www.github.com repository for this tool. You can skip that step and just install the CLI manually using the following npm command:

```
$ sudo npm install -g-g install jitsu
```

 Note that the sudo part of the command to install an npm package globally (using the -g flag) is sometimes required. Depending on your access level of the machine you are using, you may or may not need to include sudo.

Now that the `jitsu` CLI is installed, you can use this handy tool to log in to your Nodejitsu account, create an app, and deploy your project code. First, let's log in:

```
$ jitsu login
info:     Welcome to Nodejitsu
info:     jitsu v0.13.18, node v0.10.26
info:     It worked if it ends with Nodejitsu ok
info:     Executing command login
help:     An activated nodejitsu account is required to login
help:     To create a new account use the jitsu signup command
prompt: username:  jkat98
prompt: password:
info:     Authenticated as jkat98
info:     Nodejitsu ok
```

You can see that after successfully providing your username and password, you are now authenticated with Nodejitsu and ready to go.

Before we can deploy the actual application, we need to first configure the MongoDB database in our Nodejitsu dashboard. Switch back to your browser, and on the Nodejitsu **Apps** dashboard, switch sections by clicking on the **Databases** tab:

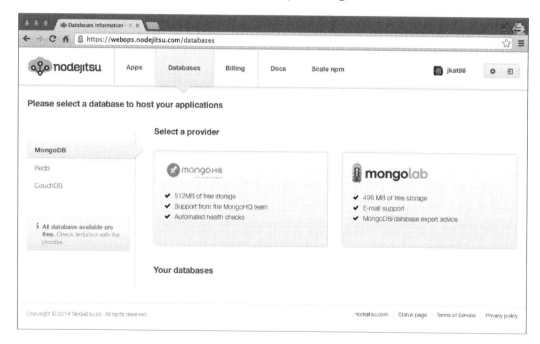

Let's choose MongoHQ for our needs by clicking on the large **MongoHQ** button. You will be prompted for a name for the new database and then it will be listed at the bottom of the screen in the **Your databases** section. The important part we need is the connection string, and there's a convenient copy link right next to it to copy it to your clipboard.

Edit the `server.js` file and update the `mongoose.connect` line to use this new connection string you copied for your Nodejitsu database:

```
[/server.js]
mongoose.connect('YOUR_NODEJITSU_CONNECTION_STRING_HERE');
mongoose.connection.on('open', function() {
    console.log('Mongoose connected.');
});
```

The only thing left remaining is to open a terminal, change directories to your project home, and execute the following command to package up your app and push it to Nodejitsu:

```
$ jitsu deploy
info:    Welcome to Nodejitsu jkat98
info:    jitsu v0.13.18, node v0.10.26
info:    It worked if it ends with Nodejitsu ok
info:    Executing command deploy
warn:
warn:    The package.json file is missing required fields:
warn:
warn:       Subdomain name
warn:
warn:    Prompting user for required fields.
warn:    Press ^C at any time to quit.
warn:
prompt: Subdomain name:  (jkat98-imgploadr) imgploadr
warn:    About to write /Users/jasonk/repos/nodebook/imgploadr/
package.json
... (a lot of npm install output) ...
info:    Done creating snapshot 0.0.1
info:    Updating app myapp
info:    Activating snapshot 0.0.1 for myapp
info:    Starting app myapp
info:    App myapp is now started
info:    http://imgploadr.nodejitsu.com on Port 80
info:    Nodejitsu ok
```

After executing `jitsu deploy`, the CLI first prompts to confirm what the subdomain will be under the `www.nodejitsu.com` domain. Feel free to change this to whatever you like (it will check to confirm availability). It will then make a few minor modifications to your `package.json` file, specifically including the `subdomain` option with whatever value you provided. Finally, it uploads your source code and performs a remote `npm install` operation. Assuming all went well, the app should be deployed and a confirmation of the URL outputs to the screen. Feel free to open that URL in your browser to view the app online!

You can also now see that the app is listed in your **Apps** dashboard:

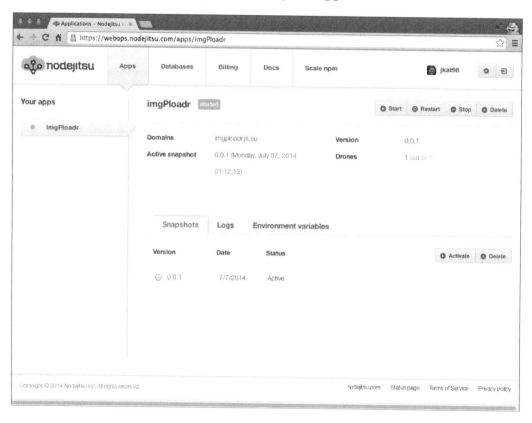

Now that the application has been successfully uploaded, launch it via its URL and give it a test run by attempting to upload a new image. The first thing you should notice is that attempting to upload an image fails with a fairly useless error (you can see the following error by accessing the **Logs** tab from your app's dashboard):

```
400 Error: ENOENT, open
'/opt/run/snapshot/package/public/upload/temp/72118-89rld0.png
```

This error is far from helpful! Basically, what's happening here is that the application is attempting to upload and save the image to the `temp` folder that doesn't actually exist! We need to add a snippet of code to our application to check for this condition and create the folders if necessary.

Edit the `server/configure.js` file and insert the following code snippet between `routes (app);` and `return app;`:

```
// Ensure the temporary upload folders exist
        fs.mkdir(path.join(__dirname, '../public/upload'),
        function(err){
            console.log(err);
            fs.mkdir(path.join(__dirname,
            '../public/upload/temp'),
                function(err){
                    console.log(err);
                });
        });
```

Here we're using the filesystem `fs` module to create both the parent `upload` folder as well as the `temp` subfolder. Don't forget to require the `fs` module at the top of the file too:

```
var connect = require('connect'),
    path = require('path'),
    routes = require('./routes'),
    exphbs = require('express3-handlebars'),
    moment = require('moment'),
    fs = require('fs');
```

> There is an npm module called `node-mkdirp` that will perform a recursive `mkdir`, which basically would accomplish the double `mkdir` we called in the preceding example. The only reason I didn't include it was for brevity and to not unnecessarily include additional instructions to install the module, require it, and use it. More info can be found at https://www.npmjs.org/package/mkdirp.

With the mentioned changes made to your code, you need to deploy your application again. Simply execute another `jitsu deploy` and a fresh copy of your code will be uploaded to your instance:

```
$ jitsu deploy
```

Open your app URL again, and this time you should be able to interact with the application and successfully upload a new image! Congratulations, you have successfully deployed your application and it is now online using the Nodejitsu hosting service!

# Heroku

Another popular cloud-based hosting provider for Node.js apps is www.Heroku.com. The one thing that sets Heroku apart from other providers is the number of powerful add-ons that are available. Any kind of service you can imagine your application will require is available as an add-on, including data stores, search, logging and analytics, e-mail and SMS, workers and queuing, monitoring, and media! Each of these add-ons can be quickly and easily added to your service and integrated into your application with ease.

Like Nodejitsu, Heroku allows you to register a free account and work within the confines of their "sandbox" pricing plans. The plans are free, but limited in scope with regard to bandwidth, processing power, and so on. Most, if not all, of the add-ons typically also offer some sort of free sandbox or trial-based plan. Just like Nodejitsu, one of the add-ons we will be using with our Heroku app is MongoHQ, a cloud-based MongoDB service provider.

To get started, first go to http://heroku.com and sign up for your free account. While registration doesn't require a credit card, in order to include any add-ons with your application, you will have to have a credit card on file (even though it won't be charged unless you choose to scale up the services). After registering, click on the link in the confirmation e-mail and provide a password; you will be presented with your **Apps** dashboard:

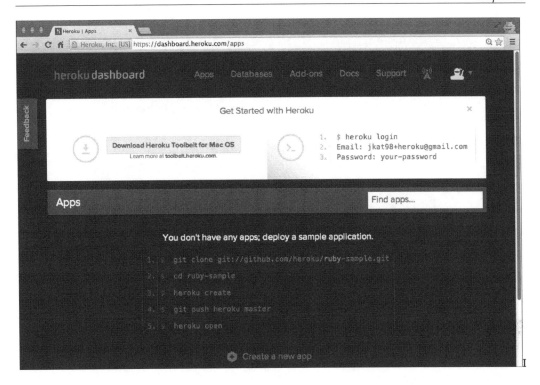

You'll notice that the first thing you need to do is download the Heroku Toolbelt (again, much like the `jitsu` CLI for Nodejitsu). Click on the **Download** button to download and install the Toolbelt. The Toolbelt is a CLI, specifically to create and deploy apps to Heroku, and gives you the `heroku` command.

Once you have the Toolbelt installed, open a command-line terminal and change directories to your project's root. From there, execute the following command to log in to Heroku:

```
$ heroku login
Enter your Heroku credentials.
Email: jkat98@gmail.com
Password (typing will be hidden):
Authentication successful.
```

Now that you're logged in, you can issue commands directly to your Heroku account and use those commands to create an application, install add-ons, and deploy your project.

The first thing you'll want to do is create a new application. Do so by executing `heroku create` from the command line:

```
$ heroku create
Creating secret-shore-2839... done, stack is cedar
http://secret-shore-2839.herokuapp.com/ | git@heroku.com:secret-
shore-2839.git
```

After creating the app, Heroku randomly assigns it a unique name; in my case, `secret-shore-2839` (don't worry though as this can easily be changed):

```
$ heroku apps:rename imgploadr --app secret-shore-2839
Renaming secret-shore-2839 to imgploadr... done
http://imgploadr.herokuapp.com/ | git@heroku.com:imgploadr.git
Don't forget to update your Git remotes on any local checkouts.
```

Let's address that last part next. Heroku relies on the Git source control on your machine in order to push your project source code up to your server, unlike Nodejitsu, which uses its own file transfer mechanism. Assuming you followed the directions earlier with regard to Git and www.github.com your project source code should be all set and committed to the master branch and ready to go. What we need to do next is add a new remote for Git on your machine to point to Heroku and specifically your new app.

Let's start with `git init` to initialize `git` in the current working directory and then execute the following command to create a new remote for Heroku:

```
$ git remote add heroku git@heroku.com:imgploadr.git
```

Before you can push your source code up to your Heroku account, we need to take care of a few things first.

A special file is required before your application will be able to run on your Heroku server. This file is called `Procfile`, and it specifically contains the command necessary to launch your application. Create this new file named `Procfile` (no extension) in the root of your project and include the following line:

```
web: node server.js
```

That's it! With that file, Heroku will use that command to launch your application. Now that you have `Procfile` set up and your project source code ready, there's only one thing left to do—install the MongoHQ add-on and configure your app to use it:

```
$ heroku addons:create mongohq --app imgploadr
Adding mongohq on imgploadr... done, v3 (free)
Use 'heroku addons:docs mongohq' to view documentation.
```

With the MongoHQ add-on added, you can now configure the database itself and retrieve the connection string (much like you did earlier with Nodejitsu). Access your `http://heroku.com` **Apps** dashboard, and it should look something like the following screenshot:

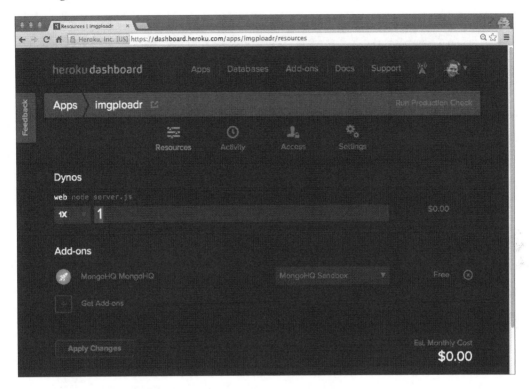

The app's dashboard screen is a great place to get a snapshot of your application and a quick glance at its current cost. Since I'm using the sandbox and/or free plans for my application and add-ons, my current estimated monthly cost is $0.00. However, you can quickly and easily scale your apps should you demand more power. Pay attention, as you can also just as quickly and easily escalate your monthly cost through the roof! (Scaling everything to maximum, I was able to get my estimated cost to roughly $60,000 per month!)

To configure your MongoHQ database, simply click on the **MongoHQ** link under the **Add-ons** section of your app's dashboard:

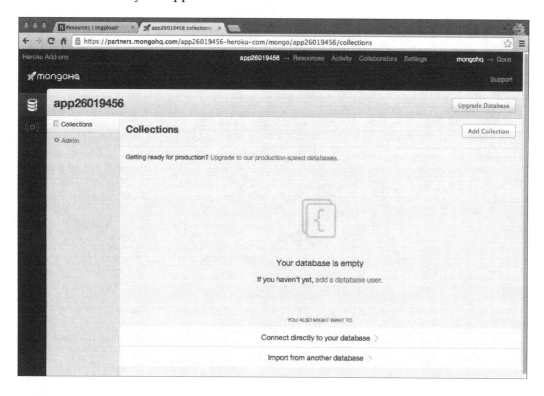

Click on the **Admin** tab with the gear icon below the **Collections** tab. Click on the **Users** tab and provide a username and password that your application will use to connect with your MongoHQ database. This will create the imgploadrdb username with a secure password. With the new user added, switch back to the **Overview** tab and copy the Mongo URI string.

Again, just like with Nodejitsu, edit the server.js file in your project and replace the mongoose.connect string with the new URI you just copied. Edit the string and replace <username> and <password> with the appropriate values based on the new user account you just created. The server.js mongoose.connect code should look like the following:

```
mongoose.connect('mongodb://imgploadrdb:password@kahana.mongohq.co
m:10089/app26');
mongoose.connection.on('open', function() {
    console.log('Mongoose connected.');
});
```

Since you just made changes to your project's source code, you need to remember to commit those changes to your Git repository master branch so that they can get uploaded to Heroku. Execute the following command to permanently commit these changes to your source code and upload your code to your Heroku server:

```
$ git commit -am "Update mongoose connection string"
$ git push heroku master
Initializing repository, done.
Counting objects: 50, done.
Delta compression using up to 8 threads.
Compressing objects: 100% (43/43), done.
Writing objects: 100% (50/50), 182.80 KiB | 0 bytes/s, done.
Total 50 (delta 3), reused 0 (delta 0)
... npm install output ...
To git@heroku.com:imgploadr.git
 * [new branch]      master -> master
```

The final step to get your application up and running is to create an instance of your server (basically the equivalent of turning it on). To do this, execute the following command:

```
$ heroku ps:scale web=1 --app imgploadr
Scaling dynos... done, now running web at 1:1X.
$ heroku open
Opening imgploadr... done
```

Success! Hopefully, your browser launched and your website is up and running. Go ahead, give it a try and upload an image! Thanks to the bug we caught during the Nodejitsu deployment, this updated version of the application should work just fine.

While deploying with Heroku seems more complicated than Nodejitsu, this is probably because it uses Git source control to facilitate the transfer of your project files. Also, because Heroku is so flexible with the power of its scaling and add-ons, the toolbelt CLI is a little more robust.

# Amazon Web Services

While Nodejitsu and Heroku can be considered developer-level service providers because they are Platforms as a Service, Amazon Web Services (and Microsoft Azure) would be considered enterprise-level services because they are more Infrastructure as a Service. The sheer volume of options and services available with AWS and Azure is staggering. These are definitely top-tier services and hosting an application like ours is kind of like using a bazooka to kill a fly!

AWS does provide its own NoSQL database called DynamoDB, but for our purposes, we want to continue to work with MongoDB and use Mongoose in our app. To do this, we can use a third-party MongoDB provider. If you recall, when we originally set up Nodejitsu, one of the MongoDB providers listed was MongoLab. MongoLab provides "MongoDB-as-a-Service", which means we can use their service to host our MongoDB database, but use all of the power of AWS to host our Node.js application (this is not unlike what's already happening with Nodejitsu and Heroku already — they just streamline the process a little better). Remember that AWS is an Infrastructure as a Service provider, so you could also just create another server instance and install MongoDB on it yourself and use that as your data source. That's slightly beyond the scope of this chapter however.

## Create a MongoLab account and database

In order to use MongoLab with our app in AWS, we first need to register a new account on http://mongolab.com and create an AWS database subscription. After you register a new account and activate it using the link they send you via e-mail, you can create your first database subscription.

From your main dashboard, click on the **Create new** button (with the lightning bolt icon):

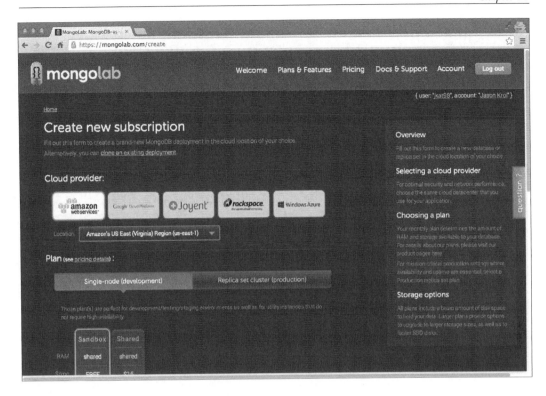

From the **Create new subscription** page, configure the following settings:

- **Cloud provider**: **amazon web services**
- **Location**: (whichever region you prefer)
- **Plan**: Select **Single-node (development)**
  - ○ Select **Sandbox** (shared/free)

- **MongoDB version**: `2.4.x`
- **Database name**: `anything_you_want` (I chose `imgploadr`)
- Confirm that the price is $0 per month
- Click on **Create new MongoDB deployment**

Going back to your main dashboard, you should now see that your new database has been created and is ready to go. The next thing we need to do is create a user account that our app will use to connect to the server. Click on the database listed on the main dashboard and then select the **Users** tab. Provide a new username and password. After the new user account has been added, copy the URI located at the top of the screen (it only appears after a user has been added) that starts with `mongodb://`.

Now that you have the new URI connection string, we need to update `server.js` to include this new connection string in our `mongoose.connect`. Edit the file and update the following code:

```
mongoose.connect('mongodb://imgploadrdb:password@ds061248.mongolab
.com:61248/imgploadr');
mongoose.connection.on('open', function() {
    console.log('Mongoose connected.');
});
```

Make sure you replace `<username>` and `<password>` with the appropriate information from the user account you created on the MongoLab dashboard.

With our application code updated to point to the new MongoLab database connection string, we need to zip up the project files so that they can be uploaded via the AWS dashboard. From your computer's file browser, locate the project root that contains all of your applications' source code files, select all of them and right-click on them to add to an archive or ZIP file. The name of the ZIP file can be whatever you choose. One thing to note is that you shouldn't include the `node_modules` folder with this ZIP file (the easiest solution might be to simply delete the folder altogether). The AWS online docs have a great write-up on creating ZIP files if you need more information (`https://docs.aws.amazon.com/elasticbeanstalk/latest/dg/using-features.deployment.source.html`).

Once your source code has been updated to use the new MongoLab connection string and you've created a ZIP file of the entire project (excluding the `node_modules` folder), you're ready to create the new AWS application and deploy your app.

# Create and configure the AWS environment

If you don't already have an account with Amazon, you're going to need one to use their AWS services. Point your browser to `http://aws.amazon.com` and click on **Sign Up** (even if you already have an Amazon account). From the screen that follows, you can log in using your existing Amazon account or register for a new account. Once you've registered and logged in, you should be presented with the entire suite of cloud services AWS has to offer.

The primary service we're interested in is **Elastic Beanstalk** (located under **Deployment and Managed** with a green icon):

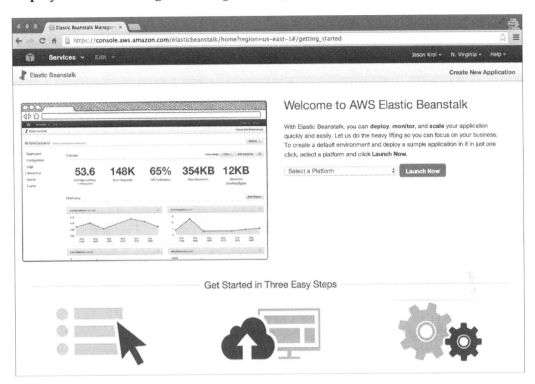

From this screen, click on the **Create New Application** link in the upper right corner. The screens that follow will walk you through a multistep wizard process where you will configure the environment in which the application will reside. Configure the following settings where appropriate:

- **Application Information**:
    - **Application name**: `anything_you_want`

- **Environment Type**:
    - **Environment tier**: `Web Server`
    - **Predefined configuration**: `Node.js`
    - **Environment type**: `Load balancing, autoscaling`

- **Application Version**:
    - Upload your own (choose the ZIP file that you created earlier)

- **Environment Information**:
  - ○ **Environment name**: `anything_you_want`
  - ○ **Environment URL**: `anything_you_want` (this is the subdomain for your app)

- **Configuration Details**:
  - ○ **Instance type**: `t1.micro`

    The remaining fields can be left blank or at their default values

- **Environment Tags**: Skip this step— it is unnecessary for this app

- The final step is to review the configuration settings and then launch the environment (by clicking on the blue **Launch** button). It might take a few minutes for **Elastic Beanstalk** to configure and launch your environment and application so you might need to sit tight:

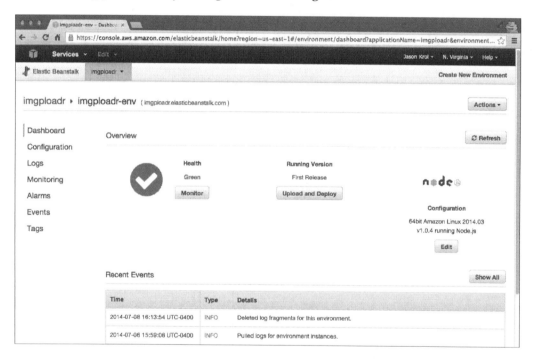

With the environment officially launched and the application online, go ahead and open your app (by clicking on the link at the top of the page) and give it a test run. Assuming everything went according to plan, your application should be up and running and working just fine!

# Microsoft Azure

Microsoft's Azure service is very similar to Amazon's AWS. Both can be considered enterprise-level services and both offer a tremendous level of flexibility and power with a really slick UI. Surprisingly, even though it's a Microsoft product, you can spin up instances of Linux environments using Azure as well as hosting your Node.js and MongoDB apps!

The first thing you're going to need, like any other service, is a registered account at `http://azure.microsoft.com`. You can use an existing Microsoft Live Login if you have one; otherwise, you can register a new account fairly easily. Once you're logged into the Azure service, the first thing you'll be presented with is your primary dashboard. The icons to the left are all of the various services and options available with Azure:

Clicking on the **+NEW** icon at the bottom-left corner will present you with the main dialog you can use to add any new service. For our purposes, we want to add a website:

1. Select **Compute, Web Site**, and **From Gallery**.

2. Select **Node JS Empty Site** from the long list of gallery options. This will create the necessary environment so that you have somewhere you can put your application.

3. On the screen that follows, provide the URL for your app.

4. Leave the remaining fields as their default values.

5. Click on the checkmark icon to complete the setup process, and your website will be created.

6. The next step is to set up the database server. Again, similar to AWS or Nodejitsu, we are going to once again select **MongoLab** as our database service provider:

7. Click on the **+NEW** icon again and select **Store** and browse the list until you find and select **MongoLab**.

8. Click on the next arrow and browse through the various plans. For our needs, we will leave **Sandbox** selected (since it's free).

9. Provide a name for your database; in my case, I entered `imgploadrdb`.

10. Click **Next** again to review and confirm the plan and monthly price (which should be 0.00 $ per month).

11. Finally, click on the checkmark icon to **Purchase** this new subscription plan.

After a few seconds, you should be taken back to your dashboard where you will see entries for both the website and database app service listed:

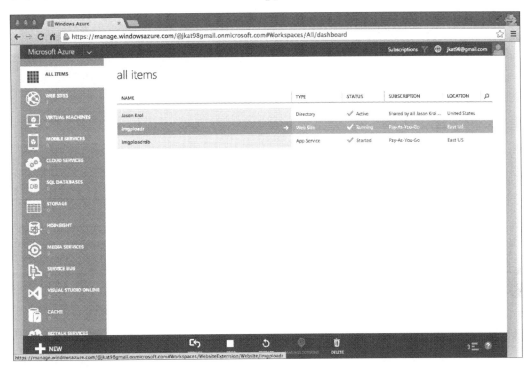

Now that the database has been created and is ready, we need to include its connection string in our application before we can upload our code:

1.  Click on the database row to select it and go to its overview.

2.  The bottom of this screen will contain a few icons, one of which is labeled **Connection Info** (and has an icon that looks like **>i**). Click on that icon to pop up a modal window that contains the connection string URI for your new MongoLab database server.

3.  Copy that URI to your clipboard.

4.  Edit `server.js` in your local app and replace the `mongoose.connect` connection string with the new string you just copied. There is no need to update `username` and `password` as Azure has already taken care of this for you by using the following code:

```
mongoose.connect('mongodb://your_specific_azure_
                  mongolab_uri');
mongoose.connection.on('open', function() {
    console.log('Mongoose connected.');
});
```

Once that change has been made, save the file and don't forget to update your local Git repository with the change, as we'll be using Git in the next section to push your code to Azure (just like we did earlier with Heroku):

```
$ git commit -am "Azure connection string"
```

Back at the Azure dashboard, click on **Web Site** in the **All Items list** (or filter by websites using the icons on the left toolbar). From this overview screen, locate the **Integrate source control** section towards the bottom and click on the **Set up deployment from source control** link. The following screenshot shows what you should see at this point:

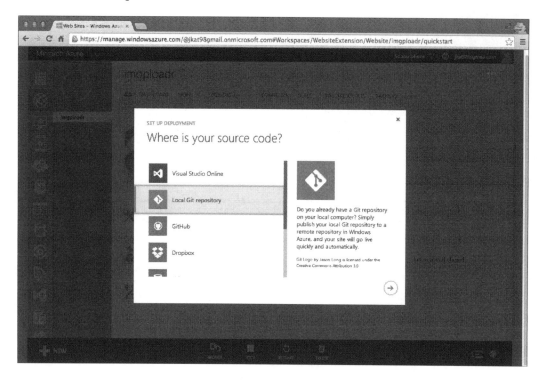

Select **Local Git repository** and then continue by clicking the next arrow icon.

The screen that follows will present instructions on how to push your local code to the remote Git repository that has just been created for your Azure website. The gist is to add a new Git remote (much like we did earlier with Heroku) that points to your Azure repository and then push your code:

```
$ git remote add azure SPECIFIC_URL_FOR_YOUR_SERVER
$ git push azure master
```

You should notice the Git information screen in your Azure dashboard update in real-time as your code starts to push up after the `git push` command. From the command line, you will see a lot of remote `npm install` output as well. Once completed, the deployment history in your Azure dashboard will update showing the information for the last active deployment:

Now that your code has been deployed to your Azure website and your website connection string is pointing to your MongoLab Azure app service, you're ready to give the website a test run! Launch it by pointing your browser to `http://yourappname.azurewebsites.net`:

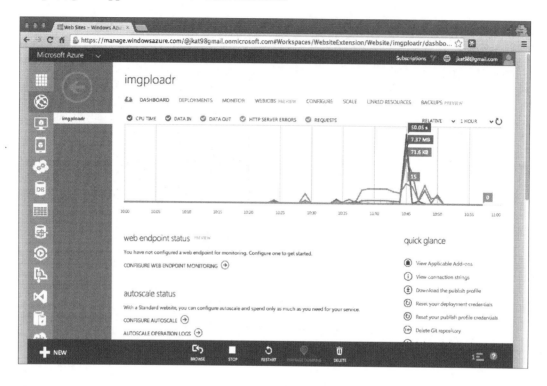

Azure does a lot of things right (UI/UX) and has some really powerful options and scaling features available! Taking a quick glance at the dashboard for a website (the preceding screenshot) you can see that there is a lot going on! There are many different configuration options as well as health monitoring and general information (FTP settings, website URL, usage metrics, and so on), so feel free to poke around and explore.

# Digital Ocean

The last service I wanted to mention and briefly take a look at is Digital Ocean `http://digitalocean.com`. Digital Ocean is a true **Virtual Private Server (VPS)** service provider and is a good example of a service that gets you just about as "close to the metal" as possible. What this means is that Digital Ocean doesn't really have all the bells and whistles that the other services we've seen offer. What Digital Ocean does offer, however, is direct unfiltered access to the Linux server instance you spin up; in this case, referred to as **Droplets**:

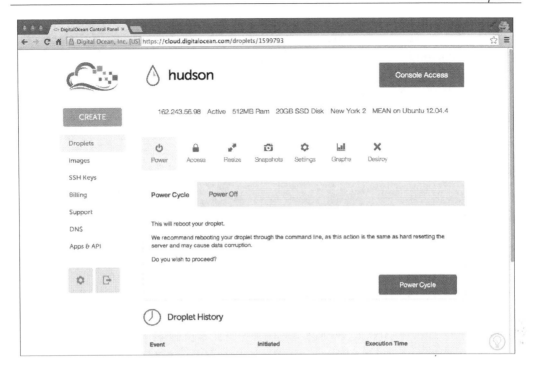

Digital Ocean allows you to boot up new Linux virtual server instances very quickly. They offer very competitive prices and they're a great service if you need to get a Linux server super fast because you only need one for a short period of time, or you want to boot up your own Linux server that you plan to use to host a production environment. The only "downside" (if I had to refer to it as such) is that you have to be pretty familiar with Linux, specifically administering a server and all the responsibilities that come with that.

You can very easily clone your project using Git on a new Droplet, but an example of the actual raw nature of a new Droplet is that Git is not installed on the server by default. You need to manually install Git before you can clone your repository. Depending on which image you decided to clone when creating a new Droplet, you might need to install and configure Node.js as well as MongoDB. Fortunately, Digital Ocean offers a number of predefined servers you can choose from when creating a new server—one of which includes the **MEAN (MongoDB, Express, Angular, and Node.js)** stack. Beyond that, actually launching your app will only run as a process during your currently logged in session—once you log out, your application will go down. You would need to further administer the server to configure your app to run as a service.

Digital Ocean allows you to connect directly to your server using the console access tool within the website itself, or using SSH directly from a terminal on your own machine:

I mention Digital Ocean only because a lot of people will find this kind of raw power quite refreshing and will want to do their own hands-on kind of configuration and maintenance of their server. Digital Ocean is an awesome service but it's not for everyone. I wanted to talk about it specifically because I feel that it rounds out and completes the list of services we've covered so far.

# Summary

We've covered the full spectrum of cloud-based hosting service providers and walked through configuring your service and deploying your project code. Nodejitsu and Heroku are great services that cater more to developers and give them a lot of power through very accessible and slick user interfaces. Amazon and Microsoft, both industry juggernauts, are representative of the kind of power and sophistication you'd expect with enterprise-level service providers. Digital Ocean is a no-frills, "close to the metal" cloud-based VPS provider that sacrifices bells and whistles for raw and direct access to the server.

All of the hosting options we covered are great and not the only choices out there. They're just a sample but speak to the power of the Cloud! Within a few minutes and very little to no cost at all, you can have an environment configured, and your website up and running online!

In the next chapter, we will take a look at the concept of Single-Page Applications and popular client-side development frameworks and tools.

# 11
# Single-Page Applications with Popular Frontend Frameworks

In this chapter, we will take a look at web application development from the frontend perspective, specifically with a **Single-Page Application (SPA)**, also referred to as thick client apps. With SPA, a large chunk of the presentation layer is off-loaded to the browser, and the browser is responsible for rendering pages, handling navigation, and making data calls to an API.

In this chapter, we will cover:

- What exactly a Single-Page Application is
- Why we use a frontend framework such as Backbone.js, Ember.js, or Angular.js
- Popular frontend development tools, such as Grunt, Gulp, Browserify, SAAS, and Handlebars
- Test-driven development on the frontend

## What is a Single-Page Application?

The current trend with sophisticated web applications is to emulate desktop applications and veer away from the "feel" of a traditional website. With traditional websites, every interaction with the server would require a full-page postback that makes a complete round trip. As our web applications become more sophisticated, the need to send and retrieve data to and from the server increases.

If we rely on full-page postbacks every time we need to facilitate one of these requests, our app will feel sluggish and unresponsive as the user will have to wait for a full round trip with every request. Users demand more from their apps these days, and if you think about the application we've written, the **Like** button is a perfect example. Having to send a full-page postback to the server just because we wanted to increment a counter by one seems like a lot of unnecessary overhead. Fortunately, we were able to easily rectify this using jQuery and AJAX. This is a perfect example of how a Single-Page Application works (only on a much larger scale).

A great example of one of the first, standout Single-Page Applications is Google's Gmail. Gmail gives you an interface that is similar to Microsoft Outlook or any traditional desktop-based e-mail client. User interaction with the application feels just as responsive as a desktop application—the "page" never reloads, you can switch panes and tabs within the application with ease, and data is constantly being refreshed and updated in real time.

Creating a Single-Page Application typically involves having a single HTML page as the source of the application that loads all of the necessary JavaScript in order to trigger a series of events that include:

- **Bootstrapping the app**: This means connecting to the server via AJAX to download the necessary startup data.

- **Rendering the screens based on user actions**: This means monitoring events triggered by the user and manipulating the DOM so that sections of the app are hidden, revealed, or redrawn, which emulates the feel of a desktop application.

- **Communicating with the server**: This means using AJAX to constantly send and receive data from the server, which maintains the illusion of a stateful connection via the browser.

# Why use a frontend framework?

We use frameworks to increase our productivity, keep us sane, and generally make our development process more enjoyable. In most of the chapters throughout this book, we worked with the Express.js MVC framework for Node.js. This framework allows us to organize our code and it extrapolates out a lot of boilerplate code, freeing up our time to focus on our custom business logic. The same should be said for the front of an application as well. Any amount of complex code is eventually going to need to be properly organized and use a standard set of reusable tools to achieve common tasks. Express.js makes our life easy while writing our backend code with Node.js. There are a number of popular frontend frameworks that you can rely on as well.

# The TodoMVC project

When deciding which frontend framework to choose for your next large scale frontend project, the decision-making process can be crippling! Keeping track of all of the different frameworks and the pros and cons of each can seem like an exercise in futility. Luckily, people have answered the call and a handy website exists to not only demonstrate the same application written in nearly every framework, but also to offer the complete annotated source code for each as well!

The TodoMVC project, `http://todomvc.com`, is a website that focuses on creating a simple, single page, to-do application, which is written using each of the proven JavaScript MVC frameworks—there's even one written in vanilla JavaScript! So the easiest way to jump into a framework would be to have a look at its TodoMVC code sample.

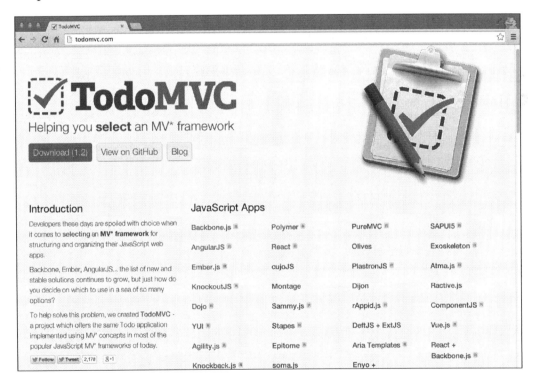

Definitely spend some time checking out the website and digging into each of the featured frameworks. You can get a really good feel of the different frameworks by seeing the same code written in completely different ways; no two are identical, and ultimately, it's up to you to evaluate and figure out which you prefer and why.

For the sake of brevity, I'm going to focus on the three that I personally like and believe are at the top of the current list of front runners.

# Backbone.js

Backbone.js is an extremely lightweight (6.5 KB in production) MV* Framework that has been around for a few years. It has an extremely large established user base, and many very large-scale web applications have been written using this framework. Some companies that have embraced Backbone.js for development of their flagship products include:

- USA Today
- Hulu
- LinkedIn
- Trello
- Disqus
- Khan Academy
- Walmart Mobile

Backbone.js is a great framework to start with if you're comfortable with jQuery and have been using it for a while and want to start improving your code organization and modularity. Additionally, Backbone.js requires jQuery and integrates it pretty tightly, so that's one less thing to worry about learning as you ease into this new world of frontend development.

Backbone.js works on the basic idea of models, collections, views, and routers.

- Models are the basic elements that store and manage all of the data in your application
- Collections store models
- Views render HTML to the screen, retrieving dynamic data from models and collections
- Routers power the URL of your application, allowing each individual section of your application its own unique URL (without actually loading live URLs) and ultimately tying the whole thing together

As Backbone.js is so lightweight, an extremely small and simple set of sample code can be put together very quickly:

```
var Person = Backbone.Model.extend();
var PersonView = Backbone.View.extend({
```

```
        tag: 'div',
        render: function() {
            var html = [
                this.model.get('name'),
                '<br/>',
                this.model.get('website')
            ].join('');

            this.$el.html(html);

            return this;
        }
    });

var person = new Person({
        name: 'Jason Krol',
        website: 'http://kroltech.com'
    }),
    view = new PersonView({ model: person });

$('body').append(view.render().el);
```

The one thing to notice is that Backbone.js by its very nature is so lightweight that it doesn't include most of the functionalities that you'd expect to work right out of the box. As you can see in the preceding code, in the `View` object that we created, we had to provide a `render` function that manually renders the HTML for us. For this reason, many people shy away from Backbone.js, but others embrace it for the raw power and flexibility it gives to developers.

Traditionally, you wouldn't put all of your code into a single file like the earlier example. You would organize your models, collections, and views into individual folders in a structure, just like how we organized the code in our Node.js application. Bundling all of the code together would be the job of a build tool (which will be discussed later in this chapter).

You can learn more about Backbone.js by visiting its official website at `http://backbonejs.org`. Also, don't forget to check out the Backbone.js implementation of the to-do application on the TodoMVC website!

 I maintain a repository on GitHub that has a boilerplate web application with complete code that uses the full stack we've covered in this book, as well as Backbone.js with Marionette for the frontend. Feel free to check it out at `http://github.com/jkat98/benm` (Backbone, Express, Node, and MongoDB).

# Ember.js

Ember.js bills itself as the *framework for creating ambitious web applications*. Ember's goal is to target fairly large-scale SPAs, so the idea of using it to build something very simple might seem like overkill but it is certainly doable. A fair assessment is to take a look at the production file size of the Ember library, which comes in at around 90 KB (versus 6.5 KB for Backbone.js). That being said, if you are building something very robust with a very large codebase, the added 90 KB might not be a big deal for you.

Here is a very small sample application using Ember.js:

```
var App = Ember.Application.create(),
    movies = [{
        title: "Big Trouble in Little China",
        year: "1986"
    }, {
        title: "Aliens",
        year: "1986"
    }];

App.IndexRoute = Ember.Route.extend({
    model: function() {
        return movies;
    }
});

<script type="text/x-handlebars" data-template-name="index">
    {{#each}}
        {{title}} - {{year}}<br/>
    {{/each}}
</script>
```

Ember.js's code looks somewhat similar to that of Backbone.js, and it's no surprise that a lot of seasoned Backbone.js developers find themselves migrating to Ember.js as their need for more robust solutions increase. Ember.js uses familiar items including views, models, collections, and routes, as well as an `Application` object.

Additionally, Ember.js features components, which is one of its more powerful and beloved features. Giving a sneak preview of the future of the Web, components allow you to create small, modular, reusable HTML components that you can plug into your application as needed. With components, you can basically create your own custom HTML tags that look and behave exactly how you define them, and they can easily be reused throughout an application.

Developing with Ember.js is all about convention. Unlike Backbone.js, Ember.js tries to get a lot of the boilerplate out of the way and makes certain assumptions for you. Because of this, you need to do things a certain way, and controllers, views, and routes need to follow a somewhat strict pattern with regards to naming conventions.

The Ember.js website features incredible online documentation and getting-started guides. If you're interested in learning more about Ember.js, check it out at `http://emberjs.com/guides/`. Also, don't forget to take a look at the TodoMVC implementation!

# AngularJS

AngularJS exploded onto the scene because of the simple fact that it's built by Google (it is open source). AngularJS is basically like putting HTML on steroids. The applications and pages that you create use regular HTML that we're all used to, but they include a number of new and custom directives that extend the core functionality of HTML, giving it awesome new power.

Another great feature of AngularJS that has seasoned non-web developers flocking to it is that it is built from the group to be heavily tested and supports dependency injection. It's a framework that doesn't makes creating sophisticated web applications feel like traditional web development. This is an extremely robust framework, clocking in at the largest file size of the three we're looking at, with 111 KB of compressed production code:

```
<!doctype html>
<html ng-app>
  <head>
    <script src=
    "https://ajax.googleapis.com/.../angular.min.js"></script>
  </head>
  <body>
    <div>
      <label>Name:</label>
      <input type="text" ng-model="yourName" placeholder="Enter a
       name here">
      <hr>
      <h1>Hello {{yourName}}!</h1>
    </div>
  </body>
</html>
```

You can see by the sample code provided that no custom JavaScript was written at all, yet the page features real-time data binding between an input field and an `h1` tag. This is stock power and functionality right out of the box, and a demonstration of the extended nature of regular HTML that AngularJS provides.

Make no mistake, however, that JavaScript still plays a huge role in the development of AngularJS. AngularJS features controllers, directives, providers, and many more features.

Learn more about AngularJS by visiting its website at `http://angularjs.org`, and take a look at the TodoMVC implementation as well!

Frontend frameworks have recently taken on somewhat religious undertones. Post a negative comment or criticism about a particular framework and it's likely you'll get blasted by its supporters. Likewise, talk positively about a particular framework and, again, it's likely you'll get attacked about how much better a different framework handles the same topic. The bottom line when deciding which framework is right for you and/or your project is typically going to be about personal preference. Each of the frameworks featured on the TodoMVC website can clearly accomplish the same goals, each in its own unique way. Take some time to evaluate a few and decide for yourself!

# Frontend development tools

Due to the sophisticated nature of Single-Page Applications, there exists a growing suite of tools a frontend developer needs to be familiar with to manage many day-to-day, and sometimes, minute-to-minute tasks.

# Automated build task managers

A build tool is just what it sounds like- a tool used to build your application. When a frontend developer creates and maintains an application, there could be a number of tasks that need to be repeated literally every time a file is changed and saved. Using a build tool, a developer can free up time and mental resources by offloading the responsibility to an automated task manager that can watch files for changes and execute any number of tasks needed. These tasks might include any number of the following:

- Concatenation
- Minification
- Uglification and obfuscation
- Manipulation
- Dependency installation and preparation

- Custom script firing
- Concurrent watchers
- Server launching
- Test automation

Some of the more popular build tools today include Grunt, Gulp, and Broccoli. Grunt.js has been around for a number of years and is very well-established in the development community. Gulp and Broccoli are fairly new but quickly gaining traction and work a little differently than Grunt. With Grunt, you define and manage your tasks using a configuration file whereas with Gulp and Broccoli, you write Node.js code and use the raw power of streams. Many developers find working with Grunt's configuration file to be fairly convoluted and frustrating and find working with Gulp to be a refreshing change. However, it's hard to dispute Grunt's history and popularity.

All three are feature-extensive ecosystems of plugins that help automate literally everything and anything you can think of with your build process.

Here is a sample output from a typical Grunt `build` command:

In a typical Single-Page Application, the build manager can be responsible for downloading and installing dependencies, concatenating multiple JavaScript files into a single file, compiling and shimming Browserify modules, linting JavaScript files for syntax errors, transpiling LESS files into production-ready CSS files, copying files to a runtime destination, watching files for changes to repeat any of the tasks again, and finally, running appropriate tests any time the code is changed—all from a single command!

Grunt can be installed using npm and should be installed globally. Execute the following command to install the Grunt CLI on your machine:

```
$ npm install -g grunt-cli
```

Refer to the getting-started guide on the official Grunt.js website for more information at http://gruntjs.com/getting-started

Additionally, feel free to check out Gulp and Broccoli as well for more information:

- http://gulpjs.com/
- https://github.com/broccolijs/broccoli

# Dependency management

There are literally millions of JavaScript libraries that exist to help you with everything from DOM manipulation (jquery) to timestamp formatting (moment.js). Managing these libraries and dependencies can sometimes be a bit of a headache. For the frontend, the dependency manager of choice is Bower.io.

Bower works almost in exactly the same way as npm; it manages the packages in the bower.json file. While working on the frontend (you need a known JavaScript library or plugin such as underscore, for example), simply execute bower install underscore and the JavaScript files will be downloaded to a local bower_ components folder in your project. From there, you can automate the inclusion of those scripts by updating your build process, or simply copying the file, including a script tag in your HTML, and then you're all set.

Bower can be installed using npm and should be installed globally. Execute the following command to install Bower on your machine:

```
$ npm install -g bower
$ bower install jquery
bower cached          git://github.com/jquery/jquery.git#2.1.0
bower validate        2.1.0 against git://github.com/jquery/jquery.git#*
bower new             version for git://github.com/jquery/jquery.git#*
```

```
bower resolve        git://github.com/jquery/jquery.git#*
bower download       https://github.com/jquery/jquery/archive/2.1.1.tar.gz
bower extract        jquery#* archive.tar.gz
bower resolved       git://github.com/jquery/jquery.git#2.1.1
bower install        jquery#2.1.1
jquery#2.1.1 bower_components/jquery
```

Visit the Bower.io website (`http://bower.io`) for more information, as well as the full directory of scripts available to be installed via `bower install`.

# Modularity

When writing large JavaScript applications, the key is to keep your source code well-organized and structurally sane. Unfortunately, JavaScript doesn't inherently support the idea of modular code right out of-the-box very well. To solve this problem, two popular libraries exist to allow you to write modular code and rely on only the modules you need within each individual piece of code.

>  An absolute must-read and incredible resource for frontend design patterns is Addy Osmandi's *Learning JavaScript Design Patterns*, which you can read for free by visiting the following URL:
>
> `http://addyosmani.com/resources/`
> `essentialjsdesignpatterns/book/`

Require.js and Browserify are two of the most popular module loaders today. Each has a very unique syntax and its own set of benefits. Require.js follows asynchronous module definition, which means each piece of code needs to define its own dependencies. Personally, I've worked with Require.js in the past, and recently I've found that I really like working with Browserify. One of Browserify's strengths is that it uses the same modular pattern as Node.js; so, writing frontend code using Browserify feels identical to that of Node. You use `module.exports` and `require` on the frontend, and you don't have to worry about syntax context switching if you go back and forth between Node and the frontend within the same application.

Using a module loader in conjunction with one of the popular MVC frameworks mentioned earlier is almost a requirement because the two go together like peanut butter and jelly!

For more information, visit the following links:

- `http://browserify.org/`
- `http://requirejs.org/`

# HTML template-rendering engines

Fortunately, we've covered the idea of HTML template-rendering engines already throughout the course of this book. The topics and concepts transfer directly to frontend applications as well. There are many different HTML template engines to choose from for use in the browser.

Many template engines will be mustache-based, meaning that they use {{ and }} for merge variables. Handlebars is currently my personal favorite, mainly because it works so well in the backend and frontend of an application, and I really like working with its helpers. Underscore.js has a built-in "lite" template-rendering engine for use with Backbone.js but its syntax uses <% and %> (much like classic ASP or ASP.net MVC Razor syntax). Typically, most frontend MVC frameworks allow you to customize the template-rendering engine and use any engine you want. For example, Backbone.js can be very easily set up to use Handlebars.js, instead of Underscore.js by default.

Here's just a small sample list of some of the currently available frontend template-rendering engines:

- **Underscore.js**: http://underscorejs.org
- **Handlebars**: http://handlebarsjs.com
- **Mustache**: http://mustache.github.io
- **Dust.js**: http://akdubya.github.io/dustjs
- **EJS**: http://embeddedjs.com

Some of these will work at the backend as well as on the frontend.

# CSS transpiling

The idea of using variables and logic within a CSS file sounds like a dream come true, right? We aren't quite there yet (in the browser, anyway), however there are a few tools that will let us use variables and logic in our CSS files and compile them during our build step. LESS and SASS are two of the most popular CSS transpilers currently available. They behave almost identically, with only slight differences in syntax and features. The big difference is that LESS was written using JavaScript and Node, whereas SASS uses Ruby; therefore, each has different requirements to get running on your machine.

Here is a sample SASS style sheet file:

```
$sprite-bg:url("/images/editor/sprite-msg-bg.png");

@mixin radius($radius) {
```

```scss
    -moz-border-radius: $radius;
    -webkit-border-radius: $radius;
    -ms-border-radius: $radius;
    border-radius: $radius;
}

.upload-button {
    border-bottom: solid 2px #005A8B;
    background: transparent $sprite-bg no-repeat;
    @include radius(4px);
    cursor: pointer;
}

#step-status {
    color:#dbdbdb; font-size:14px;

    span.active {
        color:#1e8acb;
    }

    &.basic-adjust, &.message-editor {
        width: 525px;
    }

    .icon {
        height:65px;
        width: 50px;
        margin:auto;
    }
}

@import "alerts";
@import "attachments";
@import "codemirror";
@import "drafts";
```

Looking at the sample code, you can see that we have a few new elements that wouldn't typically work in a regular CSS file. Some of these include:

- Defining custom variables for use throughout the style sheet
- Defining mixins, which act as pseudo functions for reusable styles (with dynamic parameters)
- Including mixins and variables within our style definitions
- Nesting styles with parent/child relationships

When the previous code is transpiled using LESS (or in the case of the sample code SASS), the output is a standard `.css` style sheet that adheres to all the normal browser rules and syntax.

For more information on LESS and SASS, check out the following links:

- `http://lesscss.org`
- `http://sass-lang.com`

# Testing and test-driven development

The development of a sophisticated frontend application is no different than any other software application. The code is going to be complicated and robust, and there's no reason not to write tests as well as a practice test-driven development. The availability of testing frameworks and languages for the frontend is just as robust as any other language. All of the tools and concepts we've used for testing the Node.js code that we've written in this book can be used directly on the frontend as well.

Some other tools to consider for testing your frontend JavaScript are:

- **Karma for running tests**: `http://karma-runner.github.io`
- **Jasmine for writing tests**: `http://jasmine.github.io`

## PhantomJS headless browser

One thing I'd like to point out with testing frontend code is that, typically, the test runners want to run in a browser window. This is great and makes perfect sense, but in the real world, automating your tests or quickly executing them with TDD can be a bit painful when a browser window wants to open every time your test suite runs. PhantomJS is a *headless* browser available that works perfectly in this kind of scenario. A headless browser simply means it's a browser that runs from the command line, in memory, with no actual interface (like a typical browser).

You can easily configure Karma to launch the test suite using PhantomJS instead of your browser of choice. When using PhantomJS as your browser, your tests execute behind the scenes and only errors are reported. Here is a sample output of a test suite running with Karma using PhantomJS:

```
 ⊙ ⊙ ⊙                                    2. Shell
Running "karma:test" (karma) task
INFO [karma]: Karma v0.10.9 server started at http://localhost:9876/
INFO [launcher]: Starting browser PhantomJS
INFO [PhantomJS 1.9.7 (Mac OS X)]: Connected on socket rnYQJxEmVLi1pQfZsE3G
..................................................................
..................................................................
..................................................................
..................................................................
..................................................................
..................................................................
..................................................................
PhantomJS 1.9.7 (Mac OS X): Executed 510 of 510 SUCCESS (9.404 secs / 9.285 secs)

Done, without errors.


Execution Time (2014-07-15 15:00:21 UTC)
loading tasks         2.1s    ████████ 14%
simplemocha:server   893ms    ███ 6%
karma:test            11.5s   ██████████████████████████████████████ 79%
Total 14.5s
```

# Summary

This was a whirlwind tour of some of the most common frontend tools and frameworks used when doing typical web development. We took a look at the TodoMVC project and reviewed three popular JavaScript frameworks to build robust and sophisticated frontend applications.

Popular build tools such as Grunt.js, Gulp, and Broccoli help developers streamline their workflow process by automating a lot of the repetitive tasks that need to occur every time a file is modified. From concatenating scripts into a single file, to minifying and compressing, and to executing automated test suites, the task runners can be configured to handle pretty much everything under the sun!

We took a look at two popular CSS transpilers with LESS and SASS and saw how they can make creating and managing CSS style sheets dynamic with the use of mixins, variables, and nesting.

Finally, you learned about PhantomJS, the headless browser, and using it when running frontend tests so that the tests can be executed quickly and easily from the command line using a test runner like Karma.

In the next and final chapter, we'll review some alternative frameworks to develop web applications using Node.js and MongoDB.

# 12
# Popular Node.js Web Frameworks

Throughout this book, we've focused exclusively on using Express.js as our web framework of choice, primarily because it's one of the most popular web development frameworks for Node.js. It has been around for quite a while, and is very widely used. However, there are a number of alternate frameworks available that I want to introduce you to. Some of these frameworks are much more powerful and robust than Express.js, while others are right in line or slightly less feature packed.

Most of the frameworks that exist today and discussed in this chapter are still in their early stages of development. Some have not even reached a 1.0 status. The use of these in a production environment should be considered carefully and under a fair amount of scrutiny.

In this chapter, we will take a brief look at the following frameworks:

- Koa
- Meteor
- Sails
- Hapi
- Flatiron

# Koa

Koa is a new web framework designed by the same team that created Express.js. The goal of Koa is to be smaller, more expressive, and a more robust foundation for web applications. T J Holowaychuk, who is the creator of the Express framework, is the same person who created Koa as well and you can see it focuses much of its capabilities on generators, which is a feature found in other popular programming languages such as Python, C#, and Ruby. Generators were introduced to JavaScript with ECMAScript 6. Generators prevent the standard *callback hell* that is so popular with the development process in Node.js. Koa has a lightweight architecture, so it doesn't come with any middleware, rather, it leaves the choice of implementing certain features to the developers.

The Koa website, `http://koajs.com`, is shown in the following screenshot:

More information about Koa and sample implementations can be found on its website as well as at `https://github.com/koajs/koa`.

# Meteor

Meteor is a simple and complete web framework with the goal of giving developers of any skillset the ability to build robust web applications in a fraction of the time. It features a handy CLI tool that you can use to scaffold new projects very quickly.

Meteor provides some core projects/libraries such as blaze, DDP, livequery, and so on with a unified build system. This simplifies the overall development process and yields an integrated developer experience. The overall architecture that the Meteor platform handles is shown as follows:

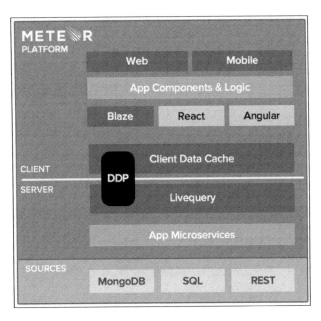

Meteor aims to build real-time applications by providing its two core features, the distributed data protocol on the server side and transparent reactive rendering on the client side. For more details, please visit: `http://meteor.com/features`.

Another notable feature of this framework is its extensive package system, named atmosphere, which has modules developed for most of the common application use cases.

It is quickly gaining traction and becoming increasingly popular every day. Currently, its GitHub repo has over 27,000 stars!

More information about Meteor can be found on its website as well as on its official GitHub repo at `https://github.com/meteor/meteor`.

# Sails

Sails is another great MVC framework for building web applications using Node.js that sometimes compares itself to Ruby on Rails. Unlike Meteor, Sails is database agnostic, so it doesn't matter which data store you choose. Sails includes some handy scaffolding tools such as an automatic RESTful API generation. Socket.io, a real-time communication framework for Node.js, is built into Sails; so including real-time functionalities in your application should be a breeze. Sails features some nice production-level automation that would typically need to be handled by a tool such as Grunt.js or Gulp (this includes the minification and bundling of CSS and JavaScript for the frontend). Sails also includes basic security and role-based authentication for your app, should you require that level of functionality. Sails could be considered a more full-fledged enterprise level framework than Express, as it has almost every feature that a popular framework such as rails has.

The Sails website is at `http://sailsjs.com`.

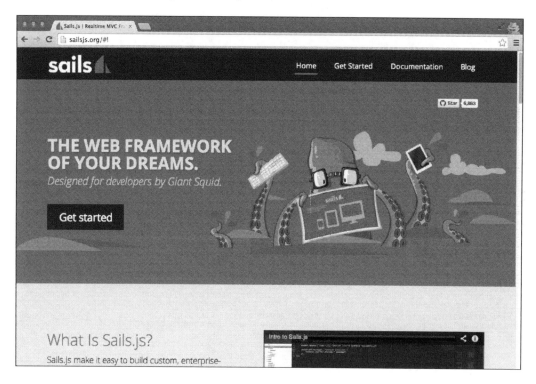

More information about Sails can be found on its website as well as its official GitHub repo at `https://github.com/balderdashy/sails`.

# Hapi

Hapi is the result of the team behind Walmart's online mobile website. The team that built that website developed a rich set of Node.js utilities and libraries that can be found under the Spumko umbrella. Considering the tremendous amount of traffic Walmart's website receives on any given day, it's no wonder that the team at WalmartLabs is on the top of their game when it comes to Node.js development and best practices. Hapi is the web framework that was born from the ashes of real-world trial and error.

The Hapi website is at `http://hapijs.com`:

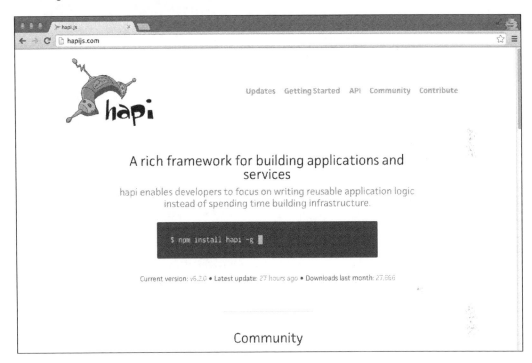

More information about Hapi can be found on its website as well as its official GitHub repo at `https://github.com/spumko/hapi`.

# Flatiron

Flatiron is yet another Node.js MVC web application framework. What sets Flatiron apart from other frameworks is its package-based approach. Since it gives the power and freedom to decide how much or how little the framework should include, developers can pick and choose the packages they want to work with and include in their project. It handles a lot of the basic data management responsibilities and CRUD for you by supplying a powerful ODM that takes care of a lot of the heavy lifting.

The Flatiron website (`http://flatironjs.com`) is shown in the following screenshot:

More information about Flatiron can be found on its website as well as its official GitHub repo at `https://github.com/flatiron/flatiron`.

# Summary

Even though we used Express.js exclusively throughout this book, there are many other options available when creating web applications using Node.js. We examined a few of those options in this chapter, including Meteor, Sails, Hapi, Koa, and Flatiron. Each framework features its own strengths and weaknesses and its own unique approach to the standard functionality that a web application requires.

That's all folks. I hope all the different facets of building a web app using Node.js and MongoDB brought the readers to a progressive way of learning and developing an awesome idea. Well, this is just the start. I would recommend you follow the developer communities of all the technologies or libraries that you are going to use in your own app.

The beauty of web development with Node.js is that there's no shortage of opinions on how to accomplish a single task. MVC frameworks are no exception, and you can see from this chapter there are a lot of really robust and feature-packed frameworks to choose from.

# Index

creating 244
screens, rendering based on user
    actions 244
**Sinon.js**
    URL 192
**Socket.io**
    real-time web application 6
**Software as a Service (SaaS) 217**
**spies 192-194**
**static methods 124**
**stats helper 154-156**
**stats module 105**
**stubs 192-194**
**Sublime Text 3 13**
**syntax basics, JavaScript 30**

# T

**template engines, Node**
    reference link 69
**templating engines 71**
**test-driven development 256**
**Test Driven Development (TDD) 187**
**test helper**
    writing 197-199
**testing 256**
**tests**
    asserting, with Chai.js 190
    running, with Mocha framework 188-190
**threads**
    reference link 3
**TodoMVC project**
    about 245, 246
    URL 245
**tools, for running frontend JavaScript**
    Jasmine 256
    Karma 256
**traditional hosting**
    versus Cloud 216

# U

**UI**
    iterating on 108-112
**Underscore.js**
    URL 254

# V

**V8 engine**
    advantages 2
**variable**
    declaring, in JavaScript 30
**variable scope, JavaScript 31, 32**
**view engine**
    Handlebars, using as 68, 69
**view models 92**
**views**
    about 52, 72
    rendering 87-89
**view-specific helpers, Handlebars 86**
**Virtual Private Server (VPS) 216, 240**
**virtual properties 124**

# W

**web application**
    booting up 58
    building 53
    designing 53, 54
    entry point, creating 56, 57
    files, organizing 55
**web application frameworks 51**
**web application request**
    lifecycle 114
**WebSockets**
    reference link 6
**Windows**
    Node.js, installing on 16, 17
**Windows 7**
    MongoDB, installing on 21
**Windows 8**
    MongoDB, installing on 21
**Windows Quick Start guide, MongoDB**
    reference link 20
**WordPress**
    URL 79

# Y

**yoeman**
    reference link 55

## Thank you for buying
# Web Development with MongoDB and NodeJS
### Second Edition

# About Packt Publishing

Packt, pronounced 'packed', published its first book, *Mastering phpMyAdmin for Effective MySQL Management*, in April 2004, and subsequently continued to specialize in publishing highly focused books on specific technologies and solutions.

Our books and publications share the experiences of your fellow IT professionals in adapting and customizing today's systems, applications, and frameworks. Our solution-based books give you the knowledge and power to customize the software and technologies you're using to get the job done. Packt books are more specific and less general than the IT books you have seen in the past. Our unique business model allows us to bring you more focused information, giving you more of what you need to know, and less of what you don't.

Packt is a modern yet unique publishing company that focuses on producing quality, cutting-edge books for communities of developers, administrators, and newbies alike. For more information, please visit our website at www.packtpub.com.

# About Packt Open Source

In 2010, Packt launched two new brands, Packt Open Source and Packt Enterprise, in order to continue its focus on specialization. This book is part of the Packt Open Source brand, home to books published on software built around open source licenses, and offering information to anybody from advanced developers to budding web designers. The Open Source brand also runs Packt's Open Source Royalty Scheme, by which Packt gives a royalty to each open source project about whose software a book is sold.

# Writing for Packt

We welcome all inquiries from people who are interested in authoring. Book proposals should be sent to author@packtpub.com. If your book idea is still at an early stage and you would like to discuss it first before writing a formal book proposal, then please contact us; one of our commissioning editors will get in touch with you.

We're not just looking for published authors; if you have strong technical skills but no writing experience, our experienced editors can help you develop a writing career, or simply get some additional reward for your expertise.

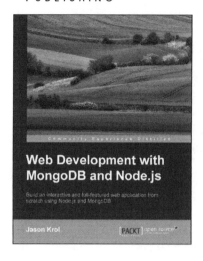

# Web Development with MongoDB and Node.js

ISBN: 978-1-78398-730-6          Paperback: 294 pages

Build an interactive and full-featured web application from scratch using Node.js and MongoDB

1. Configure your development environment to use Node.js and MongoDB.

2. Explore the power of development using JavaScript in the full stack of a web application.

3. A practical guide with clear instructions to design and develop a complete web application from start to finish.

# Node.js Blueprints

ISBN: 978-1-78328-733-8          Paperback: 268 pages

Develop stunning web and desktop applications with the definitive Node.js

1. Utilize libraries and frameworks to develop real-world applications using Node.js.

2. Explore Node.js compatibility with AngularJS, Socket.io, BackboneJS, EmberJS, and GruntJS.

3. Step-by-step tutorials that will help you to utilize the enormous capabilities of Node.js.

Please check **www.PacktPub.com** for information on our titles

## MongoDB Cookbook

ISBN: 978-1-78216-194-3          Paperback: 388 pages

Over 80 practical recipes to design, deploy, and administer MongoDB

1. Gain a thorough understanding of some of the key features of MongoDB.

2. Learn the techniques necessary to solve frequent MongoDB problems.

3. Packed full of step-by-step recipes to help you with installation, design, and deployment.

## Learning MongoDB [Video]

ISBN: 978-1-78398-392-6          Duration: 03:26 hours

A comprehensive guide to using MongoDB for ultra-fast, fault tolerant management of big data, including advanced data analysis

1. Master MapReduce and the MongoDB aggregation framework for sophisticated manipulation of large sets of data.

2. Manage databases and collections, including backup, recovery, and security.

3. Discover how to secure your data using SSL, both from the client and via programming languages.

Please check **www.PacktPub.com** for information on our titles

52126333R00167

Made in the USA
Lexington, KY
18 May 2016